Joseph Sassoon is currently a Senior Associate Member of St Antony's College, Oxford and from January 2009 a Visiting Scholar at Georgetown University, Washington. Born in Baghdad, he completed his doctorate at St Antony's College, Oxford. He has widely published on Iraq's economy and the Middle East region.

International Library of Migration Studies

1. *Migrating to America: Transnational Social Networks and Regional Identity among Turkish Migrants*

   Lisa DiCarlo

   978 1 84511 64 0

2. *Homelands and Diasporas: Greeks, Jews and Their Migrations*

   Minna Rozen (ed.)

   978 1 84511 642 2

3. *The Iraqi Refugees: The New Crisis in the Middle East*

   Joseph Sassoon

   978 1 84511 919 5

4. *Immigration and National Identity: North African Political Movements in Colonial and Postcolonial France*

   Rabah Aissaoui

   978 1 84511 835 8

5. *From Egypt to Europe: Globalisation and Migration Across the Mediterranean*

   Simona Talani

   978 1 84511 669 9

THE IRAQI REFUGEES

THE NEW CRISIS IN THE MIDDLE EAST

joseph sassoon

I.B. TAURIS

LONDON · NEW YORK

Published in 2009 by I.B.Tauris & Co Ltd
6 Salem Road, London W2 4BU
175 Fifth Avenue, New York NY 10010
www.ibtauris.com

In the United States of America and Canada distributed by
Palgrave Macmillan, a division of St. Martin's Press, 175 Fifth Avenue,
New York NY 10010

ISBN: 978 1 84511 919 5

International Library of Migration Studies, vol. 3

A full CIP record for this book is available from the British Library
A full CIP record is available from the Library of Congress

Designed and typeset by 4word Ltd, Bristol, UK
Printed and bound in Great Britain by TJ International Ltd, Padstow, Cornwall

To my Mother

Contents

	Preface	ix
	Acknowledgements	xi
	List of abbreviations	xiii
	List of tables	xv
	Map of Iraq	xvi
	Introduction	1
Chapter 1	**Internal displacement**	9
	Internal displacement	9
	Violence	14
	Minorities	23
	The Iraqi Government's reactions	27
Chapter 2	**Iraqi refugees in Jordan**	33
	Historical background	33
	Why Jordan?	35
	Profile and characteristics of the Iraqi refugees	36
	Economic situation of Iraqis and their impact on Jordan's economy	46
	Jordan's, Iraq's and international responses	51
Chapter 3	**Iraqi refugees in Syria**	61
	Historical background	61
	Why Syria?	62
	Profile and characteristics of the Iraqi refugees	64
	Economic situation of Iraqis and their impact on Syria's economy	75
	Syria's, Iraq's and international responses	79

Chapter 4   **Iraqi refugees in the rest of the world**   87
            Egypt   87
            Lebanon   92
            Rest of the Arab world   96
            Iran and Turkey   98
            Sweden   100
            Rest of Europe   105
            The USA   110

Chapter 5   **The role of humanitarian organizations**   115
            UNHCR and other UN agencies   118
            NGOs   124

Chapter 6   **Iraq's economy and its brain drain**   129
            Iraq's economy   129
            Iraq's reconstruction   133
            Corruption in Iraq   135
            Brain drain   140

Chapter 7   **Return and returnees**   153
            The myth of return   153
            Who will return and why?   155
            Restitution of land and property rights   160

            Conclusion   165

Appendix   **Iraq and the host countries – a comparative
            table**   171

            Notes   173

            Bibliography   213

            Index   239

Preface

The tragedy of the Iraqi people has spanned decades with little or no respite. The joy of many at seeing the end of Saddam's cruel regime soon turned into misery for millions of people.

As someone who fled Iraq with his family in the early 1970s, leaving everything behind, reading about the suffering of hundreds of thousands of Iraqi refugees triggered my interest in researching this subject. The feelings of being uprooted, living in exile in a new 'home', the need to adapt to a new environment, memories of the past, were all well-known to me. The inability of the world to comprehend the depth of misery of all refugees, not just Iraqis, is a fact no subterfuge can evade. At the end of 2007 there were more than 67 million refugees and displaced persons around the world.

In writing a book about a subject with a 'moving target', the purpose is to give an overview of the issues and an analysis of the different aspects of this crisis. Thus the book does not purport to be updated to the latest developments and the line is drawn somewhere in mid-2008. I have tried in many parts of the book to present comparisons from other cases of displacement and in a few instances a theoretical framework to some of the questions raised.

In researching this book, heavy use of public material was made; newspapers and tens of websites in Iraq, the Arab world, Europe and the USA; documents and publications of international humanitarian organizations; published academic research; and finally interviews with Iraqis living mainly in Kurdistan, Amman, Damascus, Cairo, Stockholm, Södertälje and a few in Western Europe. My interviews with about 50 Iraqis, some face to face, others by telephone, were not necessarily a representative sample. Sometimes it was hard to get the facts given the emotions surrounding the subject. Other times, it took a long time to gain people's confidence to tell their stories as many still live in the shadow of fear of their past. I did not mention any names of Iraqi refugees in order to protect them but all interviews are on file.

A final problem, not surprisingly, concerns the scarcity of reliable statistics. Figures presented here are mostly an indication to some of the issues discussed.

This book does not present solutions for the problems of Iraqi refugees who fled their country following the 2003 invasion. The hope is to highlight the different aspects of this tragedy so governments around the world can intensify their efforts to reduce the human suffering of millions of Iraqis.

Acknowledgements

I am indebted to many people who have helped me in researching and writing this book. Among those with whom I have discussed many of the topics here, whose advice I have appreciated and from whose written works I have learned much, are: Nadje Al-Ali, Ali Allawi, Dawn Chatty, Patricia Fagan, Philip Marfleet, Roger Owen, Avi Shlaim, Peter Sluglett, Charles Tripp and Sami Zubaida. Special thanks are due to Eugene Rogan for his support and comments on one of the chapters; Elizabeth Ferris and her team at the Brookings Institution, particularly Kim Stolz; Ala'din Alwan for his guidance and help on all matters related to the health sector; and to UNHCR, in particular the never-tiring Andrew Harper in Geneva, Sybella Wilkes in Damascus and to Susan Hopper for her help with photographs of the refugees.

Before and during my research trips, many extended their hospitality and advice; the list is too long to mention but I would like to thank Nadia Gatan in London, Zainab Mahdi in Amman and Birgitta Ombrant in Stockholm. Géraldine Chatelard deserves a special mention for her writings on the world of refugees, her advice and comments on a couple of chapters, and for her friendship.

In researching this book, I have extensively utilized journalists' reports from the region and one has to admire their courage and tenacity for allowing us to learn about Iraq and its people who fled their home. The BBC Online Monitoring was a great source to complete the picture.

My appreciation goes to Iradj Bagherzade and my editor Abigail Fielding-Smith from I.B.Tauris for their support and help.

Miriam Bradley was a tremendous help in assisting in the research and reading of the manuscripts. Her comments and knowledge were much appreciated.

I would like to thank my lifelong friend Terry Somekh for his consistent support and encouragement. I thank also my mother for her love and zest for life, and dedicate this book to her.

For the many Iraqis, in the Middle East and Europe, who took the time and trouble to answer my questions and help me with this study, I owe a particular gratitude. I sincerely hope that the difficult circumstances of many of those people will improve in the near future.

Last, but by no means least, Helen Jackson. I cannot convey in words my gratitude for her love, encouragement, her consistent support, input and suggestions, and her technical assistance throughout all the stages of the book. Without her this book would have been impossible.

List of abbreviations

BMJ	British Medical Journal
CARA	Council for Assisting Refugee Academics
CPA	Coalition Provisional Authority
CPI	Consumer Price Index
CRRPD	Commission for the Resolution of Real Property Disputes
ECRE	European Council on Refugees and Exiles
EU	European Union
FIAS	Federation of Iraqi Associations in Sweden
GAO	Government Accountability Office
GDP	Gross Domestic Product
HRW	Human Rights Watch
IACIS	International Association of Contemporary Iraqi Studies
ICMC	International Catholic Migration Commission
ICRC	International Committee of the Red Cross
ID	Iraqi Dinar
IDMC	Internal Displacement Monitoring Centre
IDP	Internally Displaced Person
IFHS	Iraq Family Health Survey
ILO	International Labour Organization
IMF	International Monetary Fund
IOM	International Organization for Migration
IPCC	Iraq Property Compensation Commission
IRC	International Rescue Committee
IRCO	Iraqi Red Crescent Organization
IRIN	Integrated Regional Information Networks
JD	Jordanian Dinar
KDP	Kurdistan Democratic Party
MoDM	Ministry of Displacement and Migration
MOU	Memorandum of Understanding
MRG	Minority Rights Group
MSF	Médecins Sans Frontières
NGO	Non-governmental organizations
NIC	[US] National Intelligence Council

OCHA	Office for Coordination of Humanitarian Affairs
OECD	Organisation for Economic Cooperation and Development
ORHA	Office of Reconstruction and Humanitarian Assistance
PKK	Kurdistan Workers' Party
PUK	Patriotic Union of Kurdistan
SANA	Syrian News Agency
SIGIR	Special Inspector General for Iraq Reconstruction
TPR	Temporary Protection Regime
UNAMI	United Nations Assistance Mission for Iraq
UNDP	United Nations Development Programme
UNESCO	United Nations Educational, Scientific and Cultural Organization
UNFPA	United Nations Fund for Population Activities
UNHCR	United Nations High Commissioner for Refugees
UNICEF	United Nations Children's Fund
UNRWA	United Nations Relief and Works Agency (for Palestinian Refugees)
USCCB	United States Conference of Catholic Bishops
VOI	Voices of Iraq, an independent news agency
WFP	World Food Programme
WHO	World Health Organization

List of tables

Table 1	Estimates of Iraqi exiles (mugtarabin)	5
Table 2	Iraqis in Jordan: household wealth and employment of household heads	46
Table 3	Employed status of Iraqis in Jordan	46
Table 4	Recognition rates for Iraqis in the EU in 2006	106
Table 5	UNHCR presence in relation to the Iraq operation	120

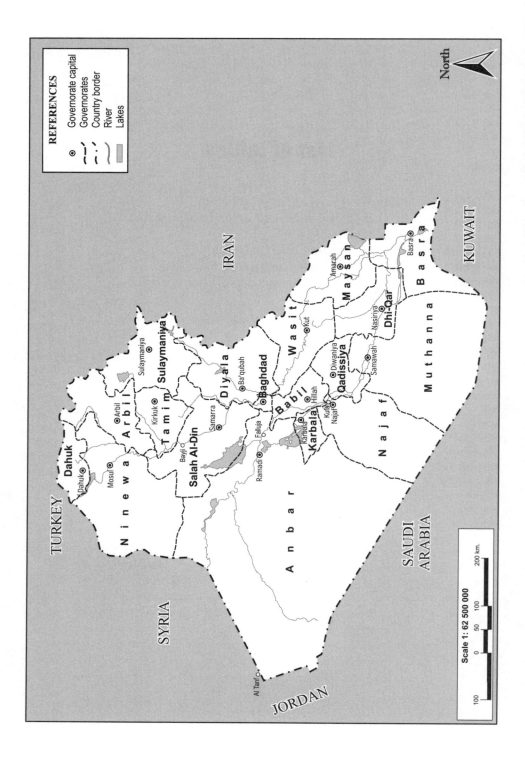

Introduction

The crisis of Iraq's refugees and internally displaced persons (IDPs) was not a surprise. Humanitarian agencies and parts of the media had warned, months before the United States (US)-led invasion began, that there would be a major displacement of Iraq's population; a humanitarian crisis would erupt as a direct effect of the war or as a result of an ethnic conflict, and both could lead to widespread abuse of human rights.[1] United Nations (UN) documents before the 2003 invasion pointed out that almost 60 per cent of the population was highly dependent on food rations and warned that the existing centralized system of food, water and sanitation would be severely disrupted.[2] An American press report five months before the war quoted UN officials who stated that Iraq was much weaker than in 1991 and that there could be a major wave of refugees to neighbouring countries, and cautioned that the majority of the population in Baghdad would have no access to clean water or electricity.[3]

Unfortunately, the US and its allies did not heed these warnings. As a result about 2.7 million people have been internally displaced and more than two million people have exited the country in search of refuge. The displaced Iraqis – 4.7 million people – are the largest displaced group worldwide, and the third largest refugee population in the world (after Afghans and Palestinians).[4] That means that more than 15 per cent of Iraq's population has been displaced, one out of every six.

Toppling Saddam Hussein and the Ba'th regime ended 35 years of dictatorship and 12 years of harsh international sanctions against Iraqis. The root causes of Iraq's mess after 2003 cannot be seen in isolation from the events and developments during Saddam's era. Iraq, in fact, had not experienced a 'normal' state of affairs for almost three decades: the carnage and disaster of the 1980–88 Iran–Iraq War; the 1991 Gulf War; the uprising in the south following the 1991 war; the numerous savage attacks on the Kurds in the north and the Shi'i in the south; and finally more than a decade of sanctions. The militarization of the economy and the Ba'th policy of concentrating power among a minority of clans and groups turned the state into the biggest single employer, and a system of economic patronage was established, reporting to Saddam himself and his close entourage.[5] The Ba'th party fostered feelings of paranoia, xenophobia and distrust to create a hegemonic state.[6]

Neither the war with Iran in the 1980s nor the Gulf War in 1991, followed by more than a decade of sanctions, led to reform or the internal collapse of Saddam's regime, but left the mass of the population in a dire situation. This is an important point to keep in mind and it will be re-examined in Chapter 6. It was only the end of the Ba'th regime that heralded the collapse of the state and the disintegration of its institutions. This was exacerbated by the US lack of pre-planning before the invasion and the mismanagement of the country post-April 2003. The result was a dysfunctional government and a political system that rewards identity politics. Intolerance, sectarianism and tribalism spread and a few power blocs began to control the country.

Sectarianism and tribalism were used as political tools at different times throughout Iraq's modern history, but rarely to the extent witnessed following the invasion. During the British Mandate, favouring one sectarian group over another was part of the divide and rule strategy. However, as Batatu explained in his classic book on the social classes of Iraq:

> Sunnī-Shī'ī [sic] dichotomy coincided to no little degree with a deep-seated social economic cleavage . . . Of course, Sunnī social dominance had its immediate roots in the preceding historical situation [i.e. Ottoman rule].[7]

Violence is also not new to Iraq. The country witnessed many bloody coups d'état before Saddam rose to power, and then during his reign violence became an integral part of running the country. Iraqi intellectuals who fled the Ba'th regime wrote about violence and its impact on daily life in Iraq, and how violence affected both the instigators and victims from social, cultural and psychological points of view.[8] After the 2003 war, the social cohesion of Iraqi society broke down as a result of the cumulative effect of suicide bomb attacks, kidnappings, killing and torture. The internecine civil war affected everyone in society and shattered existing principles of civility and humanity. Values such as pride and honour, sacrosanct in Iraqi society, became tools of degradation in this unrelenting war. In Iraq, as in other international conflicts and civil wars, sexual violence was used to torture and humiliate people and to punish or shame families or communities. Each group was committing acts of violence or revenge to such an extent that Iraqis have become deeply traumatized. As one Iraqi poet living in Syria wrote:

> Every time I return in a dream to my country to see my family and friends, the dream changes into a terrifying nightmare, with deadly pursuits across landscapes, filled with land mines and guns.[9]

During Saddam's era in the 1990s, Iraq also witnessed large waves of migration and brain drain from its territories as a result of brutal Ba'th policies and the deterioration in economic conditions during the 1990s. Some might even argue that Iraq's exodus and brain drain after 2003 is just a continuation of the pre-invasion period and thus it is not a real 'crisis'. However, there are fundamental differences. The state under the Ba'th regime functioned despite being constrained by severe and inhumane sanctions. The occupation authorities, on the other hand, dismantled the key pillars of the state before setting up new ones. As a result, many parts of the functioning machine imploded, leading to a dramatic degradation in the provision of essential services, health care, education and the civil service. Corruption, which existed before, spread and permeated all levels of government. There is no doubt that the decline in all vital sectors began in the 1990s, but after the invasion the state could barely function. Many countries that have undergone military and civil conflicts have a lot in common with the situation in Iraq. The following description of some African countries is not dissimilar from Iraq:

> Although the state dominates the social scene, it is itself an extremely weak and fragile organization with a very limited capacity for managing society and directing change.[10]

Why do people abandon their homes for an uncertain life elsewhere? Two academics tried to understand the reason and their short answer was violence. They argued that:

> People monitor the violent behavior [sic] of both the government and dissidents and assess the threat such behavior poses to their lives, physical person, and liberty. The greater the threat posed by the behavior of the government and dissidents, the larger the number of forced migrants a country will produce.[11]

The World Health Organization (WHO) defines a 'humanitarian crisis' as when four things take place: dislocation of population; destruction of social networks, including destruction of health and social systems; insecurity; and abuse of human rights.[12] All four happened in Iraq post-2003, and the common denominator of these four characteristics is violence. A good definition of refugees is therefore 'persons whose presence abroad is attributable to a well-founded fear of violence'.[13] In spite of Iraq's violent history, nothing in the past has prepared Iraqis for being refugees, and hence many of them found it difficult to adapt to their new 'homes'. Iraqis, in general, abhor the word 'refugee' (*laji'*) as they see it as a term indicating failure and the need to seek support and help from others. They also associate the word refugee with Palestinians and Afghans living in camps, and prefer the Arabic term *'mugtarab'* living in *'manfa'* (the one living in a foreign country – exile). As Edward Said explains, 'the word "refugee" has become a political one, suggesting large herds of innocent and bewildered people requiring urgent international assistance, whereas "exile" carries with it, . . . , a touch of solitude and spirituality'.[14] In this book, although both terms are used, the word refugee is predominant since it is the term used by all humanitarian and government organizations. However, the term is used somewhat loosely here. Whereas in the strict legal sense, the term 'refugee' refers only to an individual who, 'owing to well-founded fear of being persecuted for reasons of race, religion, nationality, membership of a particular social group or political opinion, is outside the country of his nationality',[15] this book employs a more general use of the term to include, for example, those who have fled from generalized violence. Furthermore, since separate statistics do not exist, most of the numbers relating to Iraqi refugees in this book include those who fled the country pre- and post-2003, and some of those in both groups may have left primarily for economic reasons.

People are forced to move in order to survive because their state is unable to meet their basic requirements and the presence of the victims abroad may be the result of 'flight to avoid harm or the result of expulsion, itself a form of violence'.[16] As will become clear later on, the Iraqi state was unable to take care of its people and in particular the displaced population. As Marfleet put it:

> It is the cumulative effect of pressures on the Iraqi population that is the key to understanding recent patterns of movement. Living standards have declined steadily since 2003, while new crises of security have led more and more Iraqis to seek 'exit'.[17]

Iraqi society has been transformed by violence and the pervasiveness of deep mistrust amongst its population. The ties, fragile as they were, that held society together, began unravelling with the explosion of ethnic violence: 'The result of this fracturing of state and society has been the devolution of power to localities and militias and the hardening of communal identities.'[18] The armed militias filled the vacuum in humanitarian assistance as the national government lacked the skills and resources to take care of their internally and externally displaced populations.

Dysfunctionality, coupled with Iraq being in the midst of a civil war for almost 18 months from February 2006 to summer 2007, created the largest displacement of population in the Middle East since 1948. As violence engulfed Iraq, it triggered the internal and external displacement of hundreds of thousands. As the Swedish Minister for Migration and Asylum Policy put it:

> 'Exodus' is a word that should be used with caution. Yet, when one observes the movement of Iraqis towards neighbouring countries, 'exodus' remains an apt description.[19]

Apart from the 2.7 million IDPs, violence and dire economic conditions drove another 2.1–2.4 million Iraqis to flee their country. While there are no exact statistics, Table 1 provides estimates of Iraqi refugees abroad.

Table 1: Estimates of Iraqi exiles (mugtarabin)

Host Country	Numbers
Syria	1,200,000–1,400,000
Jordan	450,000–500,000
Saudi Arabia & Gulf States	200,000
Yemen	70,000
Egypt	80,000–100,000
Iran	57,000
Lebanon	50,000
Turkey	6,000–10,000
Sweden	40,000
USA	6,000

Sources: UNHCR, *Iraq Situation*, April 2008; UNHCR, *Global Appeal 2008–2009*; Fafo Survey, 2007; *IRIN* 2007; *World Refugee Survey 2007*; Human rights first 2008; Interviews 2008.

Note: Numbers for Sweden and the USA refer strictly to post-2003 refugees, while for the rest there is no breakdown of pre- and post-war numbers.

The refugee movement, which began in 2004, gathered momentum throughout the next three years and peaked in late 2006.

What makes the Iraqi refugee crisis unique is the fact that many of the refugees were urban, educated middle class who fled to large urban areas, making it extremely difficult for humanitarian agencies to provide the right services and to collate accurate information from an 'invisible' refugee population. The well-off and educated were amongst the first to leave (similar to other countries which witnessed violence or fundamental changes of regime), followed by the middle class. The most vulnerable and poor (again as in other countries) stayed behind because they lack the resources to leave. Most of the earlier refugees were Sunnis and non-Muslim minorities, but as violence spread throughout the country, large numbers of Shia were also left with no option but to leave. By 2006, the refugee movement encompassed all religions and sects. In a way, the horrors of civil war and ethnic cleansing unite those refugees, and it is critical to remember that 'all refugees escape various forms of misery, leaving behind them relatives, friends, possessions' and that fundamental to their stories must be 'the central theme of loss'.[20]

The implications of Iraq's exodus could be far reaching: 'Just as the displacement of the Palestinians has influenced the politics and security of the region, and indeed of the world, for almost 60 years, the impact of the Iraqi refugee population will be felt by the international community for a long, long time.'[21] World history tells us that whenever there are large numbers of refugees, forced out from their country, instability follows. It would be correct to say that the Iraqis are not in the same position as the Palestinians after 1948, but it would be wrong to assume that the existence of such a relatively large population in two countries – Syria and Jordan – that are not willing to integrate them will be without any repercussions.

The fragmentation of Iraq's population has serious implications not only for the country but for the whole region. Iraq's relationship with its neighbouring countries and the Arab world underwent dramatic changes following the occupation, and there is no doubt that this will have an important impact on the balance of power in the Middle East for years to come. In addition, the fact that almost two million Iraqis fled to neighbouring countries and constitute about 9 per cent of Jordan's and roughly 7 per cent of Syria's population will gravely affect those countries, particularly in times of political or economic instability. The sheer number of refugees in Jordan and Syria may affect the geo-political situation in the Middle East, an area already plagued with uncertainty and discord. In general, all host countries in the region are extremely worried about Iraq's ethnic polarization and the potential contagion effects. They feel nervous of having all those Iraqis in their midst and fear they could disrupt their social fabric. These countries are also anxious that the refugees will never return to Iraq as many have lost their homes and jobs.

There are many similarities in the situation of the Iraqis living in those countries (Syria, Jordan, Egypt and Lebanon): except for Egypt, no country has ratified the 1951 Convention relating to the Status of Refugees and even Egypt has inserted so many reservations that in reality, the Iraqis do not have many rights as refugees; all four countries were and are still wary of the Iraqi population and thus very little is being done to integrate it; employment opportunities are scarce and the majority of Iraqis work in the informal economy of those countries; and as we will see, the state of most of those in exile – economically, educationally and from a health point of view – has regressed and this will not bode well for the future of the region.

The parallels between the Iraqi and Palestinian refugees are not just in the minds of these governments but among the vast majority of the Arab world. The fact that Iraqis are not living in camps is by no means a guarantee for more integration or less extremism: 'The memory of Palestinian refugee camps in Arab consciousness is undoubtedly a factor in the urban settlement pattern of Iraqi refugees in Jordan and Syria.'[22]

A modus vivendi has evolved between the Iraqi refugees and their hosts: on the one hand, the governments of Syria, Jordan and Lebanon are fearful that the Iraqis are similar to the displaced Palestinians of 1948 and 1967 and will end up staying permanently; on the other hand, the Iraqis are fearful of being deported or of new measures that will make their livelihoods even harder. How long will this arrangement last? No one really knows as it would be significantly affected by the internal situation in those countries and the political-economic developments in the region.

The displacement of Iraqis has increased Sunni–Shi'i tensions and there is no doubt that this has raised alarm in all Arab countries. How will this affect the region in the future? Again, the answer to this question depends largely on regional developments – particularly with Iran, and the coexistence of Sunnis and Shia in a unified Iraq.

This study begins by looking at the internal displacement in order to put the external displacement in context. It then considers the situation of the Iraqi refugees who left their country after the 2003 war in their different host countries – Jordan, Syria, Egypt, Lebanon and Sweden – with a brief look at other countries. The book examines the plight of these refugees, their predicaments, their economic conditions and social networks. Threaded through these chapters is an examination of the repercussions of exile on women, children, education, health and the economic impact of the Iraqis on their host countries. The reactions of the Iraqi government and the governments of the neighbouring countries are analysed. The book also discusses the role of the international organizations and non-governmental organizations (NGOs) in helping the refugees. Iraq's economy is assessed in light of the brain drain that took place, and corruption in Iraq is analysed to gain an understanding of how the current system in central and northern Iraq is operating. Finally, the book addresses the question of return and the prospects of the refugees as they return from exile.

Chapter 1

Internal displacement

> Oedipus: *What sort of cleansing? And this disaster – how did it happen?*
> Creon: *By banishment – or atone for murder by shedding blood again.*
> *This blood brings on the storm which blasts our state.*[1]

The main focus of this book is on those Iraqis who have fled the country, rather than those who have been displaced internally. However, the internal displacement is intertwined with the external in a number of ways; it is the same violence and the same economic situation that have caused people to flee their homes, whether to another location within Iraq or across the border to another country.

This chapter examines the situation in Iraq since the 2003 invasion. It considers the internal displacement and its effect on the country; explores the violence and its consequences for women, children, health and education; assesses the situation of minorities; and lastly reviews the reactions of Iraq's government and politicians.

Internal displacement

The history of internal displacement in Iraq dates back to long before the 2003 invasion. Under Saddam Hussein, expulsion of people from their homes was a state policy intended to punish recalcitrant populations. Ethnic cleansing was a central part of the Ba'th regime's policy towards certain minorities, in particular the Kurds. Displacement prior to 2003 took place in north and south Iraq throughout different periods. Accurate statistics do not exist on the displacement that took place during Saddam's era due to the regime policy of systematically controlling and manipulating information. For the north, estimates of the number of IDPs were between 630,000 and 800,000 individuals.[2] During the period 1974–87, 46 per cent of the population were thought to have been expelled as part of the Arabization campaign, and another 28 per cent were victims of the *Anfal* campaign which occurred in 1988.[3] In the south and central regions of Iraq, estimates of IDPs stood at around 300,000 to

400,000 individuals as the Marsh Arabs and Shia were targeted by the regime.[4] In all areas, expulsions were based on wielding overwhelming power or threats of using force unless targeted families comply with the wishes of the regime's security agencies. In certain instances, large-scale projects such as the draining of the southern marshes were implemented in order to accomplish political aims. Another procedure used during the expulsion process was the confiscation of property and ration cards. A testimony recorded by a UN agency describes the typical experience of a family subjected to forced displacement:

> Once the decision is taken to expel a family, Baath [sic] Party members present themselves at the residence of that particular family and order them to leave the area within 24 to 48 hours. In order to ensure that the family will effectively move, Baath Party members usually withhold the identification cards of the members of the family. In some cases a member of the family is put in detention in order to accelerate the process. Once the family is ready to leave their home, they need to pass by the local police station and fill in a form stating that they are voluntarily changing their residence. Their identification cards are only then returned to them and if a member of the family was detained, only then is he or she released.[5]

Often, these families left all their property and belongings due to the short notice they were given to leave. This issue is critical to understand and Chapter 7 will deal with the question of property claims.

The factors behind the displacement were not just due to the policy of the regime. 'They go to the heart of the struggle for power in Iraq, to the fundamental issues of Iraqi politics: water, land, oil, minority and majority rights, citizenship and national allegiance.'[6]

In the immediate aftermath of the invasion in 2003, and contrary to UN and US expectations, there were no major displacements of population. Internal displacement after the fall of Saddam can be divided into three phases: from May 2003 to February 2006; from the destruction of Al-Askariyya Mosque (the shrine of the Two Imams) in Samarra on 22 February 2006 until the summer of 2007; and finally the phase where the surge of American troops began to lead to a reduction in violence.

In the first phase, displacement was caused mainly by military campaigns against insurgents by the US-led forces and their Iraqi allies, and internal communal tensions which began to bubble to the surface. A growing number of Iraqis fled Baghdad's neighbourhoods and suburbs, especially mixed areas, to move to areas in which their own community predominated. This pattern began in early 2004, gathered momentum in 2005 and intensified in 2006. A journalist reported in November 2005 that the 'deep divides that have long split Iraqi society have violently burst into full view'.[7] But even the reporter felt that the 'evidence is so far mostly anecdotal'.[8] The Iraqi government and media paid very little attention to these outbursts of sectarian violence, and apart from some international organizations, there was little or no focus on the displacement of population.[9]

Another reason for displacement during the first phase was the return of Iraqi refugees (mainly from Iran) who had fled the country during Saddam's era and felt secure to return. United Nations High Commissioner for Refugees (UNHCR) estimated that 300,000 Iraqis had returned to the country.[10] While an American report boasted that US-funded programmes helped approximately 300,000 refugees 'reintegrate into their communities between 2003 and 2006',[11] a survey by a UN mission found that in 2004, 65 per cent of 56,700 returning refugees found themselves in a situation of internal displacement.[12]

UNHCR was providing assistance to returnees, and noted that 'return is complicated by scarce resources and prevailing instability'.[13] During 2004 and 2005, 80 per cent of the returnees in northern Iraq and more than 35 per cent in the south 'ended up internally displaced upon return', mainly due to lack of housing, social services and growing unemployment.[14]

Major military operations such as the siege of Falluja in November 2004 led to the vast displacement of almost 200,000 civilians over a ten-day period. Needless to say, mechanisms providing health care and water broke down during these military operations.[15] Some displacements were short-term and civilians returned to their homes at the cessation of military operations; others, such as in Falluja, endured a more prolonged displacement.[16] Meanwhile, attacks on minorities began to occur, paving the way later for more intensified ethnic cleansing. A report as early as November 2004 indicated that 350 Assyrian Christian families wanted to move back to homes in northern Iraq out of fear, following 'two coordinated attacks on Christian churches, one in August against five churches, four in Baghdad, one in Mosul and another attack in October on up to seven churches'.[17]

In the face of growing sectarian violence and attacks on minorities, institutional restraints began to erode. At the end of 2005 one report succinctly summed up the year: '2005 will be remembered as the year Iraq's latent sectarianism took wings, permeating the political discourse and precipitating incidents of appalling violence and sectarian cleansing.'[18] During that year, a growing insurgency with Sunni Arab overtones, feeding on Sunni dissatisfaction with the Americans and the interim Iraqi government, increasingly destabilized the country.

The pervasiveness of violence caused intolerance and mistrust to spread, particularly among the youth. This culminated in the bombing of Al-Askariyya Mosque in February 2006, thus opening the second and more intensified phase of displacement. Sectarian violence became the leading cause of displacement as people were being forced from mixed areas to single-sect ones. Numbers of displaced families began to increase exponentially. According to the Iraqi Red Crescent Organization (IRCO), the number of IDPs increased from about 46,000 in March 2006 to roughly 200,000 by August 2006 and to 400,000 by the end of the year.[19] It is important to keep in mind that tracking and identifying displacement in Iraq was challenging due to the absence of massive population movements and big camps: 'People were fleeing on a daily basis, often family per family and taking refuge in relatives' homes and within host-communities.'[20] Unlike the first phase when a good percentage of Iraqis managed to return to their homes at the end of military operations in their areas, large numbers during the second phase realized that the chances of return were very slim and families began to try to sell their homes.[21]

By mid-2006, the forced displacement of Iraq's population had become, as in other civil wars, a deliberate strategy of the warring parties. Displacement became an objective in the military struggle between the Sunnis and Shia: 'a way of consolidating territorial and political control'.[22] The insurgency in Iraq had developed, in the words of one observer, into a 'war after the war' that divided the country and essentially created a full-scale civil conflict,[23] and the dispossessed became the hapless pawns caught up by 'ethnic cleansing'.

There were five categories of people being displaced by sectarian violence:

1) Sunnis from Shi'i majority areas
2) Shia from majority Sunni areas
3) Sunnis and Shia settled by the Ba'th in Kurdish areas
4) Minority groups from both Sunni and Shi'i areas
5) Sunnis from conflict areas between insurgent and US forces.[24]

A good description of the state of affairs that prevailed in Iraq was provided in a testimony to the Senate Armed Service Committee by Lt. Gen. Michael Maples, Head of the US Defense Intelligence Agency:

> The perception of unchecked violence is creating an atmosphere of fear, hardening sectarianism, empowering militias and vigilante groups, hastening a middle-class exodus, and shaking confidence in government and security forces. The sectarian violence, an inexperienced and weak central government, immature institutions, problems in providing basic services, and high unemployment are encouraging more Iraqis to turn toward sectarian groups, militias, and insurgents for basic needs, threatening the unity of Iraq. Moreover, robust criminal networks act as insurgent and terrorist force multipliers. Many Sunni Arabs, motivated by fear, financial incentive, perceptions of marginalization, and exclusion from Iraqi government and security institutions, act as insurgent sympathizers, capable of supporting the insurgency.

He then went on to assess the conflict between Sunnis and Shia:

> Conflict in Iraq is in a self-sustaining cycle in which violent acts
> increasingly generate retaliation. Insecurity rationalizes and justifies
> militias, in particular Shi'a [sic] militias and increases fears in the Sunni
> Arab community.[25]

The number of internally displaced individuals continued to mount
steadily; according to IRCO there were 2.2 million by October 2007 and this
number of IDPs oscillated slightly until March 2008. Other agencies had a similar estimate of 2.25 million in September 2007 (800,000 in the northern
provinces, 740,000 in the central provinces and 715,000 in the southern
provinces).[26] However, a report by the IDP Working Group (whose members
are UNHCR, the International Organization for Migration (IOM) and other
UN agencies) estimated that by the end of March 2008 there were 2.78 million
IDPs and that although displacement is at a lower pace compared with 2006,
secondary displacement has been reported in Baghdad.[27] Some of the displaced tried their luck by moving to Kurdistan. According to UNHCR in Arbil,
there were about 40,000 displaced families (an average family is composed of
six individuals) in the Kurdish areas. Out of those 240,000 IDPs, only 30,000
were Iraqi Arabs, while the rest were Kurds escaping from Mosul and southern
Iraq. Iraqi Arabs moving to Kurdistan face many hurdles: each family must
have a Kurdish guarantor residing in the city where they want to move to and
the guarantee (*kafala*) is renewed every two months. In Camp Kalawa on the
outskirts of Sulaymaniya, I saw scattered tents in a small, squalid area where
about 60 Arab families reside. Opposite the camp, there was a dilapidated
block of flats where Kurdish IDPs live.[28] It is important to keep in mind that
some of the figures show many families move twice or thrice based on availability of city services or schools for their children.[29] Statistics on the displaced
families indicate that the majority came from Baghdad and its suburbs (69 per
cent), followed by the province of Diyala (15 per cent) and then Anbar (7 per
cent); 64 per cent of the displaced are Shia, 32 per cent are Sunnis and 4 per
cent are Christians.[30] By early 2008, there were 1.2 million displaced people in
the capital and 58 per cent of them were children under the age of 15.[31]

The third phase of displacement began towards the end of September 2007
when three developments led to a reduction in violence: the increased number
of American troops on the streets of Baghdad; a huge increase in the number
of Sunni Arabs who have turned their guns on jihadists instead of American
troops due to tactical alliances between some Sunni tribes and US forces; and
finally a six-month halt to military action by the Shi'i militia leader Moqtada
Al-Sadr. By then, segregation in the fullest sense had already taken place and
was most evident in Baghdad. It was reported by a US official that whereas

Baghdad had a 65 per cent Sunni majority in 2003, it had become 75 per cent Shi'i by September 2007.[32]

By the end of 2007, internal movement of population, in spite of the security gains, had become more difficult. Most of Iraq's 18 governorates had imposed informal and formal restrictions on IDPs' entry and residence. Additionally, the imposition of restrictive entry requirements by Iraq's neighbours actually created more pressure on internal displacement towards the north.[33] Also, new waves of displacement took place as a result of the Turkish bombing of Kurdish villages in November and December 2007 in pursuit of Kurdistan Workers' Party (PKK) rebels.[34]

It is too early to predict whether there will be a political reconciliation and the trends of lower violence will continue. At the end of 2007, the Iraqi government was reluctant to make significant concessions to the Sunnis or to include large numbers of tribal and insurgent fighters in the regular Iraqi security forces. American military leaders realized that their military gains will come to a halt without a political solution. General David H. Petraeus, the top American military commander in Iraq, cautioned in December 2007 that the reduction in attacks by 60 per cent were 'tenuous' and 'fragile' and needed political and economic progress to cement them.[35] Analysts warn that Iraq is in the midst of a cease-fire rather than a transition to lasting peace, and that all the recent changes may be reversed.[36]

Violence

In a survey by the International Organization for Migration (IOM), 63 per cent of those assessed reported that they fled as a result of direct threats to their lives and over 25 per cent said they had been forcibly displaced from their property; 89 per cent of those targeted said it was due to their religious/ sectarian identity.[37] The most common factor for both those who have been internally displaced and those who have fled the country is violence. To understand the history of violence in Iraq is outside the scope of this book.[38] However, it is important to look at the ethnic hatred that has erupted in its ugliest form after the occupation of the country. Once the state had collapsed and its institutions, which were run mainly by a secular urban cadre, had disintegrated, ethnicity and tribalism took over.

Tribalism (*Al-qabaliyya*) and kinship underwent major changes under Saddam Hussein; from a total rejection during the early days of Ba'th, to the legitimization of the tribal system and sharing of power later in the 1990s.[39] Thus, when the state stopped functioning and violence began to rise, people turned to their communities and ethnic groups for help and protection. Interestingly, during the initial phases of occupation, only a small minority of Iraqis (4.5 per cent) questioned in a survey indicated that in choosing a political party, they should select one from their own religious group.[40] But as Marfleet wrote:

> With most Iraqis increasingly desperate about jobs, income and access to food, fuel, water and electricity, sectarian parties and communalist networks exerted a much stronger influence. In the absence of a strong state, resources came increasingly through links to family, clan, religious institutions and parties.[41]

Very few of the tribal and religious leaders fulfilled their responsibility of calming things down.[42] On the contrary, they have used sectarianism as a way of garnering and building more power. Radical armed groups were the main drivers of sectarian displacement, and as al-Khalidi and Tanner pointed out, there are many parallels between such groups on both sides. For example, both sought to spread violence in mixed neighbourhoods where inter-communal relations were previously good; and both sides used mosques for military operations.[43] As intolerance began spreading, exacerbated by the fact that Sunni and Shi'i tribal leaders were calling for revenge for members of their community killed by the other side, violence reached unprecedented levels. It is hard even to imagine the scale of the brutality and killings that were taking place.

The intensity of the violence is reflected in the dramatic increase of deaths from injuries. Overall the proportion of deaths from injuries increased from 10.5 per cent before the invasion to 23.2 per cent after the invasion. The increase was most dramatic among men between the ages of 15 and 59, where deaths from injuries more than doubled from 31.2 per cent to 63.5 per cent after the invasion and became 'the leading cause of death in this age group'.[44]

John Lee Anderson, a journalist from *The New Yorker*, filed a powerful story from Baghdad, which portrayed how frenzied revenge became uncontrollable when a man decided to avenge the killing of his brother. The man told the journalist:

> Jaafar [the killed brother] had ten fingers; each one of his fingers was worth ten *Jaish Al-Mahdi* [the Mahdi Army] guys . . . So I decided to take my revenge against a hundred of them. So far, I have taken my revenge against twenty.[45]

Not only did their mother know and support her son for his acts of revenge, but she asked him to bring her parts of the dead men's bodies to place around Jaafar's grave in order 'to be completely comforted'.[46] Sectarian hatred, violence, distrust and vendettas together formed a lethal combination that shattered neighbourhoods and towns around the country:[47]

> Here [in Sunni neighbourhoods], as in so much of Baghdad, the sectarian
> divide makes itself felt in its own deadly and destructive ways. Far more
> than in Shiite [sic] areas, sectarian hatred has shredded whatever remained
> of community life and created a cycle of violence that pits Sunni against
> Sunni as well as Sunni against Shiite.[48]

As noted in the Introduction, the social cohesion of the society has broken down, and in Iraq, as in other civil wars, sexual violence has been used to humiliate opponents. In Bosnia, for example, up to 50,000 women were subjected to sexual violence and 40 per cent of Liberia's population suffered similar abuse.[49] Although the majority of victims in these conflicts and in Iraq were women and girls, men and boys have also been targeted to achieve the same effect of humiliation. Victims of sexual violence suffer physically and psychologically and have to face the serious socio-economic consequences of being stigmatized and marginalized by their society.

Women

Before 1991, female literacy rates in Iraq were the highest in the region (only 8 per cent illiteracy in 1985) and Iraqi women were widely considered to be among the most educated and professional women in the Arab world. The 2002 Arab Development Report, based on 1995 data, ranked Iraq the highest in terms of women's empowerment. However, as Nadje Al-Ali explains, after 1991 'a radical shift took place in terms of women's diminishing participation' in labour, access to education and social services, and hence the demise of women's gains began in the 1990s.[50] Since the invasion of 2003, the political process in the country did not reverse the trend of the 1990s, and in fact, it allowed a marked deterioration in their status. Women in Iraq are, undoubtedly, one of the groups that have suffered the most since the invasion, and their ordeal came in all shapes and forms. Displacement actually brings to the forefront not only socio-economic differences but also gender differences. It not only 'underlines unequal relations between men and women but also places women and girls in extreme danger'.[51]

A report by the international women's organization, MADRE, emphasizes the sharp rise in abduction, rapes, sexual slavery and coerced withdrawal of girls from education throughout Iraq. In addition, it underscores the dramatic increase of 'honour killing'. Male relatives supposedly acting to restore 'family honour' tarnished by women's 'immoral behaviour' perpetrate these murders.[52] Another form of 'punishment' for those who are allegedly committing adultery is burning. In most cases, families report that the burnings were 'accidental'. The nature and scale of the injuries suggest that most of the burnings are deliberate and many of the bodies bear the unmistakable signs of having been subjected to intense heat. A women's organization based in Kurdistan reported that, just in Sulaymaniya, there were 400 cases of burning in 2006.[53] United Nations Assistance Mission for Iraq (UNAMI) expressed serious concerns over the rising incidence of 'honour' crimes in Kurdish areas and noted that 255 women had been killed in the first six months of 2007, three-quarters of them by burning.[54] Numbers of abductions, another form of violence against women, have also increased sharply. Although accurate statistics are not available, an estimated 3,500 women have gone missing since 2003 and it is thought that a high percentage have been traded for sex work.[55]

In general, physical violence is relatively high in Iraq. According to the Iraq Family Health Survey (IFHS) Report, more than 21 per cent of married women in Iraq experience physical violence at home, and 33 per cent suffer from emotional violence. There are marked differences, however, between Kurdistan (10.9 per cent) and southern/central Iraq, where 22.7 per cent reported at least one form of physical abuse.[56]

Iraqi women are squeezed between 'the attempt to start a new Iraq that diverges from the policies of the previous regime' and the attempt of Islamist militias to impose new policies.[57] Women are not only facing an imposition of dress codes but also the threat of gender segregation at universities.[58] In fact, violence against women has become 'a primary weapon in the arsenal of fundamentalists of various religions, who seek to impose their political agenda on society'.[59] Women interviewed by the BBC said 'they no longer dared venture on to Basra's streets without strict Islamic attire'.[60] Basra city's police chief told Integrated Regional Information Networks (*IRIN*), the UN agency dealing with humanitarian news and analysis, in an interview:

> Basra is facing a new type of terror which leaves at least 10 women killed monthly, some of them are later found in garbage dumps with bullet holes while others are found decapitated or mutilated. The perpetrators are organized gangs who work under religious cover pretending to spread instructions of Islam but they are far from this religion.[61]

On every front, the position of Iraqi women has regressed despite US and UK rhetoric about women's rights. As we will see later in Chapter 6, professional women are systematically threatened and killed.

On the educational level, the low school attendance of girls is creating a huge educational gap. According to the Ministry of Education, the ratio of girls attending schools in the southern provinces has dropped from two girls to three boys to one to four. The girls are being kept at home either due to the security problem or because they are being forced by their families to 'assist in household chores'.[62]

Prostitution has also increased dramatically (this topic and the position of Iraqi women will be further discussed in Chapters 2 and 3). As Iraqi families continue to fall on hard times, some have been forced to make the most painful of decisions: selling their daughters. According to the Organization of Women's Freedom in Iraq, 15 per cent of Iraqi women widowed by the different wars have been desperately searching for temporary marriages or prostitution, either for financial support or protection in the midst of sectarian war.[63] This 'temporary marriage' or what is called euphemistically 'marriage of pleasure' (*muta'ah*) is nothing but another cover of forcing girls into prostitution. Women are 'offered' in short-term marriage contracts for Shia during a trip to another city or pilgrimage to the holy cities of Najaf and Kerbala.[64] These 'marriages' can last from one day to six months.

Children

The youth and children of Iraq are not faring much better than the country's women. Children were the collateral damage of the conflict as the ongoing violence has had a devastating effect on them. An estimated two million children face daily threats including poor nutrition, disease and interrupted education. Iraqi children are caught in the crossfire of conflict and more than 125 children were killed and 107 injured between 2005 and the summer of 2007 in direct attacks on schools. These numbers do not include children killed or injured on their way to and from school.[65] According to UNICEF, the United Nations Children's Fund, an average of 25,000 children per month were displaced due to violence or intimidation.[66] Additionally, one in eight children dies before their fifth birthday and 9 per cent are acutely malnourished (which is double the number prior to 2003).[67] The IFHS Study Group reported that the total number of deaths of children below the age of 15 increased from 2.82 per 1,000 in 2002 to 4.37 per 1,000 after the invasion. These deaths were not only due to violence (0.34 per 1,000) but to the dramatic surge in deaths from communicable and non-communicable diseases.[68]

Given the collapse of the system, international organizations reported that four million people in Iraq need food assistance. Thus children are being forced to assume income-generating roles because their families are suffering from acute poverty.[69] Children orphaned by violence are extremely vulnerable to abuse and exploitation. Estimates of the number of orphans range from three to five million. The situation is exacerbated by the government's inaction and by bureaucratic measures such as the closures of private orphanages.[70]

There is no doubt that the daily violence and insecurity has an adverse affect on children's behaviour and psychological development. The stories of these children are heart-rending; one humanitarian worker describes the scene:

Once I was called to an explosion site. There I saw a four-year-old boy sitting beside his mother's body, which had been decapitated by the explosion. He was talking to her, asking her what had happened. He had been taken out shopping by his mom.[71]

No wonder, then, that a survey of 2,250 youngsters in a Baghdad neighbourhood by the Iraqi Ministry of Health showed that about 70 per cent of primary school pupils suffer symptoms of trauma-related stress such as bedwetting or stuttering. The Association of Iraqi Psychologists reported that, in early 2007, it was estimated that over 90 per cent of 1,000 children analysed had learning difficulties, mainly due to the climate of fear and insecurity.[72] Many children have to pass dead bodies on the streets of Baghdad and no doubt this is a hard situation for anyone, but especially for children, to adapt to.[73] The long-term impact on those children's behaviour is far from clear. An Iraqi psychiatrist accurately states that no one is 'certain what will become of the next generation, even if there is peace one day'.[74]

Traumatized young Iraqis have turned more and more to hard drugs. The Ministry of Health reported a huge increase in the consumption of drugs in the first two years after the invasion. According to the Ministry's statistics, the numbers have doubled; in suburban Baghdad the number of registered drug addicts rose from 3,000 in 2004 to 7,000 in 2005.[75]

It is not just the children's mental health that is suffering; in fact, the whole health system of the country is enduring a major crisis.

Health

Estimates of deaths during and after the 2003 war vary widely depending on the source. However, the first epidemiological survey, conducted by academics from Johns Hopkins University, of excess mortality during the 18 months after the invasion, based on cluster sample methods, indicated an excess mortality of 98,000. Over half the deaths recorded in this study were from violent causes and about half of them took place in Falluja as a result of the siege. A follow-up survey conducted in May–June 2006 (and published in *The Lancet*) estimated 654,965 excess deaths since 2003 (equivalent to 2.5 per cent of the population), of which 600,000 were due to violence and the balance of roughly 54,000 stemming from the worsening of health status and access to health care.[76] A national household survey conducted by the Iraqi government and WHO estimated that 151,000 Iraqis died as a result of violence between March 2003 and June 2006.[77] This number is below that of the previous study but much higher than the estimate of Iraq Body Count which uses media reports, whereas the two former studies were based on cluster surveys. Iraq Body Count has been criticized for underestimating the number of people killed (47,668 between March 2003 and June 2006) because its sources are not necessarily reporting all the scattered killings taking place all over Iraq.[78] Although the WHO study interviewed five times more households than *The Lancet* survey, its researchers were unable to go to more than 10 per cent of households they planned to visit, mainly in Baghdad and Anbar province, because of the violence. The other caveat about this study is that it finished only three to four months after the Samarra bombings when violence began to spread dramatically. Calculating death tolls in Iraq or in any violent conflict area has been notoriously difficult.[79] It seems that the right number for excess mortality in post-invasion Iraq is somewhere between the WHO and *The Lancet* figures.

Iraq is currently rated by WHO as a country with high adult mortality comparable to that in much poorer countries like Afghanistan, Sudan and Yemen. According to a document by the then Minister of Health, Ala'din Alwan (one of the few independent ministers with impressive professional credentials), a number of factors contributed to this state of affairs: a sharp rise in poverty; poor sanitation and water supplies; poor nutrition; a serious decline in accessibility and quality of health services; and a decline in educational enrolment and attendance.[80]

Poverty rates in Iraq increased sharply during Saddam's era. Absolute poverty increased from 25 per cent in urban areas and 33 per cent in rural areas in 1988 to 72 per cent and 66 per cent respectively by 1993.[81] A study in 2004 by the UN World Food Programme (WFP) found that approximately 21 per cent of Iraq's central/southern population were chronically poor or unable to meet their basic needs over long periods of time. By September 2004, 6.5 million people, or 25 per cent of the population, were dependent on food rations.[82] Based on a survey, which included 16 governorates, almost 60 per cent of the population were either extremely poor or poor. (The definition of extremely poor is a household spending less than $30 per annum.)[83] Needless to say the high unemployment, which will be discussed later, contributes to this poverty. As a result of household poverty, children (like orphans) are prompted to leave school to support their families.

From 1991 to 2003, access to safe drinking water in Iraq decreased. Before the 1991 Gulf War, 95 per cent of urban Iraqis and 75 per cent of the rural population had access to clean water. By 2003, these figures had declined to 60 per cent in urban areas and 50 per cent in rural areas.[84] In spite of the investments that the USA allocated to the water sector, the deterioration has continued since 2003, partly due to insurgents' attacks and partly due to mismanagement of projects. By the end of 2005 only 32 per cent of the total population had access to potable water compared with 50 per cent pre-war and only 19 per cent had sewage access compared with 24 per cent prior to the 2003 invasion.[85]

UNICEF reported that the lack of sanitation and water supply were the reasons for the outbreaks of cholera in the summer of 2006.[86]

As mentioned, Iraqi children suffer from malnutrition and there are indications that child malnutrition rates rose from 19 per cent before the 2003 invasion to 28 per cent by summer 2007.[87] Before the war, per capita protein and per capita food availability had already decreased and vitamin A deficiency existed throughout the country. Following the war, and as a result of looting and destruction, the food inspection system has been severely shaken and this has led to increased infection.[88]

Health systems in conflict settings are among the first to become disrupted in what are now called 'fragile states'. Often health systems in such countries were already weak prior to conflict and subsequently become dysfunctional as a result of conflict. In Iraq, where the health system, already weakened as a result of the two earlier wars and sanctions, has been dysfunctional since the 2003 war, access to health services is now in a catastrophic situation in the capital and across the governorates. While several immunization campaigns have been successfully undertaken by the Ministry of Health, many people, and in particular the dispossessed families, are unable to receive treatment.

The state-owned medical supply company (Kemadia) is unable to provide for the hospitals and health care centres. Similar to other governmental institutions, Kemadia has been crippled by corruption, mismanagement and lack of distribution capacity.[89] By 2006, 90 per cent of the 180 hospitals countrywide lacked basic medical and surgical supplies.[90] Médecins Sans Frontières (MSF) reported that former general hospitals are now performing complex emergency surgery with only the most basic equipment and drugs.[91] Health care facilities are also overstretched due to the increasing number of victims of violence and of the related extreme deprivation.[92] In many cases, desperate families of victims have to look for blood themselves. Agents and sellers congregate in front of hospitals and blood centres offering to sell their blood to these distressed families. In the context of very high unemployment, selling 350 cubic centimetres of blood at $20–30 was an 'attractive' option for many.[93]

Pollution is also contributing to the deterioration in health. According to the Ministry of Environment, there are up to 400 polluted sites in Iraq that are serious health hazards to the population. Ongoing violence and lack of funds are hampering clean-up efforts. An oncologist at a hospital in the capital informed *IRIN*, the UN news agency, that the number of cancer cases has increased dramatically over the past five years, partly as a result of exposure to polluted materials over the previous 25 years. The Ministry of Health maintains that about 52 per cent of all cancer patients in Iraq are children younger than five years of age.[94] A final but critical factor affecting the health system is the depletion of Iraq's human resources, whereby a very large proportion of highly-qualified health professionals have left the country. This will be discussed in more detail in Chapter 6. Health systems in a conflict setting can support a healthy life or, by their absence or ineffectiveness, can undermine it and perpetuate health inequality, as evident in Iraq post the 2003 invasion.[95]

Closely connected to the deterioration in the health system is the decline in educational enrolment and attendance. The problem of increasing poverty, declining levels of health and a failing health service affects all of the population. However, for children and young people, their consequences are particularly worrying, and are compounded by the deterioration of the educational system.

Education

The education system in Iraq was highly regarded until the early 1980s. Improvements were registered at all levels of education and primary schools achieved nearly universal enrolment. But two wars and sanctions throughout the 1990s led to a steady decline, driven by the lack of resources and politicization of the system. By 2003, one-quarter of all children were not in school, facilities were dilapidated, curricula outdated and teachers underpaid.

Following the collapse of Saddam's regime, a comprehensive study on the condition of schools in Iraq was released in October 2004 by the United Nations Educational, Scientific and Cultural Organization (UNESCO) in collaboration with the Iraq Ministry of Education and the Ministry of Higher Education & Scientific Research. Given the fact that the infrastructure of schools and universities was severely hit by the violence since the invasion, UNESCO documented the serious shortage of accommodation for schools and the need to improve those that did exist: 47 per cent of schools were partially damaged, 23 per cent were in very poor conditions and 10 per cent were totally unsafe.[96]

As the situation deteriorated in 2005 and 2006, there were reports that schools in certain communities were becoming shelters for displaced families, forcing the pupils to either remain at home or study in difficult conditions.[97] The civil war led to interruption of studying so that only 28 per cent of Iraq's 17-year-olds sat their final exams in summer 2007, and only 40 per cent of those taking the exams achieved a passing grade in south and central Iraq.[98] The enrolment of girls, as discussed previously, has dropped due to insecurity, lack of water and sanitation and the pressure on girls to support their families.

Illiteracy among the IDPs is growing. Although internally displaced children, in principle, have access to education on a par with the general population, in reality they face a number of particular problems:

1) Due to lack of documentation, refugee returnees (mainly from Iran) and IDP families face difficulties enrolling their children in schools, in particular in southern Iraq.
2) Many returnee children were born in Iran and Arabic has not been their primary language of education.
3) IDPs and returnee children usually lack grade equivalency and are therefore often placed in grades several years below their age.[99]

UNICEF estimated that in 2007 as many as 220,000 displaced children of primary school age had their education interrupted, adding to the estimated 760,000 children (17 per cent) already out of primary school in 2006.[100] For university students life has been abominable. The journey between home and university has been fraught with danger. As one student put it: 'From the moment I get out of my house, I think of inevitable death, at any moment . . . that I may not see my family again and they fear the same.'[101] There is no doubt that violence and the fear of violence has corroded educational standards in Iraq. Violence can come in the shape of intimidation as universities from Basra in the south to Kirkuk and Mosul in the north have been infiltrated by militia organizations, and female students are regularly intimidated for failing to wear the hijab.[102]

The targeting of academics and the departure of many talented professionals from the country left a huge dent in the university educational system, as will be examined later.

The violence has not only affected women and children, but the cornerstones of civil society such as health and educational systems have also been negatively impacted in a substantial way. Another group that has been severely affected is the minorities.

Minorities

Iraq's minority communities include both Muslim and non-Muslim groups. The main Muslim minority are the Turkomans, who are either Sunnis or Shia, and constitute 3–4 per cent of the population; then there are the Faili Kurds, who are Shia, and the Shabaks, also predominantly Shi'i. Non-Muslim minorities make up 4–5 per cent of Iraq's total population and include: the Chaldean (followers of the Eastern Catholic Church); Assyrians (Church of the East); Syriacs (Eastern Orthodox); and Armenians (Roman Catholics or Eastern Orthodox).

Other religious minorities include the Mandeans (or Sabean-Mandeans) who follow Gnostic traditions, Yazidis, Bahais and a handful of Jews.[103] These minorities, together with their Sunni and Shi'i neighbours, once formed the intricate fabric of Iraq's modern state.

During Saddam's era almost all of these minorities faced some kind of persecution and harassment. Apart from its war on the Kurds in northern Iraq,
the Ba'th government expelled and persecuted Kurds, Turkomans and
Assyrians and imposed a policy of 'Arabization'. Other minorities faced, at
some point or another, and, for different reasons, arbitrary arrests, mock trials
and torture.[104] Currently, these minorities find themselves on the fringes of
society, enduring endless violence and brutal attacks on their buildings and
institutions.

The Turkomans live in towns and villages in northern Iraq and are the third
largest ethnic community in Iraq after Arabs and Kurds. Although they suffered alongside the Kurds during Saddam's *Anfal* campaign, they are now
under tremendous pressure from the Kurds to support them in what is called
'the battle for Kirkuk'. The Kurds want the city to be part of Kurdistan and the
Arabs have sworn that the city will never be a Kurdish one. A referendum on
the fate of the oil-rich city has been postponed a few times, but unfortunately
for the Turkomans they are squeezed from both sides, each of which is hoping
that Turkoman support will swing the balance of power in its favour.[105] Kirkuk
was relatively peaceful in the first two years after the fall of Saddam, but since
2005 the city has been witnessing an increase in bloodshed as political tensions
rise: 'The wave of violence is terrifying residents and testing to the limit their
fragile relations among its Kurdish, Arab and Turkoman residents.'[106]

In a statement to a UN working group on indigenous populations, the Iraqi
Turkmen [sic] Human Rights Foundation pleaded to the UN to intervene to
stop the violence against Turkomans: 'Ethnicity should not be consecrated as
the basis for territorial division.'[107] The Foundation claimed that in the
Turkoman district of Telafer, there have been 1,350 killed and 2,650 wounded,
thousands arrested and a large number of houses demolished or robbed and
4,685 families forced to move to other cities.[108]

The other Muslim minority, the Faili Kurds, have lived in Iraq since the days
of the Ottoman Empire. Many of the Faili Kurds were successful merchants
and businessmen, and under the Ba'th regime they were targeted, stripped of
their citizenship and a large number of the community was expelled to Iran.
The Ba'th government claimed they were Iranians and therefore had no right
to be citizens of the country. After the fall of Saddam, the Faili Kurds living in
Iran began to return to Iraq, hoping to regain their citizenship and recover the
homes they had lost. But their ethnicity and religion (and lack of documents)
are once again exposing them to violations of their human rights.[109]

Attacks on religious minorities began, as we saw before, soon after the invasion and accelerated in the next three years. Christian business owners have
been targeted systematically; shops selling alcohol, owned almost exclusively
by Christians and Yazidis, have been bombed and looted.[110] Following threats
by Islamic extremists, 95 per cent of these shops were closed, though some

reopened in September 2007 following the lull in violence.[111] Attacks on churches and Christian-owned buildings such as schools were planned so as to have maximum impact. A rocket attack was launched against a convent in Mosul as early as 2003, and on a Sunday in August 2004, there were almost simultaneous attacks on four Christian churches in Baghdad and Mosul.[112]

The Patriarch of the Chaldean Church complained that the forced expulsion of Christians, particularly in southern Iraq, has not encountered any serious reaction from the Iraqi government or the USA. In an interview with the Iraqi newspaper *Azzaman*, he remarked that there are only 400 Christians left in Basra out of 35,000 before the 2003 invasion, and estimated that 250,000 Christians have fled the country. In March 2008, the Archbishop of the Chaldean Church in Mosul was killed after being kidnapped a few weeks earlier and all attempts to negotiate his release failed.[113] According to the Patriarch, the Iraqis and Americans are unwilling to halt the campaign taking place in Baghdad to force the Christians either to convert to Islam or pay the special tax for non-Muslims (*jizya*) and abandon their homes.[114] One Christian resident of the Dora neighbourhood in Baghdad, in which many Christians lived, described his ordeal:

> I saw a family being killed in front of me because they refused to leave their home. Insurgents shot dead the couple, an elderly woman and two children and left a message by their side saying that it [the killing] was just to show what would happen if any other [Christian] family insisted on remaining in the Dora district.[115]

According to a local Christian association, some Christian children had been kidnapped since 2005 by Sunni insurgents and were used either to fight the Shi'i militias and US troops or to finance the purchase of weapons through the ransoms paid for their release.[116]

The exact number of Christians who have fled Iraq is hard to determine. A spokesman for the Christian Peace Association said that about 450,000 Christians remain in Iraq out of 800,000 estimated before the 2003 invasion. The Association stated that nearly half have left the country and the other half are still in Iraq because they cannot flee or they have been denied visas to other countries.[117] A large number of Christians managed to flee to Jordan and Syria, as we will see in Chapters 2 and 3. As one senior Christian in the Kurdish regional government predicted, 'if it continues as it has, Baghdad and Mosul will be emptied of Christians'.[118] Wijdan Mikhail, a Christian, who was appointed in the first Iraqi government after the fall of the Ba'th regime as Minister of Human Rights, argued that the country is losing its Christians:

The process started before the war but it has accelerated. In the schools the
children say that a Christian is a *kaffir* [unbeliever], that he is different from
the Muslims. And that means he can be treated differently. In 20 years there
will be no more Christians in Iraq.[119]

The situation for the Mandeans has also deteriorated markedly since the
invasion and is exacerbated by the fact that their religion forbids the use of
violence or carrying of weapons and therefore its adherents are effectively prevented from defending themselves. Traditionally the Mandeans work as gold
and silversmiths and religious rulings (fatwas) have been issued by Sunni
teachers claiming they are 'impure'. In Baghdad the number of Mandean
families in April 2003 was 1,600 and in Nasiriya 950, but by April 2006, the
numbers shrank to 150 and 320 families respectively.[120]

The Yazidis also had their share of suffering. In August 2007, four suicide
truck bombers struck at least two villages, killing close to 600 including many
children.[121] But even before that, the community endured a spate of assassinations and kidnappings. The sect, the majority of whom live in northern Iraq,
is under pressure from both Arab and Kurdish Muslims who want them to
convert to Islam. A radical Sunni Arab group issued a fatwa that 'Yazidis should
be killed wherever found'.[122] It is estimated that 70,000 Yazidis out of a total
population of 500,000 had fled the country by summer 2007.[123] The Yazidis
capitalized on the few months of relative stability in late summer 2007 to take
over the liquor stores in Baghdad after their Christian owners fled the country
to escape death threats by religious militants.[124]

Other smaller minorities, such as the Assyrians (mostly living in the north)
and the Bahais, have also been subjected to arrests and harassment
whether for religious reasons (Bahais are considered 'apostates' or heretics
under Sharia law due to their beliefs) or for territorial reasons, as in the case of
the Chaldo-Assyrians. Some of the latter's villages in the Dahuk province were
occupied by the Kurds, while others have had their houses confiscated in
Mosul.[125] The Assyrians are singled out 'for retribution because many worked
for the UN prior to 2003 and because the Americans have made use of
their skills'.[126] Many Assyrians worked as interpreters or construction workers
and commuted to the Green Zone and to US bases, and some felt betrayed by
the US lack of protection for their community. One Assyrian who worked
for the US army, but had to flee after his family was threatened, wondered 'why
doesn't the Christian world care about us? The US went to war with a Christian
rhetoric, but they left Iraq's Christians to die.'[127]

The minorities are more vulnerable than the rest of the population because
there is no 'larger tribe' or clan to protect them and they do not have militias.
When the state and society are fractured, as in Iraq today, there is devolution
of power to localities and militias, and if one neither belongs to them nor is

supported by them, then he or she will, by definition, be defenceless and susceptible to violent attacks.

The Palestinians, although theoretically not a religious minority as they are Sunni Arabs, have also been subjected to persecution and attacks. Like the minority groups, they also have no one to 'protect' them or to turn to. Palestinian refugees came to Iraq in three main waves: in 1948, in 1967 and in 1991. Their population in 2003 was estimated at 34,000 and the majority lived in Baghdad and its suburbs. Under Saddam Hussein, they received subsidized housing and, to the belief of the Shi'i in particular, preferential treatment. Thus the Palestinians were among the first victims of reprisals by Shi'i militias.

According to Human Rights Watch (HRW), the Iraqi security forces have been implicated in arbitrary arrests and killing of Palestinian refugees, some of whom have been expelled from their homes and ended up living in tents.[128] Palestinians are now obliged to register in Baghdad once a month, treated as non-resident foreigners instead of residents or recognized refugees. But as one journalist described, 'merely to approach the (Shiite-dominated) Ministry of the Interior to register is to risk kidnapping, torture and murder'.[129] The attack on Al-Askariyya Mosque in 2006 led to a wave of attacks on Palestinian housing projects in Baghdad, killing at least ten Palestinians. These assaults, abductions and tortures continued throughout 2006 and 2007.[130]

Palestinians seeking to flee Iraq face far greater obstacles than do Iraqi citizens, including other minorities. Neighbouring countries like Jordan, Kuwait, Saudi Arabia and Syria refuse to admit them. (Their plight in Jordan and Syria will be discussed in Chapters 2 and 3.) Meanwhile, Iraqi security forces and armed militias continued raiding the Palestinian compounds, driving them to head to the border. But given the closed borders, they have ended up stranded in border camps in horrendous conditions.[131] Thus, they have become second-time, and for some, third-time refugees with no end in sight.

The Iraqi Government's reactions

Given the mass internal displacement and the exodus of refugees, the deterioration in the situation of the country's women and children, the awful state of the health and education systems and the persecution of Iraq's minorities, the question that begs itself is: what have the politicians, the parliament and, to a certain extent, the media in Iraq done to ameliorate those conditions and halt the fracturing of the society?

When the USA invaded Iraq, the state collapsed and its power structures disintegrated, and there was nothing to replace them. The Americans, through the Coalition Provisional Authority (CPA), had grandiose plans which never materialized. The USA has focused principally on the insurgency and not the failed state, and there was no strategy 'to rebuild the state and end its chronic dysfunctions'.[132] When the CPA passed the mantle to the new Iraqi government, ministers began making bombastic statements about imminent improvement in services, but neither they nor the ministries over which they presided 'could deliver a fraction of what they had publicly promised'.[133]

In the context of all the problems Iraq is facing, the government has been unable to demonstrate that it has an effective ministerial structure, or the ability to govern in many areas. In an assessment by the US National Intelligence Council (NIC) made in the summer of 2007, after a marked reduction in violence compared with the previous 12 months, it lamented the fact that 'Iraq's sectarian groups remain unreconciled', and that, 'to date, Iraqi political leaders remain unable to govern effectively'.[134]

From the point of view of this book, the functionality of certain ministries is more important than others. Since violence is the fundamental reason for internal and external displacement, it is logical to start by looking at the Ministry of Interior and the Police which is under its authority. A 2007 report, prepared by a commission of retired senior US military officers and headed by retired marine General James Jones, concluded that:

> The Ministry of Interior is a ministry in name only. It is widely regarded as being dysfunctional and sectarian, and suffers from ineffective leadership. Such fundamental flaws present a serious obstacle to achieving the levels of readiness, capability and effectiveness in police and border security forces that are essential for internal security and stability in Iraq.[135]

As for the Police, the commission's conclusions were as harsh:

> The Iraqi Police Service is incapable today of providing security at a level sufficient to protect Iraqi neighbourhoods from insurgent and sectarian violence.[136]

UNAMI was concerned about continuing reports of torture and ill-treatment of detainees held at pre-trial detention facilities under the authority of the Ministry of Interior. It felt that there is 'no discernible change in approach by the Government of Iraq towards the issue of detainee abuse and the importance of holding perpetrators criminally liable for such crimes'.[137] Sectarianism had infiltrated most of the ministries and the Ministry of Interior 'had fallen under the control of the [Shi'i] militias, and the state was now being used to settle scores and run a campaign of intimidation, abductions and assassinations against innocent Sunni Arabs'.[138] Hence the Iraqis do not feel safe and secure and cannot rely on the protection of the rule of law when the ministry itself abducts rather than protects its citizens.

The other ministry that deserves our attention is the Ministry of Displacement and Migration (MoDM). The ministry was set up in August 2003 with a mandate to address the needs of refugees, IDPs and returnees (the latter in terms of repatriation, relocation, resettlement and reintegration) and to coordinate with the international agencies such as UNHCR and IOM in relation to IDPs and refugees. When it was set up, the emphasis was on Iraqis returning to Iraq, and IDPs from Saddam's era returning to their homes. But as a new crisis developed with huge numbers of new IDPs and tens of thousands fleeing the country, the effectiveness of the ministry was limited. Apart from grabbing headlines on its website defining its mandate to 'develop strategies to create durable solutions for internally displaced people in Iraq', it is difficult to see any concrete steps that had any real effect for those who had been displaced.[139] The Minister of Displacement and Migration in 2007, Dr Abed Al-Samad Rahman Sultan, wrote that the ministry has only 650 staff, including guards, yet it is responsible for a wide range of activities. He acknowledged that the ministry 'is without any administrative legacy or institutional knowledge in the field of migration and displacement'.[140]

It is also important to examine the functions of the Ministry of Health. After the departure of Dr Alwan as a minister in March 2005, other Ministers of Health brought with them the process of politicization and began administrative displacement or the deliberate transfer of mainly Sunnis to different job locations on ethnic grounds.[141] Some of the 'officials' trusted with taking care of the health of the people were arrested for the killing and kidnapping of hundreds of Sunnis, 'many of them snatched from hospitals by militias'.[142] The investigation, the first of its kind, confirmed long-standing fears by the Sunnis that hospitals had been turned into hunting grounds for Shi'i militias determined to spread fear among local Sunnis and drive them out of the capital. Apart from politicization and sectarianism which is pervasive within Iraq's government, there is another issue plaguing the system: high turnover. In its annual report, WHO in Iraq complained that between 2003 and the end of 2006, six different ministers have been appointed to lead the Ministry of Health. In addition, the 'majority of senior/middle level managers have been rotated or replaced by newly appointed officials'. The report added that in such a situation of continuous staff turnover, the ministry's 'capacity of promoting changes and reforms and to build its own capacity, has been inevitably weak'.[143]

'Capacity building' in government ministries is a key objective of consultants and international organizations currently working in Iraq. The IOM, for example, began in 2004 a programme for 'Capacity Building in Migration Management' to 'assist the Iraqi authorities in defining and aligning interministerial roles and responsibilities in the field of migration'.[144] Allawi bluntly defined the 'capacity' issue as 'the catch-all word that implied that the Iraqi government was not necessarily what it was cut out to be'.[145]

The real problem, however, is that sectarianism has become embedded in Iraq's political system, leading to paralysis and dysfunctionality. An Iraqi newspaper summed it up:

> The government of [Nouri Al-] Maliki fails the simplest test to measure the success of any government in the world. It is weaker than the militia force of any of the political factions in the country. . . . It cannot provide proper public service. It has drastically failed to reinstate security.[146]

The Iraqi parliament has also been ineffective as it has failed to pass many laws. Another Iraqi newspaper described the working of parliament by saying:

> Despite blaming the current political process and the deep disputes between political factions for the weak performance of the parliament, Iraqi legislators have a personal and collective responsibility for the delay in the adoption of many laws.[147]

The Iraqi parliament is composed of 275 members and a quorum needs 138 members. Many sessions supposedly dealing with critical issues such as violence and displacement could not take place because of the absence of a quorum.[148] A senior US military commander complained that Iraqi politicians appear out of touch with everyday citizens because they do not venture out of the Green Zone and as a result 'they don't know what the hell is going on the ground'.[149]

A tragic but critical point is that the Iraqi authorities are reluctant to recognize and admit that there is indeed a humanitarian crisis, and do so only under pressure from international organizations and media.[150] Even in September 2007, the *Azzaman* newspaper accused the government of being 'in total denial about the daily killings, the uprooting of millions of Iraqis . . . and even the imminent imploding of a whole nation'.[151] The truth is that even the Iraqi media was late in covering the unfolding tragedy and, during the years 2004–06, one can find only scant mention of the refugees' plight.

Violence in Iraq and its civil war are related to the lack of an effective rule of law. Crime, corruption (which will be discussed in detail in Chapter 6) and a dysfunctional government, all form a complex web within the realm of violence to such an extent that it is difficult to distinguish whether the perpetrators of the attacks are common criminals or are part of a militia or an extremist group.

The 2.7 million IDPs are running out of coping mechanisms given the cataclysmic circumstances since 2003. Intolerance is pervasive as in other ethnic and civil wars. A senior UNHCR official summed up his assignment in Kosovo by telling the press that 'there was from the start an environment of tolerance for intolerance and revenge. There was no real effort or interest in trying to stop it.'[152]

The same can be said of Iraq; the brutality and cruelty are beyond imagination, and as is often the case with these violent conflicts and ethnic cleansing, 'it is clear that whoever is behind the violence wants displaced people to relinquish all thought of ever returning home'.[153] Indeed, those behind the violence succeeded in fulfilling their aims.

The responses of the Iraqi government and the politicians have not been up to the challenges faced by the country. They could neither protect the millions of people who were forcibly displaced nor provide the necessary services to the population. Thus began Iraq's exodus.

Chapter 2

Iraqi refugees in Jordan

I always found the name false which they gave us: Emigrants.
That means those who leave their country. But we
Did not leave, of our own free will
Choosing another land. Nor did we enter
Into a land, to stay there, if possible for ever.
Merely, we fled. We are driven out, banned.
Not a home, but an exile, shall the land be that took us in.[1]

This chapter considers the history of Iraqi refugees in Jordan prior to the 2003 war and analyses the factors that led those Iraqis to choose Jordan as a place of refuge. It looks at the profile and characteristics of both pre- and post-2003 Iraqi refugees in Jordan and assesses the situation of women, children and minorities. It then examines the economic situation of Iraqis in Jordan and their impact on the host country, and finally appraises the response to the crisis by both the Jordanian and Iraqi governments as well as the world at large.

Historical background

Throughout the 1990s hundreds of thousands of Iraqis fled their country, mainly due to Saddam's brutal repression of Iraqi Shia and Kurds. Iran took the bulk of those refugees but by 1995, Iraqis also began to head to Jordan either to settle there or to use Jordan as a transit base to other countries. Although there are no accurate statistics on Iraqi refugees in Jordan before the 2003 war, it was estimated that by 1996 there were 100,000 Iraqis. By 2003, their numbers were put at 250,000 to 350,000 and only 30,000 were legally permanent residents in Jordan.[2]

Jordan has the highest ratio of refugees to total population of any country in the world,[3] and is host to the largest number of Palestinian refugees under the mandate of the United Nations Relief and Works Agency (UNRWA). Jordan acted generously towards these refugees, granting them fully-fledged citizenship while UNRWA provides health and education services for the

Palestinian refugee camps. An important effect of the Palestinian refugee issue from the point of view of this book is that Jordon and Syria, the two main host countries of Iraqi refugees, have not adopted the 1951 Convention, and have not devised a framework to deal with mass influxes of refugees: 'In the Arab Middle East, except for the Palestinians, forced migrants have almost been left in a legal abyss.'[4]

Géraldine Chatelard, who carried out in-depth fieldwork in 1999–2001, profiled the Iraqi refugees living in Jordan from a socio-economic perspective. Her findings, although based on a survey of about 150 individuals and specifically related to those accessing UNHCR, provide an interesting comparison with the post-2003 refugees who are the focus of this book. According to her estimates, 56.3 per cent were men and 43.7 per cent were women, and two-thirds in her survey were between 25 and 39 years old. A sizeable majority of the respondents (66.8 per cent) were Shia, followed by Christians (13 per cent) and Sunnis (11.7 per cent).[5] Many of these Iraqis were middle class, including doctors and teachers. Chatelard highlights two key points: first, the lower class or the impoverished Iraqis did not have the financial means to emigrate (this is also true of the refugees who have fled since the 2003 invasion); and second, most of the migrants pre-2003 sold all their properties and brought large amounts of money with them which indicated that they were not planning to go back to Iraq (the same cannot be said of the post-2003 refugees, many of whom were unable to plan ahead in such a way given the violent circumstances prevailing in Iraq after the invasion).

With regard to employment, only 7.2 per cent of the male respondents of Chatelard's survey indicated they did not work, but at the same time only 2.3 per cent had work permits. The majority of the men worked informally as manual workers such as cleaners or painters and the rest worked as vendors on the streets of Jordanian cities.[6] While the percentage of post-2003 refugees able to find work is much lower, the kinds of jobs done by those who have found work are strikingly similar.

By late 2002, with the signs of a new war in Iraq approaching and UN agencies predicting at least a million refugees, the Jordanian government was deeply worried that there would be a mass influx of refugees. A Jordanian Minister warned that his government 'won't allow huge floods of refugees' as 'we simply can't absorb them'.[7] Jordan indicated at the time that it would only admit refugees who were in transit to a third country.[8]

It should be noted that although Jordan is not party to the 1951 Convention relating to the Status of Refugees, its 1952 Constitution prohibited extraditing 'political refugees ... on account of their political beliefs or their defence of liberty'.[9] That in itself, however, did not change the fact that there is still no legal definition of refugees. In addition, Jordan signed in 1998 a Memorandum of Understanding (MOU) with UNHCR, affirming its commitment to the principle of non-refoulement and whereby refugees are granted temporary asylum for a maximum period of six months, renewable at the discretion of the Jordanian authorities. If this is not renewed, then they become illegal aliens, subject to daily fines and at risk of being deported.[10]

With the toppling of Saddam's regime in April 2003, a new chapter in the history of Iraqis' exodus to Jordan began. In the next sections an analysis of the reasons behind choosing Jordan, followed by a description of the characteristics of the Iraqi population in Jordan, will be presented.

Why Jordan?

The first chapter of this book has explored why so many Iraqis have fled the country, with the paramount factor being the all-encompassing violence. An Iraqi survivor of abduction and torture summed up his (and others') reasons for exiting Iraq:

> The truth is, I am someone who loves his country. I was forced to leave because of the bad security situation. In addition, there are no services, no electricity, no water, no security. I and my family and many other families were forced to leave.[11]

Additionally, as was shown in the previous chapter, all the basic services that citizens normally expect from their country had crumbled, thus creating a situation whereby leaving becomes one of the few options left.

The Hungarian writer Paul Tabori writes in his classic book *The Anatomy of Exile* that 'an exile is a person compelled to leave or remain outside his country of origin on account of well-founded fear of persecution for reasons of race, religion, nationality, or political opinion'.[12] Once a family decides to flee, the next decision is where to. The first consideration in choosing a country is whether that country will be willing to take them or at least if they have a good chance of gaining entry to that country. As we will see in Chapter 4, certain neighbouring countries were not widely considered by Iraqis due to the severe restrictions they imposed on Iraqis entering their territories. The second consideration is whether the chosen country can offer peace and stability, and has a history of treating refugees – and Iraqi refugees in particular – well. In 2004, when Iraqis began to flee their country in large numbers, Jordan did not require prior entry visas from Iraqis, treating them as it treats nationals of other friendly Arab countries such as Egypt, Yemen and the Gulf States.

The third factor in choosing a country of destination such as Jordan is the presence of relatives, family members or co-religionists. Sometimes, the unity of the family takes precedence over the safety factor to the extent that some

Iraqis returned to unsafe Iraq to reunite with their families whom they could not bring to a safe refuge. Indeed, this was an important consideration for both the pre- and post-2003 exiles. As Chatelard concluded in her survey of Iraqi refugees in 2002, 'it well seems that both the ethnic and religious affiliation of Iraqi migrants determine the direction of their migration'.[13] Even when these refugees do not intend to return to Iraq (while violence reigns), they feel comfortable being in a country close to Iraq where they can easily reunite with their relatives. A fourth reason for coming to Jordan is the hope of finding employment, particularly for young men and those with education. However, prior to 2003, Chatelard's survey indicated that the majority of migrants had a distorted vision of the economic opportunities in Jordan.[14]

Finally, some refugees came to Jordan as a transit point, with the hope of going on to a third country. After the 2003 invasion, many Iraqis, and in particular minorities such as the Christians and others who fled because they were targeted for working with the US or other Coalition forces, had high hopes of getting to Europe, North America or Australia.[15] Interestingly, surveys prior to 2003 indicated that only a minority had heard of UNHCR and its activities, and some of those who were aware of UNHCR and other international agencies were reluctant to register.[16] This is an important point to keep in mind and one which we will come across time and time again: Iraqis, similar to other refugees (particularly those who left without proper documents or whose residency status was or became illegal), are recalcitrant about identifying and 'exposing' themselves, whether to international organizations or to survey takers.

Profile and characteristics of the Iraqi refugees

In the immediate aftermath of the 2003 invasion, the first waves of Iraqis to flee were similar to the initial groups of refugees in the 1990s: businessmen and former government officials who supposedly brought with them billions of dollars. A Jordanian weekly described how Amman had become a major destination 'for Iraqis of all factions who are fleeing their country and seeking shelter from the hell of the occupation'.[17] The newspaper named politicians from Saddam's regime and post-Saddam who came to Jordan to settle down. Al-Jazeera reported from Amman that it was common to see former members of Saddam's Ba'th party climb 'out of long, black sedans and sidle into the fanciest restaurants'.[18] These wealthy Ba'th party members were dubbed 'Mercedes Refugees' by the diplomatic community and the press.[19] Two of Saddam's daughters, Rana and Raghad, also settled in Amman and, according to Al-Jazeera, Raghad shops for designer clothes and jewellery in Amman's fanciest shopping malls, 'paying cash from a black leather briefcase carried by a male Iraqi bodyguard'.[20]

One of the issues facing international humanitarian organizations and research institutions is the fact that the Iraqi refugees, unlike refugees in many other war-torn areas, are not living in camps or tents; the vast majority of them are urbanites heading to urban centres. This 'urban caseload',[21] as one organization refers to it, presents a challenge to the humanitarian NGOs as it is difficult to discern and work with a population that is totally scattered among the local population. The most comprehensive survey of Iraqis in Jordan and their characteristics was conducted by the Norwegian-based organization Fafo. The Jordanian Foreign Ministry and Department of Statistics contracted Fafo to undertake this survey, and the results were published in November 2007.[22] A few issues and caveats have emerged regarding the survey and its methodology.

The unwillingness of refugees, particularly when they do not have a legal status, to be surveyed or interviewed by any international organization or quasi-governmental agency has already been discussed. It is essential to take this into account when interpreting not only this survey but also any other set of statistics on refugees (education, health, employment, etc.). The sad reality is that for these vulnerable groups, there is very little upside in answering questions posed to them by those organizations that have no power to help them improve their situation. As a consequence, surveys such as Fafo's are skewed in favour of those less vulnerable and with the right legal status. Not surprisingly, this survey found that a high percentage of Iraqis in Jordan own their houses and have overall a higher quality of life than the average Iraqi in Jordan. The proof that the sample is slanted derives from the fact that Fafo found that among those Iraqis surveyed, 56 per cent had valid permits.[23] If it was a representative sample, this would translate into at least 250,000 Iraqis having a legal status in Jordan, and by the time of Fafo's survey that was definitely not the case. It would be reasonable to expect that a high percentage of Iraqis who have residency permits are middle-class professionals or arrived before 2003. This expectation is supported by the Fafo survey which indicates that close to 80 per cent of the wealthiest group of Iraqis have valid permits, compared with only 22 per cent of the poorest class of the population.[24]

Fear and avoidance of international organizations is not a new phenomenon in the history of Iraqi forced migrants in Jordan. During Saddam's era, for example, refugees in Jordan had serious concerns that UNHCR and other organizations were infiltrated by Iraqi agents.[25] Since the 2003 invasion, the concern is that by registering themselves or being surveyed, refugees may be exposed to the Jordanian security forces and that in turn could mean deportation.

There were also unconfirmed rumours that the Jordanian government wanted Fafo to focus on demographics rather than total numbers, 'the implication being that the government had problems with the numbers'.[26] This suspicion of 'fiddling' with the total number of Iraqis stems from the belief that the report was finished six months before publication and then negotiations between the Jordanian government and Fafo took a few months until a number was agreed. One diplomat in Amman told me that the Jordanians wanted Fafo to reflect a higher number in order to be able to receive more aid, and to counter the large number of Palestinians.[27] A Jordanian official, whom I interviewed, told me the delay was due to 'bureaucratic' matters. The same official agreed that Fafo's sample was biased towards west Amman which has more middle-class Iraqis.[28] Fafo relied on estimates given to it by the Jordanian authorities and Fafo conceded that 'it may not have been able to provide an estimate for the number of Iraqis currently in Jordan on its own'.[29] For example, Fafo used data provided to it by the Jordanian telephone companies (reaching an estimate of 481,000 residents), but these data do not differentiate 'between Iraqis on short visits on the one hand, and those who have been, or intend to stay, for longer periods of times'.[30] Another caveat is that the report ignored important aspects of Iraqis' lives in Jordan: health, prostitution and child labour. The Jordanian official responded to this criticism by saying that fertility aspects were discussed in the report but other issues such as health were not studied for 'budget reasons'.[31]

Fafo's study concluded that there were between 450,000 and 500,000 Iraqi residents in Jordan as of May 2007, 77 per cent of whom came to Jordan after the 2003 invasion. Fafo's survey showed that the vast majority (68 per cent of those surveyed) were Sunnis, 17 per cent were Shia and 12 per cent Christians, the rest being Sabeans and Yazidis.[32] The average size of an Iraqi household in the sample in Jordan is 4.1 persons, while 26 per cent are below 15 years of age and roughly 18 per cent are between 15 and 24 years of age.[33] That such a high percentage of the displaced population are children and young people has serious ramifications for education, and this will be discussed in more detail later. The population of Iraqis in Jordan is almost exclusively urban, with the majority living in the capital. Interestingly, 76 per cent of those surveyed by Fafo indicated that they came from Baghdad.

Many Iraqis have faced serious hardships since their arrival in Jordan. We will look at some sections of the population – women, children, minorities – and examine the state of health and education among all Iraqis.

Women

According to Fafo's study, 80 per cent of the economically inactive population stated their economic status as housewives, 20 per cent of households are female-headed, and these are amongst the poorest households.[34] During 2003–07, 25 per cent of Iraqi women in Jordan between the ages of 15 and 50 gave birth, and around three-quarters of these births took place in private hospitals.[35]

Iraqi women were vulnerable in Iraq and, for some, arriving in Jordan made them even more defenceless as the challenges to their survival and wellbeing intensified. The report of the Women's Commission for Refugee Women and Children on Iraqi women in Jordan was disturbing:

> Every Iraqi woman the Women's Commission interviewed said they knew women who were experiencing violence at home and that the problem is getting worse – a result of the stressful frightening and increasingly desperate situation families are in. They also said that women and girls inside Iraq were becoming targets of violence, including rape, trafficking and prostitution. Many refugees are traumatized by the violence they experienced or saw in Iraq and need psychological assistance, which is rarely available.[36]

Iraqi women and girls had to cope with the effects of violence they encountered in Iraq and had to face the difficult circumstances of being illegal refugees in Jordan. In a different report, the Women's Commission stated that most of the women they surveyed 'raised concerns about domestic violence, including marital rape, which is not illegal in Jordan'.[37] Unsurprisingly, the stress of living in cramped quarters, mostly unemployed with no legal status, has contributed to the upsurge in domestic violence. One refugee woman described her home life to the Women's Commission:

> We are having this situation [of domestic violence] here. Nobody is patient with the other. Even the youngest, he wouldn't accept any kind of criticism. Everybody is tense. . . . The women bear the brunt of the anger.[38]

In fact, a specialist in the field felt that the biggest worry is the increase in domestic violence among Iraqi households. In many refugee situations, displaced women demonstrate greater adaptability and resilience than displaced men. Certainly in terms of stress and anxiety, Iraqi women seem to cope far better than the men. The explanation possibly lies in the fact that most of these women continued in Amman with their traditional roles as mothers and wives, albeit in worse conditions than before.[39] Poverty, lack of jobs and depletion of savings are all pushing vulnerable women to sexual abuse and exploitation. Destitute women and girls are being forced into prostitution as families struggle to survive. The Women's Commission found that 'sex work among Iraqi refugees was a growing problem' and that 'in Jordan customers usually come directly to women's homes or to other private venues'.[40] However, there are indications that the number of Iraqi prostitutes has dropped since 2007 due mainly to the restrictions imposed by the Jordanian authorities on entry to the country, but also to the fact that some of these women managed to move to the Emirates.[41]

Women with education and from the middle class 'have also encountered difficulties in surviving in Jordan, particularly those who are single or non-Muslim minorities'.[42] Many tell of similar stories: after leaving their jobs and homes in Baghdad (due to violence) and fleeing to Jordan, they cannot legally work, live on their dwindling savings and cannot afford proper education or health care for their children. As a result, mental stress within the family reaches a breaking point and violence erupts.[43] One huge hurdle facing young graduates – both men and women – who leave Iraq after their graduation is that the Iraqi authorities refuse to furnish them with the certificates and documents of their studies and graduation, in an effort to prevent them from working outside Iraq and thus forcing them to remain in Iraq.[44]

The Women's Commission was concerned that Iraqi women refugees 'are not receiving critical reproductive health care because of poverty, lack of services and religious policy restrictions at the main clinics for refugees'.[45] The Commission found that 'clinical care for rape survivors, which includes emergency contraception to prevent pregnancy and medicine to reduce HIV transmission, was not available at the clinics or hospitals the team visited'.[46]

Although maternity services in Amman for Iraqi refugee women are generally good, women 'must present a marriage certificate to receive care at the faith-based clinic that serves refugees'.[47] Abortion is illegal in Jordan except to save the life of the mother.

Aware of this desperate state of affairs and the deteriorating conditions of those women, about 15 per cent of resettlement referrals by UNHCR in Jordan (and Syria) are 'Iraqi women at risk'.[48]

Children and education

The Iraqi children, like the women, are in a precarious position and probably among the worst affected by their displacement. Having gone through the trials and tribulations of living in Iraq, they arrived in Jordan to face uncertainty. For the years following the 2003 war and until September 2007, Jordan's policy towards Iraqi children enrolling in Jordanian schools was ambiguous, some say deliberately.[49] The policy was that Iraqi children whose families were not registered were not permitted to enrol in public school but allowed to attend private schools. According to HRW, Jordan's 'deliberate policy of misstatements and mixed signals has left Iraqis without residency permits confused and apprehensive about their children's rights'.[50] Displaced by force, leaving their jobs and social networks behind, families faced the agony of not knowing whether they could provide their children with education.

The confusion in the policy stemmed from the fact that a few days before the 2006–07 school year, the Jordanian Prime Minister stated that his government was taking measures to facilitate residency permit procedures to enable

Iraqi children to attend school. But these remarks 'were too late, too vague, and too poorly publicized to inform Iraqi parents'.[51] The result was that Iraqi children felt isolated, thus exacerbating their trauma stemming from displacement and violence. As one 14-year-old refugee girl in Amman told the Women's Commission:

> I studied to the 8th grade. I would like to go to school, but I don't have any papers so I can't. I stay in this room all day and clean it. I have no friend. I don't leave [the house].[52]

Away from their crowded homes, those Iraqi children who do attend school in Jordan found that the school is 'the only place they breathe fresh air' away from the anxieties and tensions at home.[53]

Under coordinated international pressure, the ambiguous Jordanian policy was finally changed before the 2007–08 school year when it was confirmed in August 2007 that Iraqis will be allowed to access all types and levels of public education regardless of their parents' residential status. Even with the change in rules, many children still did not enrol due to a number of reasons. First and foremost, as registration means giving personal details and addresses, many parents 'were often reluctant to allow their children to leave the house because they feared deportation'.[54] A second reason is that many Iraqi children have been out of the school system for one to three years which meant it is very difficult for them to return to formal education. In fact, it was estimated that as many as 62 per cent of school-aged children may have been out of school for over a year.[55] A third reason is that Iraqi children had experienced bullying which made them reluctant to attend classes.[56] Among other obstacles to registration is the financial element, whereby many families cannot afford the expenses (registration of 20–40 Jordanian Dinars, cost of books and transportation); lack of appropriate documentation; and religious concerns felt by minority groups.[57]

Statistics about enrolment among Iraqi children aged 6–17 years differ greatly. According to UNHCR, there were 250,000 school-aged Iraqi children residing in Jordan by summer 2007, and that even with the Jordanian government's new open-door policy to allow all children to enrol, it would be impossible to accommodate all Iraqi children into schools for the 2007–08 school year.[58] UNICEF reported, based on estimates by the Jordanian government, that 19,000 Iraqi children are enrolled in public and private schools and 50,000 are out of school.[59] Amnesty International, on the other hand, stated there were less than 10,000 Iraqi children in private and public schools.[60] While the Amnesty numbers look somewhat low, Fafo's statistics seem rather high. Its survey indicates that 78 per cent of Iraqi children aged between 6 and 17 were enrolled by 2007 in public and private schools.[61] This means that, based on

Fafo's tables, 60,000–70,000 Iraqis are attending school which indeed seems optimistic. This almost certainly reflects the fact that the Fafo survey seems to have encompassed more of the middle/wealthy classes and less of the vulnerable/poor classes. Three in four of those children surveyed by Fafo attended private schools (among Jordanians only 20 per cent attend private schools), and the report acknowledges that private school is 'particularly common among the wealthier parts of the Iraqi population'.[62]

The life of the youth over 17 is also precarious. Those from the lowest classes take to the streets of Amman to sell newspapers, perfumes, etc., while others try to be absorbed in Jordan's relatively small (compared to Syria and Iraq) informal economy. The theme of uncertainty dominates their stories.[63] With no schooling or proper jobs, the youth fill this vacuum either by staying at home (especially the girls and young women) or taking to the streets. Some who had to stop studying because of their displacement feel their lives have come to an end, as described by a 20-year-old Iraqi refugee woman:

> When I stopped studying, it was like someone killed me. I was studying computers and engineering [at Baghdad University]. . . . All my friends are still in Iraq. I lost connections with my friends there. . . . Now I am sad. My country is damaged. I need education to build my future.[64]

Finally, two general comments: first is that there is no doubt that the educational level of Iraqi children is below most of their parents, which is indeed a major worry for Iraq's future; second is that most Iraqis interviewed in Jordan find it difficult to accept that education standards in the first decade of the twenty-first century are higher in Jordan than in Iraq, due to 20 years of wars and sanctions. In fact by 2003, illiteracy rates in Iraq stood at 26 per cent for the population aged 15 and over compared with 9.7 per cent in Jordan (which has one of the lowest rates among Arab countries). Similarly, average years of schooling for Jordanians aged 15 and over was almost double the average in Iraq (6.9 versus 3.95).[65]

Health

Jordan's public health-care system is state-subsidized, including government hospitals and clinics; 70 per cent of the Jordanian population is covered by health insurance, while the remaining 30 per cent has no health insurance coverage at all. According to WHO, Jordan has about 100 hospitals of which 30 are government ones and the rest private (58) or military (11).[66] Unfortunately the subsidized public health-care system is 'overburdened and provides only basic care'.[67] Fafo's survey indicated that only one in eight Iraqis has valid health insurance, whether the insurance is private or governmental. In order to get insurance it is necessary to provide personal details to insurance agencies and, as discussed before, Iraqis are extremely reluctant to share such information. Interestingly, there is no huge disparity between the wealthiest groups and the poorest ones as both are highly uninsured.[68] Consequently, many Iraqis not carrying medical insurance are not able to cover even the state-regulated fees.

The Jordanian government, in coordination with international organizations, agreed in summer 2007 to allow Iraqis access to primary health care, similar to that provided to insured Jordanian citizens, with the commitment that Iraqi patients will not be asked about their residency status. However, two issues remain. The first is the lack of trust on the Iraqi side to receive any government services; even in the light of this agreement, those without the necessary papers fear they are at risk of deportation. The second, and more important issue, is that the Iraqis have to pay for treatment of chronic non-communicable diseases such as cancer, diabetes and cardiovascular problems. Jordan's private medical system is expensive but considered to be good, and in fact medical tourism revenues have been rising since 2005, with Sudan, Iraq, Palestine, Saudi Arabia, Libya and Yemen being the countries that send the highest number of patients to Jordan.[69]

Access to health care for Iraqis is provided through government health centres, Caritas Internationalis (a confederation of Catholic relief, development and social service organizations) and the Jordanian Red Crescent. One of the issues facing Iraqis is that Caritas Internationalis provides health care only to Iraqis registered with UNHCR, including those recognized as refugees and who are awaiting resettlement,[70] but by the end of 2007, only 10 per cent of Iraqis were registered with UNHCR. Similarly, the Jordanian Red Crescent facilities are only accessible to Iraqis who are registered officially either with the Jordanian government or with UNHCR. As a result, the majority of Iraqi refugees cannot access those facilities.[71]

Of the Iraqis living in Jordan and surveyed by Fafo, 90 per cent said they use the private sector clinics and hospitals rather than the government ones.[72] There are two possible explanations for this: one, as discussed before, is that Fafo's survey encompasses the less vulnerable groups who can afford the private health care system; and two, many of the Iraqis who lack legal status in Jordan are fearful of being identified and reported if they were to use the government sector. The Women's Commission found that many refugees do not seek care because they cannot afford to pay for medical care and medicine even when they are subsidized.[73]

In spite of the high percentage of Iraqis using only private sector medical care, the number of Iraqis using Jordanian government-subsidized services has been sufficient to have badly stretched personnel and facilities and increased costs to the Jordanian government.[74] Thus, major humanitarian organizations (United Nations Fund for Population Activities (UNFPA), UNHCR, UNICEF, WFP and WHO) launched a joint appeal to ameliorate the health conditions of displaced Iraqis in Syria, Jordan and Egypt. These organizations are concerned that although those governments have agreed that displaced Iraqis should be eligible for health care services similar to health care services received by the local population, 'the reality is that there are huge difficulties in meeting this commitment and severe problems of access in practice'.[75] One general objective of the appeal, therefore, is to advocate for provision of equal access for Iraqis, 'particularly for primary health services, including immunization, emergency services, reproductive health services, child health services, school health, mental health, access to essential drugs ... '.[76] The total budget for the appeal is about $85 million of which one-third (about $28 million) is allocated for Jordan, mainly to improve access to health services.[77]

Given the fact that there are no serious studies of risk factors of non-communicable diseases such as hypertension or diabetes, WHO used the comprehensive survey it carried out in Iraq in 2006 as a base for understanding the health of the Iraqi community in Jordan.[78] Some of the findings of this report, if they are accurate, are alarming: 40 per cent suffer from hypertension; 10 per cent from diabetes; 37 per cent have high cholesterol levels; and almost 67 per cent are overweight or obese.[79]

It is important to keep in mind that the health situation in Iraq deteriorated after the 1991 Gulf War: 'Lack of water, electricity, food and medical services led to the spread of infectious diseases and to an increasingly high percentage of children suffering severe or moderate malnutrition.'[80]

Iraqi refugees face another health challenge: many of those who were displaced had to face uncertainty and hardship in their new refuge and now suffer psychological problems. Some are traumatized by what they went through or witnessed in Iraq. Furthermore, for those without jobs and living on depleted savings, they and their families are under tremendous strain. The shock of fleeing one's country and the harsh realities of one's new life are leading to psychological problems. In a small survey of 354 Iraqi respondents conducted in Amman, it was found that almost 60 per cent suffer in one way or another from psychological problems.[81] Many of those displaced do not seek treatment, particularly in light of the fact that mental health and psychological services are severely lacking in Jordan.[82] Thus these refugees have no real professional support system to cope with trauma. As one specialist explained, 'family and faith are the only two support systems'.[83] Some foundations, such as Al-Himaya Foundation for trauma recovery, growth and resilience, have been established to create a resource centre to help some of those refugees.[84]

Minorities

There are no accurate statistics about Iraqi minorities living in Jordan. According to Fafo, non-Muslim minorities constitute roughly 16 per cent of the Iraqi population (which equates to about 75,000 to 80,000 individuals). In Fafo's sample, about 12.5 per cent are Christian (8.2 per cent Catholic, 3.6 per cent Orthodox, 0.7 per cent Assyrian and 0.1 per cent Protestant); 2.5 per cent Sabeans; and 1.1 per cent Yazidis and others.[85] Akin to other Iraqis, non-Muslim minorities came from all socio-economic classes. Their stories of suffering and turmoil endured inside Iraq match the stories of other Iraqis and have been discussed in Chapter 1. After they arrived in Jordan, they faced the same issues of trying to find housing and employment and provide education and health care for all members of their families. Once their entry visas expired and they live illegally, they begin to move from one neighbourhood to another depending on the jobs they can find and the state of their savings.[86] One report described a day in the life of an Assyrian:

> Martin [the refugee] spends his days sitting in the *Souq*, Amman's
> supermarket, waiting for a recruiter to give him a job for the day.
> Sometimes he is lucky but his time goes mostly to waste. His younger
> brother Michael is a tea-boy and earns 70 Dinars a month. The rent is 120
> Dinars and they live on alms from relatives in Australia.[87]

An interesting aspect of the displaced Iraqis in Jordan is how Muslim and non-Muslim minorities live side by side and coexist as though the ethnic cleansing and the pervasive violence they lived through have not affected their attitudes towards each other. Muslims and non-Muslims work together and play sport together in a way not seen in Iraq since the 2003 invasion. Most Iraqis interviewed agreed that the common identity of being a refugee and trying to create a new life has reduced the ethnic and religious tensions, but not deleted them totally. There are, however, indications that among the lower and poor classes who have suffered most, coexistence is less common due to accumulated hostilities towards the other sects. While Amman is not an ethnically segregated city, there is a geographical clustering of the Iraqi Christians and Mandeans in the capital.

One difference between the Muslim and non-Muslim minorities is that the latter have been more successful in the resettlement process. Although international organizations are very reluctant to point out ethnicity or religion in their resettlement procedures, there are many indications that non-Muslim minorities constitute a high percentage of those referred for resettlement relative to their percentage in the refugee population as a whole. This can be attributed to two facts:[88] first, with the rise of Islamic extremism in Iraq, their chances of return to Iraq have been acknowledged as significantly reduced; and second, many of those minorities have relatives in Europe, Australia and North America which makes it somewhat easier to receive visas.

Having outlined the demographics of the Iraqi population in Jordan and highlighted the situation of some particular groups, we will now assess the economic situation of Iraqis living in Jordan and their impact on Jordan's economy, and then analyse Jordan's reactions to these refugees.

Economic situation of Iraqis and their impact on Jordan's economy

Fafo used a sample of 1,690 respondents to create a wealth index based on five quintiles:

Table 2: Iraqis in Jordan: household wealth
and employment of household heads
(in %)

	% of Sample
Lowest Wealth	21.5
Low Wealth	19.8
Middle Wealth	13.3
High Wealth	11.0
Highest Wealth	34.5

Source: Fafo, *Iraqis in Jordan*, Table 1.19.

Fafo found that more than 70 per cent of Iraqis in Jordan are of working age (15+) and of these, about 30 per cent are actually participating in the workforce. For women, it is even lower with only about 14 per cent being active in the labour market (see Table 3).

Table 3: Employed status of Iraqis in Jordan
(in %)*

	Employed	Unemployed	Not Economically Active
Total	21.5	7.8	70.7
Male	42.3	8.5	49.2
Female	6.2	7.4	86.4

Source: Fafo, *Iraqis in Jordan*, Tables 1.19 and 1.5.
* Fafo, unfortunately, used different numbers of respondents for almost every one of their tables which makes it extremely difficult to aggregate and summarize the tables.

Of those surveyed with current employment, 10 per cent want to change their jobs given the fact that they felt their jobs did not fit their qualifications.[89] This probably reflects the frustration of the middle class who fled Iraq to find themselves living on the margins of society.

Among those who left Iraq in large numbers were doctors. Senior Iraqi doctors, who were top specialists in their own country, found themselves working as junior doctors in Jordan.[90] A group of those doctors wrote to an Iraqi network blog called *Al-Perleman Al-Iraqi* that there were in September 2007 about 5,000 Iraqi doctors in Jordan, and complained that after all the sufferings they endured in Iraq, they faced in exile the prospects of working below their qualifications. Some, such as junior doctors who are working to specialize in Jordanian teaching hospitals, are not paid any salary as these hospitals take advantage of the fact that most of these doctors do not have legal residency permits and thus are not eligible to work.[91] For example, an Iraqi neurologist who escaped to Jordan in July 2005 found various clinic jobs until he managed to upgrade his visa to a one-year residence permit. He then succeeded in getting a job as a specialist in a large public hospital but at the salary of a junior doctor. He told HRW that 'Jordan is a quiet country, and things are easy for us', but he added that 'the Jordanians exploit us. If I could I would return to Iraq because I have 14 years seniority there as a doctor'.[92] Another recurrent problem facing these doctors is the accreditation of their Iraqi certificates by the Jordanian medical board which, at times, can be a tedious and bureaucratic process.[93] In certain Jordanian hospitals such as the Al-Isra Hospital in Amman, Iraqi doctors constitute the majority of doctors in certain areas and, in addition to their normal load and responsibilities, they see a large number of Iraqi patients who tend to trust them more than any other doctors, and whom they treat outside their hours of work.

Engineers, artists and other Iraqi middle-class professionals tell the same story: gratitude for being in a safe place but deep frustration and anxiety from a professional and financial point of view.

Of the Iraqis working in Jordan, 61.4 per cent are employees, about 15 per cent are self-employed, and roughly 23 per cent are employers (only 2.6 per cent of working women are employers). Of those who are employers, 62 per cent come from the high wealth and highest wealth groups.[94]

Given the low levels of employment among Iraqis in Jordan as reflected in Table 3, it comes as no surprise that about 64 per cent rely for their livelihood on transfers of income from Iraq and/or from a third country (42 per cent from Iraq and 22 per cent from other countries), with the middle, high and highest wealth quintile groups receiving almost 70 per cent from transfers.[95] Needless to say, those who are surviving on remittances from Iraq are vulnerable to depletion of savings and cessation of transfers for different reasons. Indeed, this is one of the major factors leading to increased poverty and pushing certain groups to engage in crime and prostitution. Many of those middle-class Iraqis arriving in Jordan originally believed either that the violence would be over in a few months and thus they would be able to return to Iraq, or that they would be on their way to a third country. As the months wore on, these families were left stranded, burning through their savings and facing a painful new reality in their lives.[96]

Many Iraqis have been forced by their financial circumstances to move to poorer parts of Amman and there are many reports that some Iraqis – including children – have resorted to begging.[97]

On the other hand, there is no doubt that a good proportion of Iraqis fleeing their country, before and after the 2003 invasion, managed to bring money with them, as reflected by the fact that Fafo's survey indicates that 25 per cent of Iraqi households in Jordan own their dwellings.[98] Household wealth plays a factor in home ownership; 60 per cent of the households in the highest wealth group own their houses, whereas only 1 per cent of the poor households do.[99]

In fact, with the passage of time, a real gap in wealth and status has evolved among Iraqis in Jordan. While there are stories of successful entrepreneurs whose business is booming,[100] thousands of other Iraqis are relying on humanitarian aid for food and blankets.[101]

Some of the better-off groups have investments in and outside Jordan, and some even kept their investments in Iraq. Again, the survey shows a strong correlation between the household's economic status and the size of their investments. Within the households in the highest wealth group, 40 per cent have investments in Jordan, 28 per cent have investments outside Jordan and 25 per cent of that group kept investments in Iraq.[102] Interestingly, the Fafo study indicates that there is no wide gap when it comes to wealth between Sunnis and Shia in Jordan. However, Muslim households have more investments in Jordan and in Iraq in comparison with the Christians living in Jordan.[103] Jordanian data confirms that among non-Jordanians, Iraqi investors are the group with the highest investments in the country. In 2006, for example, about 3,900 Iraqi investors invested the equivalent of about $120 million, representing 12 per cent of overall foreign investment in Jordan.[104] During the years 2000–05, total Iraqi investments in Jordan reached $345 million.[105] It is interesting to note that about 63 per cent of all Iraqi households surveyed by Fafo felt that their economic situation was worse or much worse compared with 2002.[106]

Apart from purchasing their own houses to live in, some Iraqis invested in the property market which is considered one of the backbones of Jordan's economy. From 2002–05, the value of Iraqi transactions in the Jordanian housing market has doubled each year, rising from about five million Jordanian dinars (JD) to JD 100 million (one Jordanian dinar is equal to $1.4). The value of Iraqi transactions as a percentage of all foreign transactions also increased dramatically from 21 per cent in 2002 to 68 per cent in 2005.[107] Obviously, these purchases boosted property prices in Jordan and added to the inflationary pressures in the housing market. This created deep resentment among local Jordanians as there is no doubt that 'Amman housing prices have risen dramatically, as the supply of housing has been unable to keep pace with the hundreds of Iraqis arriving'.[108]

Indignation and resentment of Iraqis in Jordan stem from a number of reasons, some real and some unsubstantiated. One issue that local officials describe as a major problem is that the huge influx of Iraqis has caused the creation of a black market for jobs that is undercutting the wages of ordinary Jordanians and 'robbing them of their jobs'.[109] As discussed before, educated Iraqis are being hired in an illegal fashion, underpaid, and asked to work longer hours without proper compensation. Jordan's official unemployment rate was about 15.5 per cent in 2005, up from 13.5 per cent in 2004. The Ministry of Labour's report on unemployment for 2005 criticized Jordanians for 'refusing to take jobs performed by foreign workers'.[110] The over-qualified Iraqis ended up taking menial jobs that Jordanian citizens refused to do due to 'low pay and a culture of shame'.[111]

But the biggest resentment is centred on inflation: the war in Iraq and the subsequent arrival of such a large number of Iraqis has caused prices to go up for purchasing and renting houses, for staple commodities, for fuel and electricity. As a result of this enhanced inflation, Jordanians are suffering across the board. But the problem of inflation is somewhat more complex than blaming the influx of Iraqis. A study conducted by the Center for Strategic Studies at the University of Jordan concluded that the Iraqi refugees and the 2003 war, in a broad sense, contributed to Jordan's inflation rate to rise from 1.6 per cent in 2003 to 6.5 per cent in 2006, but the presence of the refugees is only one of many factors. In the researchers' opinion the dramatic surge of food and fuel prices has caused most of the inflation increase.[112] Food prices rose by more than 20 per cent during those four years. Prior to the 2003 invasion, Jordan imported subsidized oil from Iraq which in turn kept prices low. After the 2003 war, these subsidies were ended or reduced dramatically, and thus Jordan's spending on fuel increased sharply. At the same time Jordan began exporting large quantities of food (fruits, vegetables and milk) to Iraq (partly to feed the US Army), while imported food has become more expensive. The Jordanian producers (and one assumes with the encouragement of the Jordanian government) are taking advantage of the increased demand and higher prices paid by the US Department of Defense than the local buyers.[113] In addition, two global phenomena, which have no connection whatsoever to Iraq and its refugees, dominated world markets: a falling US dollar and a spiralling increase in oil prices. As the Jordanian dinar has been pegged to the US dollar since 1995 (in fact, since 1993 hovering around the $1.4 level), a lower US dollar caused imports to become more expensive. Higher oil prices (with reduced subsidies) led to a rise in production costs for local manufacturers.

Reports from Jordan that discuss the deterioration of the socio-economic situation due to the increase in the prices of staples such as lentils and bread, which has had a severe impact on Jordan's poor population, suggest, explicitly or implicitly, that the Iraqi refugees are the cause of this deterioration.[114] Yet the Jordanian study demonstrates that the Iraqis are not the main cause of inflation by pointing out that inflation in Amman (where most Iraqis are located) is lower than Jordan as a whole from 2002–06, and for certain periods lower than many other governorates in Jordan.[115] The conclusions of the authors are clear-cut:

> ... it is important to emphasise that the Iraqis in Jordan are not responsible
> for most of the economic challenges that Jordanians are currently facing,
> and their return to Iraq would do little to alleviate inflation in Jordan.[116]

During 2004–06, the Jordanian economy witnessed strong gross domestic product (GDP) growth rates of 8.4 per cent, 7.2 per cent and 6.3 per cent respectively. The reasons for this growth have more to do with external and regional factors than government reforms. Among those reasons were the ramifications of the Iraq war, increased wealth and savings in the oil-producing Gulf countries which led to a rise in foreign flows into Jordan.[117] This growth, coupled with higher inflation, led the government to increase interest rates from 7.59 per cent in 2004 to 8.56 per cent in 2006. However, it should be noted that interest rates had actually been much higher prior to 2004 and were almost 10 per cent in 2002.[118] The increase in the cost of borrowing led to higher prices in the rental market.

One of the engines behind the impressive growth of GDP is the construction sector, which has grown by an average of 10.7 per cent each year from 2003–07 to meet the demand for housing by the new wave of refugees.[119] *The Jordan Times* estimated that the arrival of Iraqi families in 2004 and early 2005 pumped $2 billion into the Jordanian economy, and that 'clearly contributed to accelerating the cycle of the economy'.[120]

Apart from property, the Iraqis invested heavily, particularly before 2005, in Jordan's industry, and to a lesser extent in its hotels, hospitals and agriculture. According to the Center for Strategic Studies at the University of Jordan, Iraqi investments accounted for approximately 6.5 per cent of total investment in Jordan's industrial sector between 2004 and 2006.[121] Interestingly, Iraqi investments in Jordan's stock exchange are relatively small (only JD 211 million), which constitutes less than 1 per cent of the overall value of the stock exchange as of April 2007.[122] In fact, prior to 2006, Iraqis were not even among the top ten categories of nationalities as investors in Amman's stock market.[123]

In other words, Iraqi investments are active (industry) and not passive (stock exchange) which, by definition, leads to higher employment.

Jordan's population is just under six million people and its informal economy is small (relative to Syria or Iraq), and there is no doubt that the influx of so many Iraqis in a period of two to three years has put tremendous pressure on the quality of the infrastructure and the level of government services, particularly in Amman. This issue is critical and will be revisited in the next section to understand Jordan's official (and non-official) reactions to, and methods of dealing with, the Iraqi refugees. Overall, the net economic impact of Iraqis in Jordan has been positive, and they should by no means be blamed for the economic ills of Jordan. It is important to point out that Jordan's economy overall benefited from the waves of immigrants in 1990–92, when three waves of involuntary immigration took place: large numbers of Palestinians fled Kuwait with its invasion by Iraq in 1990; a second wave of Palestinians came to Jordan after the end of that war; and a third wave of Palestinians and Jordanians returned to Jordan due to new residency regulations in Kuwait, Saudi Arabia and the Gulf States. During those two years, Jordan received about one million people, mostly educated professionals, who brought with them skills and capital and helped stimulate the economy.[124] Thus, the economic contribution of the Iraqi refugees came in spite of the fact that their capacity to invest and employ other Iraqis has been impeded by their legal status or absence of it. The fact that the Palestinians, holders of Jordanian passports, could be employed created its own dynamics of having more investments by Palestinian entrepreneurs.

Jordan's, Iraq's and international responses

Jordan's response

Jordanian policy towards the Iraqi refugees is based on two principal issues – security and economy – and within security one also can include the ramifications of the Palestinian issue for the Hashemite Kingdom of Jordan. In fact, historical studies show the intertwining of these two issues whereby Jordan's economy and the combination of its revenues played a critical role in its foreign policy decisions. In particular, Iraqi and Jordanian economies became increasingly interdependent from 1996 with the introduction of the UN 'Oil-for-Food' agreement, and the Jordanian Red Sea port of Aqaba was, until 2003, the centre for exchange of Iraqi oil exports in return for the imports of food supplies and humanitarian goods.[125]

After the invasion of 2003, Jordan adopted a policy of allowing Iraqi refugees in as 'guests' of the Kingdom. Jordanian officials refused to admit there was a refugee problem. One Jordanian official encapsulated what HRW described as the government's nonexistent refugee policy when he told the humanitarian agency that Jordan was not facing a refugee problem, but rather one of 'illegal immigration, no different from what the United States faces with Mexicans'. And given that Jordan refuses to recognize the problem and therefore ask for international help to address it, HRW fittingly described this policy as the 'Silent Treatment'.[126] Pre-2003, it was portrayed as 'a "semi-protectionist" policy toward Iraqi migrants', which meant 'letting them in but depriving them of status . . . and of means of livelihood'.[127] The main determinant of this policy is the Palestinian issue: 'In Jordan, the word "refugee" is an extremely loaded term, and a legal, social and political category that is almost exclusively the preserve of Palestinians.'[128] The Iraqi influx was seen by the Jordanians as an element straining the nation's fragile political-demographic make up. The notion that new 'refugees' will add to the 1.8 million Palestinians living in the country is truly worrisome for the Jordanians. Thus the policy fundamentally was the same before and after 2003.

As Chatelard points out, for the Jordanians, the issue of Palestinian refugees is 'prominent both on the domestic security and foreign policy agendas', and as such, their policy towards refugees is coloured by their concerns about the ramifications of the Palestinian question.[129]

Jordan acted generously by opening its doors to Iraqis in accordance with the strong traditions of Arab hospitality and brotherhood. But it is clear that in Jordan, there is 'a strong determination not to establish arrangements that might lead to permanence'.[130] This policy is, in many ways, similar to those of other Arab governments. For the Arab countries, the 'admission of Arab nationals in the governments' perception does not amount ipso facto to the granting of asylum, but instead is meant to be a mere gesture of hospitality'.[131]

One Jordanian official whom I interviewed in Amman made his country's policy very clear:

> The solution is in Iraq. We refuse to accept that the solution will be outside Iraq. They [the Iraqis] are not happy anywhere else. Everything we do towards Iraqis is temporary, simply to make their lives easier. We cannot make it [Jordan] a natural place to stay.[132]

Referring to the Palestinian refugees, the same official explained that Jordan has been generous both to the Palestinians and Iraqis, but there is a limit, otherwise Jordan will be known, in his words, as 'The Hashemite Kingdom of Refugees'.[133]

Thus the Jordanian Ministry of Interior divided Iraqis into categories such as guests, investors, residents and refugees, with the latter term seldom used. Jordanian officials at the Ministry of Interior insisted that there were only

'20,000 Iraqi refugees' in Jordan at the beginning of 2007.[134] Affluent Iraqis could obtain a residency permit (*iqama*) on a yearly and renewable basis, but this category of *iqama* requires, inter alia, a deposit of about $150,000 in a local bank.

There is little doubt that Jordan wants Iraq to be stable, moderate and unified and a good trading partner. However, the influx of refugees into Jordan has caused alarm to the Jordanians from a security point of view. First and foremost, Jordan was perturbed about the spreading violence and the possibility of a contagion effect in the sense that external unrest can lead to internal turmoil. This fear was amplified in August 2005 when two US warships in Aqaba Bay were attacked by Jordanian affiliates of Al-Qaeda. The real turning point in the Jordanian attitude towards Iraqis came in November 2005 following the bombing of three hotels in Amman by Iraqi nationals, which led to the deaths of about 60 people.[135] Restrictions followed these bombings. From 2006, Jordan barred single men and boys between the ages of 17 and 35 from entering; then Jordanian authorities insisted that Iraqis produce newly-issued passports of what became known as the G category, as many forgeries were discovered in the then existing passports. This, of course, led to many delays for Iraqi families attempting to take refuge in Jordan as the Iraqi authorities were issuing only 3,000 G passports every month.[136]

Iraqis are constantly talking about the Jordanian *Mukhabarat* (security forces) and the country's obsessiveness about security. Iraqis, like all foreigners living in Jordan, are banned from forming a *Jam'iyya* (society) or a club to prevent the gathering of a large number of people. As one Iraqi facetiously told me, 'we have to thank the dead people. Only in *Majlis Al-'Aza* (gathering for condolences) are we allowed to gather in the hundreds.'[137] Needless to say, the prohibition of civil society groups hinders the provision of assistance for the neediest Iraqis by the Iraqi community itself.

The Jordanian government had to deal with pressure from both the media and politicians. Some made virulent attacks on policies allowing masses of Iraqis to come to Jordan. One journalist commented:

> As the Palestinians, the Iraqis bring with them security risks to the country's unique stability, if only because of their own sectarian differences and because their recent political history was bloody and violent.[138]

A former Jordanian lawmaker went further by claiming that 'Jordan is being invaded by Iraqi looters and prostitutes' and that the Iraqis are 'all alien to our culture and traditions'.[139]

An important issue in the configuration of relations between Jordan and Iraq and related to security is the Shi'i factor. The Jordanian public, with implicit and explicit encouragement from the government, has become increasingly distrustful of Shi'i Iraqis. King Abdullah warned before Iraq's elections of January 2005 of an emerging 'Shiite Crescent' that would destabi-lize Gulf countries with Shi'i populations, and charged Iran with using its influence and money to manipulate the elections.[140] Jordan has been consis-tently and vehemently against a possible break-up of Iraq as fragmentation could mean a southern state under Iranian Shi'i domination.[141] Throughout 2006, Jordanian officials began turning back large numbers of Iraqis seeking entry at the land border of Al-Karama.[142] Shia, in particular, were singled out and there were reports that Jordanian soldiers would ask Iraqis for their ethnic affiliation before allowing them to cross the border. One man told HRW that when his parents – one Sunni, the other Shi'i – arrived at the Jordanian bor-der, they permitted his Sunni mother to enter, but refused entry to his Shi'i father (as a result, not wanting to be separated, the couple returned to Baghdad).[143] The US Committee for Refugees and Immigrants reported that the Jordanian General Intelligence Department was increasingly targeting Iraqi Shia for deportation.[144]

While the bias against Shia was magnified after the 2003 war, it definitely existed before. In the 1990s, when Iraqi Shi'i clerics in exile in Jordan applied to the Ministry of Religious Affairs to obtain official recognition of their com-munity, they were turned down. Thus Shi'i refugees were left in 'a legal abyss, unable to obtain any official document when a change occurs in their personal or family situation'.[145] Chatelard argued that 'as a whole, Jordanian public opinion holds Shiites [sic] in suspicion and sees all Iraqis as *ghuraba* (strangers or aliens) and not as Arab or Islamic brethren'.[146]

The Jordanian authorities stopped issuing six-month visas and commenced issuing one-month visas with the possibility of renewal. Conditions for entry were becoming more stringent throughout 2007 and by December 2007, Jordan began demanding that Iraqis wishing to enter the Kingdom have first to secure entry visas. This was portrayed as a way to 'help' the Iraqis avoid long hours of waiting at the borders, but in reality this was another serious block to their entry. By early 2008, very few Iraqis were allowed to enter Jordan. Exceptions were being made for students who had been accepted to Jordanian universities, businessmen or sick people with the right documentation – and all with enough funds to cover their costs during their stays.[147]

The second central issue in shaping Jordan's policy towards Iraq's refugees is the economy, and Jordan's economic vulnerabilities are intertwined, as men-tioned before, with its security concerns. At a meeting in UNHCR's headquar-ters in Geneva in April 2007, Jordan's then Minister of Interior claimed that his country was spending $1 billion a year on Iraqi refugees.[148] The Jordanians were worried about many economic issues, but first and foremost is the impact of hundreds of thousands of refugees arriving in their country over a relatively short period. As King Abdullah explained in one interview:

They [the Iraqis] have come to Jordan because of the dire conditions in their own country, and Jordan has provided them with all the facilities they need to lead a dignified life. But we fear at this point that we may witness a greater flow of Iraqi people into Jordan. This will be extra burden on our country, because our resources and capabilities are limited.[149]

Jordan has not been helped by the sharp rise in oil prices since mid-2007 and 'it has forced the government into a delicate balancing act in order to preserve political and fiscal stability'.[150] As Jordan's public deficit rose from 4.4 per cent of GDP in 2006 to an estimated 5.6 per cent of GDP in 2008, the government was forced to eliminate fuel subsidies entirely, thus risking political instability. The issue of the impact on Jordan's scant resources comes up time and again whether by officials or the media: 'The acceptance of the principle of the Iraqi refugees makes the host countries assume a burden above their own means.'[151] A study published in 2005 in Amman argued that although there are positive aspects to the arrival of Iraqi refugees in Jordan – such as the availability of cheap and trained labour, growing investments and a bustling transport sector – these favourable aspects do not offset the negatives of the situation, where the Iraqi 'guests' are placing too much pressure on Jordan's meagre resources.[152]

As mentioned in the previous section on the economic situation of Iraqis, a number of topics were high on the agenda of the general public and the managers of Jordan's economy: unemployment, dramatic increases in property prices, inflation (reflected in basic commodities) and the strain on public utilities such as gas and water. There is little doubt that the media created pressure on the government with articles blaming the Iraqi refugees for Jordan's problems:

Even those Iraqis who are rich disrupted the stability of Jordan's real estate market and caused the prices of land, houses and apartments to rise beyond the means of the Jordanian middle class. The extra demand on consumer products, especially fruits and vegetables, raised their prices sharply, disrupting the budgets of limited-income groups of Jordanian families.[153]

Taxi drivers in Amman, similar to taxi drivers in other major urban centres worldwide, are a good barometer of the sentiments prevailing on the street. Unfortunately, most of them in Amman are quick to blame the Iraqis for the economic problems facing Jordan. Any deterioration in economic conditions in Jordan could lead to further resentment of Iraqi refugees. The government is fully aware that 'it cannot afford to have the public opinion turn massively against the Iraqis as this could be dangerous to its security'.[154] Some journalists, although unhappy about the impact of Iraqis on Jordan, still did not advocate, publicly at least, closing the doors or expelling them. But many did insist that Jordan should be compensated by the USA and Britain.[155] Others, however, called for putting 'a limit to the Iraqi influx to Jordan', given the fact, in their opinion, that Jordan 'cannot bear or absorb more migratory waves because its ability to bear has reached its limits'.[156] It seems that the subject of the wealthy Iraqis and their behaviour in Amman aroused intense indignation among those journalists as they complained that the Jordanians were 'beginning to sense a kind of patronizing arrogance among some Iraqis due to their financial status'.[157] This is not dissimilar from when the Palestinian returnees to Jordan after the 1991 Gulf War were characterized by many Jordanians as a wealthy class of middlemen.[158] Some journalists got their facts mixed as one claimed that 'unemployment among the Iraqis in Jordan is small, including the poor among them'.[159]

Connected to the economic and security concerns discussed above, there are three other strategic issues that are interrelated to those two pillars of Jordanian policy: oil, trade and water. Since the 1980s and until 2003, Saddam guaranteed most of Jordan's oil needs at below-market prices and, as mentioned before, Jordan benefited significantly from the 'Oil-for-Food' programme that came with the sanctions imposed on Iraq during the 1990s. After the fall of Saddam, Jordan had to look for alternatives and turned mainly to Saudi Arabia and to the Gulf States to secure its oil needs at subsidized price levels.[160] These concessionary arrangements, however, lasted only for a limited time and by 2006, Jordan's imports of fuel from Iraq came to a halt.[161] As a result, imports from Iraq have become insignificant and Jordan maintains a trade surplus with Iraq. Consequently, Iraq stopped being the most important trading partner of Jordan and was replaced by the USA.[162]

The third strategic aspect, in addition to oil and trade, is water. Jordan is one of the most water-poor countries in the world, and its renewable water-resources are less than 200 cubic metres per capita compared to the recommended 1,000 cubic metres of the World Bank.[163] This meant that the influx of Iraqis has strained Jordan's ability to deliver water to its population, especially given the fact that these refugees arrived in Jordan over such a short period. The real problem, however, lies in the fact that most of the water network is worn-out and figures indicate that at least 45 per cent of the water in the supply network is lost due to leaks. Reports abound of thousands of Jordanians suffering from illnesses related to water contamination in villages and towns across the Kingdom.[164]

It is worth noting that the media did not offer the government any solutions such as recognizing that these Iraqis are refugees rather than 'guests'. Some journalists described, in a Panglossian manner, how this problem will be resolved:

As soon as the ordeal of the occupation, Iranian intervention, and domination by sectarian and racist forces ends, the Iraqis will return to their country and Amman will become their summer resort and second business centre, while our guests will serve as a Jordanian lobby in the Iraq of the future.[165]

Iraq's response

As these tragic events are affecting more than half a million Iraqis, the question that begs itself is: how did the Iraqi government respond to this crisis in its neighbour's territories? Apart from declarations of sympathy for its citizens who were fleeing the violence, there were very few practical measures. One would have expected the Iraqi government to give significant aid to Jordan and the refugees, but the amounts were indeed pitiful compared with the sums stolen and embezzled since 2003. For example, in November 2007, the Iraqi government announced it would give Jordan $8 million to 'help host the estimated 500,000 Iraqi refugees'.[166] That equates to little more than $15 per refugee. There were also announcements that Iraq would sell oil to Jordan at $18 below world prices and it was mentioned that Jordan would import about 70,000 barrels per day.[167] Needless to say, these measures did not alleviate either Jordan's economic problems or the suffering of the Iraqi refugees.

The Iraqi government, it seems, does not feel 'responsible' for these refugees because, in its opinion, these people 'deserted' Iraq and no government official had told them to do so. A more cynical interpretation also points to the fact that at the time the wave of refugees began in earnest in 2004 and 2005, the vast majority were Sunnis. It is claimed by some that the Shi'i-controlled government not only did not feel any obligation towards the fleeing Sunnis but was also somewhat relieved that they were leaving Iraq.

Among the Iraqis living in Jordan, the predominant feeling is that not only the Iraqi government does not care for them, but as one family told me:

Each time an Iraqi official visits Jordan, the majority of Iraqis hold their breath worried that the official is putting pressure on the Jordanians to force Iraqis, and in particular the young [university] graduates to go back.[168]

Conspiracy theories are rife among the community, which is again natural when people live under stress and anxiety about the future and when a large proportion of them are not working.

International response

There are two kinds of international response to the Iraqi refugees in Jordan: by international humanitarian organizations and by governments (other than the Jordanian and Iraqi governments). A large number of UN agencies, local and international NGOs are located in Jordan, and some of these organizations have had a base there for a long time to cater for the Palestinian refugees. Due to its relative safety and good infrastructure, Amman attracted many other organizations after the 2003 invasion, to help the Iraqis in Iraq and in Jordan. UNHCR is the major humanitarian organization with emphasis on community training, capacity building, health, education and legal assistance to refugees. By summer 2007, the UNHCR office in Amman had more than 100 staff and was working in partnership with the United Nations Development Programme (UNDP), WFP, UNFPA, UNICEF and WHO. Among its national partners were Mizan (the law group for human rights), Jordanian National Alliance Against Hunger, Jordan Red Crescent, Ministry of Interior and Ministry of Planning.[169] There are at least ten other organizations with similar activities but some with different emphasis (women, children, health, nutrition, psychological counselling, Christians and legal counselling). These organizations include CARE International, French Red Cross, International Catholic Migration Commission (ICMC), Save the Children, Middle East Council of Churches, Relief International, Quaker Service, Caritas Internationalis, Islamic Relief Worldwide and United Nations Office for Project Services.[170]

Unfortunately for the Iraqi population, the effect of assistance is limited by three key constraints. The first is the reluctance of Iraqis to come forward and be assisted by these organizations. Another reason is the lack of budgeting channelled to Iraqi refugees, especially in the first couple of years after the influx of refugees began. Last but not least, the Jordanian government's 'silent treatment' of the refugee issue prevented adequate international aid resources from reaching Jordan. This is indeed an important issue to point out that Jordan fundamentally refused for a long time aid for refugees per se. (This is in stark contrast to Syria.) Jordan wanted the aid to be directed at a sector as a whole and not specifically to refugees. For example, aid can be given to the health sector in Jordan, for the benefit of all citizens, but cannot be directed just to improve the health of the Iraqis. As a result, the Jordanian government discouraged humanitarian organizations 'from projects that establish a refugee category and is ambivalent with regard to an expanded UNHCR role based on donor funds for assistance activities'.[171] It is important to emphasize that Jordan began to change its attitude in 2007 due to the attention of the international media to the refugee crisis which, in turn, prompted some governments to bring up the issue with Jordan. Thus the net result, until 2007, was summed up by HRW: 'Iraqis throughout the Middle East remain unregistered, uncounted, unassisted and unprotected'.[172] Needless to say, without these humanitarian organizations, the situation of the refugees (particularly in the fields of health, education and children) would have been much worse.

By mid-2008, UNHCR had managed to register about 54,000 Iraqis living in Jordan, 31,000 of whom were registered in 2007 itself. It is important to keep in mind that the relationship between the Jordanian government and UNHCR suffered numerous setbacks, as will be discussed in Chapter 5. The long wait to be registered has been reduced from three or four months to two or three days. By December 2007, UNHCR had also referred around 8,000 Iraqis for resettlement in third countries and 1,459 had actually left Jordan (only 18 per cent were actually given visas by third countries).[173] Fafo's study indicates that only 21 per cent of those Iraqis surveyed in Jordan had plans to emigrate, but the percentage is much higher among the Christian and other minority groups.[174] Nevertheless, it is interesting to point out that the survey shows that 58 per cent did not have plans to go back to Iraq, and again within Christians and minorities, the percentage of those wanting to stay in Jordan is much higher.[175]

With regard to governmental responses to the crisis, very few countries have helped. Sweden (which will be discussed later in Chapter 4) is the exception and has taken the lead in accepting Iraqi refugees. Australia, New Zealand, Ireland and Canada have also resettled a number of Iraqis. However, the combined efforts of all these countries has only relieved Jordan of a small part of the burden given the high numbers of Iraqi refugees remaining in the country. The role of the USA will be examined in Chapter 4, but it is essential here to underline an important point: although the USA is a major donor to Jordan, 'a relatively small portion of its Jordan foreign aid package is devoted to refugees'.[176] For example, the US aid to Jordan in 2005 averaged about $700 million but less than half a million dollars was earmarked for refugees in Jordan, and that was channelled through the US multilateral donation to UNHCR.[177]

Unfortunately it was not only the USA that all but neglected the plight of Iraqi refugees. In fact, from a financial perspective, the UK and other European countries have contributed even less than the USA to Iraqi refugees in Jordan. (Their policies towards Iraqi asylum seekers will be discussed in Chapter 4.) Most countries (including some Arab countries) continue to pay lip service to the importance of helping Jordan cope with the refugees but in reality, and considering their wealth and power, they are doing little to solve the crisis. What is most remarkable is that both the USA and the UK have strong current and historical ties to Jordan, and one would have expected these two countries (even aside from the moral imperative deriving from their military involvement in Iraq) to come to the aid of their ally with financial help and do their utmost to prevent any destabilization of the country. Alas, this has not happened.

Although this chapter raised a number of negative elements and criticisms of Jordan's policy towards the Iraqi refugees, the fact remains that Jordan has been and continues to be one of the region's most welcoming countries towards refugees in general and Iraqis in particular. Between 500,000 and 750,000 Iraqis found refuge and relative security in a neighbouring country and succeeded, at least, in leaving the inferno of Iraq behind them. While the negative impact of Iraqi refugees in Jordan has been overstated and the positive impact almost entirely obscured, the fact remains that the influx of Iraqis has placed a burden on Jordanian resources, infrastructure and utilities, and Jordan has borne this burden without substantial help from other governments.

Chapter 3

Iraqi refugees in Syria

I have no place to hide; I have neither a civilized country, nor am I comfortable here or free.[1]

Historical background

Throughout the twentieth century, Syria hosted refugee groups such as Palestinians and Armenians in large numbers and Syria's pan-Arabism policy since the 1960s meant an open-door policy to Arab exiles. According to estimates by Fafo and other agencies, there were about 280,000 to 300,000 Palestinian refugees in Syria in 2000.[2] What is interesting from this book's perspective is Fafo's conclusion, that the 'Palestinian refugees have been better integrated into Syrian society than in Jordan, and especially in Lebanon where lack of social and economic rights have produced excessive poverty and desolation...'.[3]

Syria received many waves of Iraqis going back all the way to 1933 when Christians and Yazidis from Mosul arrived in Syria. Later on, communists, Sunnis, Shia, Kurds and Assyrians were welcomed there. During most of Saddam's era, relations between Iraq and Syria were strained, and many of Saddam's opponents lived in Syria and used the country as a base for political opposition activities. Among those who found refuge in Syria were some of the current politicians in Baghdad who returned to Iraq after 2003.

After the Gulf War of 1991 and the repression of Shia in southern Iraq, Syria closed its border with Iraq and the border remained closed until 1997.[4] There are indications, however, that the number of Iraqis entering Syria began to increase from 1999 onwards. Estimates put the number of Iraqis in 1999 at about 58,000, increasing to about 187,000 in 2001, and to roughly 250,000 by 2003.[5] The large numbers of Iraqis in Syria before the invasion is due to the fact that Syria replaced Iran, from 1999, as the political base for the Iraqi opposition.

Like Jordan, Syria has not signed the 1951 Geneva Convention. The 1973 Constitution prohibits the extradition of 'political refugees' because of 'their

political principles or their defence of freedom', but Syria does not have a procedure for granting asylum.[6] With regard to the Palestinian refugees, a 1956
law provides that Palestinians residing in Syria are considered as Syrians in all
matters pertaining to the laws and regulations, but does not include rights to
naturalize or vote.[7]

Why Syria?

As discussed in Chapter 1, the predominant factor for Iraqis to leave their
country after the 2003 invasion was the pervasive violence. Again, in the case
of Syria, those who left Iraq because of sectarian and other violence comprise
Iraqis from all sects and religions. In a survey conducted by a team from the
Brookings Institution among 192 Iraqis, sectarian violence or other forms of
violence such as kidnapping, being threatened with assassination (the inter-
viewee or his family), having a family member killed, displaced from their
homes or simply fear of violence (respondents called it 'the bad situation in
general') accounted for more than 70 per cent of the reasons for leaving Iraq.[8]
Almost all of the Iraqi refugees in Syria interviewed by Amnesty International
were victims of 'serious human rights abuses' in Iraq and had felt they had no
choice 'but to leave the country'.[9] For many Christians and members of other
minorities (Sabean-Mandeans, Yazidis) the rise of radical religious groups
who 'targeted their livelihoods and imposed draconian restrictions on how
they could worship or even live their everyday lives' prompted them to flee
Iraq.[10] Interestingly, some Sunnis and Shia decided to leave Iraq because they
did not want 'to live under the restrictive religious and social edicts' imposed
by the religious militias, even of the same community.[11]

For those associated with the previous regime (Ba'th party members,
government officials and military officers), Syria was a safe haven from the
radical Shi'i militias and the post-2003 Iraqi government. For others, affiliated
or perceived to be affiliated with the Coalition forces, fleeing to Syria from the
radical Sunni groups became a necessity to protect their lives.[12]

As in the case of Jordan, middle-class professionals such as doctors,
academics, journalists and lawyers began to flee to Syria from 2004 as their
jobs put them at high-risk with radical groups, both Sunni and Shi'i, when
they became lucrative targets to be kidnapped for ransom. An Iraqi woman
who fled to Syria and whose husband, a doctor, was murdered recounted to a
journalist what the Iraqi police 'investigating' the murder told her: 'He [her
husband] is a doctor, he has a degree and he is Sunni, so he couldn't
stay in Iraq. That's why he was killed.' Not only were his murderers not
arrested but she received, two weeks later, a letter ordering her to leave her
neighbourhood.[13]

There were also Iraqis who left Iraq for economic reasons. For some, such as shopkeepers, craftsmen, artisans and small business owners, their livelihoods collapsed. In certain cases, businesses were physically destroyed or simply collapsed due to the ongoing violence and the deteriorating market conditions. Barbers, for example, had to close their shops under pressure and threats from Shi'i militias who believe beards should be left to grow, and Western-style haircuts must be avoided.[14]

Like all refugees, once a decision is made to flee, the next decision is to where? In the first two to three years after the invasion, there was a choice: Jordan or Syria. From 2007, the availability of choice shrank drastically. Most of the reasons behind choosing Syria are not dissimilar from those discussed in the previous chapter on Jordan. Based on the Brookings' field-report and other interviews with Iraqis, the reasons for choosing Syria can be summed up as:

1) The geographic proximity to Iraq: it is easier to get to Syria than to Jordan. This was particularly true for Shia who had to cross the Sunni Anbar province to get to Amman. Overall, the roads to Syria are safer than those to Jordan.

2) Arab nationals, including Iraqis, could enter Syria freely and stay for three months, after which time they had to request a residence permit from the Syrian Department of Immigration and Passports.[15]

3) As discussed in Chapter 2, the integrity and security of the family is of the utmost importance to Iraqi refugees: 'Security concerns are collective because Iraqi exile migration is rarely an individual undertaking.'[16]

4) Syria's informal economy is much larger than Jordan's and the cost of living is much lower than in Jordan. These two economic aspects played important roles for Iraqis, particularly the poorer ones, in choosing Syria rather than Jordan.

5) Syria is less homogeneous than Jordan in the sense that it has always had large minorities and has been the friendliest to Shia among destination countries. The 'Alawis, to whom the ruling family of Al-Assad belong, are themselves a minority.[17] Given the strengthening relations between Syria and Iran, Shia enjoy the help of Shi'i charitable institutions, some of which are supported directly by Iranian religious groups. This is a critical factor for Shia given the fact that no such setup exists in Jordan. According to the Brookings' report, Syrians have a better reputation among Iraqis than other Arabs; many Sunnis cherish the fact that Syria is not pro-America, while Shia perceive the Syrians differently from the Jordanians and Palestinians who had preferential treatment from Saddam Hussein's

regime.[18] Overall, Syria's record of integrating Iraqis, and Arabs in
general, is definitely better than other countries.

6) Interviews with Iraqis indicated that access, or at least partial access,
to health and education services in Syria is far easier than in Jordan
or other neighbouring countries, and for them this was a significant
consideration.

Iraqis seem to be escaping from everything as the fundamentals of security
and stability collapsed. As one Iraqi put it:

> It is not just politics or one tyrant that you have to avoid; it is also religion,
> your sect, your neighbourhood, all the Sunni and Shia [sic] leaders, and
> everything else. And still, you can never tell if you will escape being killed
> or not; you cannot tell if your children will be spared or not.[19]

Getting to Syria was hazardous even before the 2003 invasion as notorious
gangs attacked passengers on the roads leading to Syria. But after the fall of
Saddam's regime, the lines between attacks by the *mujahidin* (insurgents) and
by bandits became blurred as 'the same group or individuals may often carry
out both sets of activities, with the determining factor being the identity of the
victim'.[20] Iraqis are targeted even before they reach the borders, with the insur-
gents/looters obtaining information from drivers and travel companies about
the potential targets among their passengers. The Iraqis tell horrendous stories
of their journeys through the circles of hell from the violence in Iraq via
dangerous roads to the border until they get the approval to enter Syria and
begin a new chapter in their lives.

Profile and characteristics of the Iraqi refugees

There are no accurate data on the number of Iraqis living in Syria, but estimates put it at around 1.2 million to 1.4 million by the end of 2007.[21] The
Syrian government, for its own political reasons, has insisted that there are at
least 1.5 million refugees.[22] Estimates are problematic and the 'vexed question
of counting refugees, and the ways in which this task is complicated by politics, is never more evident than in urban areas'.[23] To put this in context, Iraqis
constitute roughly 6.5 per cent of the overall population in Syria, estimated at
the end of 2007 to be 19.4 million.[24] As in Jordan, Iraqi refugees headed to
urban areas in Syria. There have been two relatively large assessments and surveys of Iraqi refugees in Syria, but one has to be cautious given that the 'hidden, marginalized nature of urban refugees makes it difficult to make accurate
estimates'.[25]

The first assessment was conducted by UNHCR and other UN agencies in 2005 and was published in March 2006.[26] It estimated that there were around 450,000 Iraqis in Syria, 48 per cent of whom were children under the age of 18. The second survey, conducted in the latter part of 2007 by Ipsos market research agency in conjunction with UNHCR in Syria, found that the number of Iraqis had increased dramatically. The assessment which involved 75 interviews found that only 7.5 per cent of respondents had arrived in Syria prior to 2006, while 30 per cent arrived in 2006 and 62.5 per cent in 2007 – with the bulk coming in mid-2007.[27] Although these percentages might not reflect the real picture, they definitely indicate that as the violence spread through Iraq, the number of forced migrants increased sharply.

Of those interviewed by Ipsos, 78 per cent were from Baghdad and the rest from different parts of Iraq. As in Jordan, the urban refugees headed to cities, with roughly 80 per cent living in the Damascus area. Large numbers of Shia live in the suburb of Sayyidah Zainab, built around the tomb of the granddaughter of the Prophet Mohammad. Hundreds of thousands of pilgrims pay an annual visit to the tomb and as a result the population in Sayyidah Zainab increased from 800 people in 1960 to almost 100,000 by 1996.[28] Following the 2003 invasion, the area (which is only nine kilometres from the capital) has become the centre of the Iraqi exile community given its low rents, thus attracting also a large number of Sunnis. In fact, Saudi Arabia is building a huge *waqf* (endowment) adjacent to the Sayyidah Zainab shrine to provide services for the local population.

Christians and Sabeans tend to live in the suburb of Jarmana. Many Sunnis headed to Aleppo which has a long history of trade ties with Iraq. Given that Aleppo has a sizeable Christian population, it also attracted a significant number of Iraqi Christians.[29]

Ipsos found that 63 per cent of interviewees had family abroad; with the highest percentage (28 per cent) in Sweden, followed by the USA (18 per cent).[30] With regard to religious affiliation, Ipsos did not enquire about this and the UN agencies' assessment of March 2005 seems somewhat unrealistic (57 per cent Shia and 21 per cent Sunnis).[31] A better guide is probably the numbers provided by UNHCR of those registered in Syria (204,000 individuals representing roughly 15 per cent of the overall estimated Iraqi population). According to UNHCR, the breakdown by June 2008 was as follows: 57 per cent Sunnis; 20 per cent Shia; 15 per cent Christians; 4 per cent Sabean or Mandean; and 3 per cent under the category of 'Islam unspecified'.[32] (These percentages do not necessarily reflect accurately the proportions of the religious categories of Iraqis in Syria. Obviously far more minorities registered with UNHCR with the hope of resettlement in a third country.)

With regard to living conditions and income, 98 per cent of those interviewed by Ipsos rent a house and 2 per cent own their homes. This is in a marked contrast to better off Iraqis who purchased their houses in Jordan. Ipsos numbers of owning and renting are not far off those of the 2005 assessment; 15 per cent of respondents share their apartment with another family.[33] An average furnished apartment for one family is approximately 6,000 Syrian Pounds per month, roughly $120 ($1 equals 51 Syrian Pounds). Iraqis found it easy to let their houses in Iraq and pay rent in Syria. This led many Syrians to believe that Iraqis are rich. In the course of 2006 and 2007, two factors affected the ease with which Iraqis could afford rental property in Syria: rental yields in Iraq began dropping as violence encompassed many areas; and rental prices in Syria increased with the temporary arrival of Lebanese refugees in summer 2006 as a result of the Israeli invasion.[34]

According to the survey, the population demographic is 44 per cent male and 56 per cent female, but only 35 per cent said the main income provider is the male head of the household, while 36 per cent indicated that the main provider is the female head of the household. As in Jordan, Iraqis are not allowed to work. However, the informal economy is much larger in Syria and hence it can absorb a larger number of refugees. Still, 37 per cent of refugees surveyed said that their main source of income is savings, another 24 per cent were relying on remittances from relatives, 12 per cent on pension and only 24 per cent from current salaries. Not surprisingly, and considering the precarious conditions in Iraq where most of the remittances and pensions are derived, 33 per cent of those surveyed expected their money to last less than three months.[35] This is a critical point which will be discussed in Chapter 7 when the issue of returns to Iraq will be analysed. Due to the relative poverty of the Iraqi refugees in Syria (certainly poorer than their brethren in Jordan), 10 per cent of school-aged children are working to support their families.[36]

Given this situation, it is unsurprising that Iraqis living in Syria feel despondent about their lives and the future of their families. One refugee, in a documentary by Al-Jazeera TV, described how he sees his life:

> We are not refugees; rather, we are homeless vagabonds amid total Arab and international silence over an Arab state's tragedy. They sold us in a slave market and here we are now, as witnessed by history. Are there undeclared political reasons for this silence?[37]

Iraqis in Syria faced hardships and the basic tenets of life – earning a livelihood, access to education and health – became major hurdles that they had to deal with almost on a daily basis. We will look at the different sections of Iraqi society in Syria such as women, children and minorities, and examine the state of health and education.

Women

In both Jordan and Syria, many Iraqi women assumed the role of the head of their families or households after their husbands were killed, imprisoned or kidnapped following the invasion of 2003. This phenomenon is more widespread in Syria than in Jordan as more poor families headed to Syria. The financial responsibilities for these women meant dependence mainly on informal employment in Syria given that they probably brought little capital with them, and with time that capital was depleted.

The Ipsos survey indicated that more than half of the female-headed households have between two and three children and that 65 per cent of those children are not enrolled in Syrian schools as their mother had to prioritize child labour over education.[38] Half of the female heads of households have secondary or higher education and are between 35 and 50 years of age. Nearly half of them have no individual or household monthly income, with savings, loans, donations and remittances being their main source of income, and according to the survey, they expected this assistance to last between one and three months only.

Many of these women are facing destitution, and such desperation can often lead to sex work. Nearly every major conflict breeds prostitution as displacement takes place and local taboos no longer exist. It would be wrong, however, to link the rise in prostitution in Syria only to incoming Iraqis. Even before the 2003 invasion and the Iraqi exodus, there was increasing prostitution with women from Syria, Turkey, the former Soviet republics and Russia. Nevertheless, the influx of many women with the responsibilities of taking care of their children and families has definitely expanded prostitution in Syria. As one UNHCR official explained, it is difficult to gauge the coercion and the actual 'trafficking'; he felt that 'this situation isn't triggered by trafficking – trafficking just takes advantage of the situation'.[39] In a report by UNHCR Damascus, filed at the end of 2007 with an update on sexual and gender-based violence (SGBV), it was mentioned that 270 survivors of SGBV had been identified between February and the end of October 2007 and that each week two to three cases of SGBV are highlighted.[40] Other forms of SGBV that were mentioned by UNHCR were: girls as young as 12 are forced into prostitution by their families to secure income for their families; girls are sold in Iraq and brought to Syria to be used as prostitutes;[41] women are resorting of their own free will to prostitution for economic reasons; economic and sexual exploitation in the workplace, especially at factories and shops outside Damascus. The UNHCR office also reported that during field visits, UNHCR officials observed that networks of organized gangs – mainly young Iraqi men – are involved in this business.[42]

Prostitution is a sensitive issue, particularly for women in the Arab world, and gathering accurate information is very difficult. In the UN agencies' assessment of Iraqi refugees in March 2006 and based on information from NGOs, local authorities and religious leaders, sex work in Syria by Iraqi refugees is divided into three types: prostitution on an individual level, on a family level, and on the level of organized networks. At the individual level, sex work implies the practising of prostitution by a girl or woman without the knowledge of her parents or siblings due to severe needs. At the family level, some or all family members are involved and sex work of this nature 'may be highly exploitative and coercive'. The UN agencies gathered many sources confirming the presence of the head of the family in the house when clients are brought in. As for organized networks that provide girls to tourists and nightclubs, some are sophisticated networks who find the girls and manage their business. Reports were received that some of these networks even involve doctors and other medical staff to perform abortions.[43]

The media carried many stories about the lives of those women. A nun at a convent in Damascus who helps Iraqi refugees explained that some of the women 'seeking work outside the home for the first time and living in a country with high unemployment, find that their only marketable asset is their bodies'.[44]

There are no official statistics or information about prostitution in Syria but the founder of the Iraqi women's group Women's Will puts the figure at 50,000 Iraqis, a number which seems quite inflated.[45] Whatever the real number is, there is little doubt that the percentage of prostitutes within the Iraqi population in Syria is far higher than in Jordan or other host countries due to the fact that many Iraqis who fled to Syria were less affluent and more susceptible to destitution than their compatriots in Jordan. Syrian authorities have begun clamping down on some of the clubs which are basically brothels as a result of international pressure, and following media reports that inexpensive Iraqi prostitutes have helped make Syria a popular destination for sex tourists from the Gulf States and Saudi Arabia. One journalist reported that nearly half the cars in the car park of the club she visited had Saudi license plates.[46] Overall, Syrians are officially silent on the subject, but Amnesty International said they have voiced concerns in private.[47] Anecdotal evidence suggests that security officials who receive bribes are engaged in 'protecting' these prostitutes from being detained or deported. Lip service is sometimes paid when, for example, the official Syrian news agency reported that the Syrian Minister of Interior assured an Iraqi women's delegation that his country is doing its utmost to provide 'all possible facilitation to Iraqi refugees despite the economic, social and security burdens'.[48]

Shame plays a critical role in preventing women who want to leave the business from stopping or returning to their families as they 'had brought shame on the family's name'.[49] Shame also impedes many of these women from turning to NGOs for help and, together with fear, rules out asking for protection from the police authorities.[50]

As in Jordan, Iraqi women are experiencing other hardships: domestic violence, deterioration in health conditions, trauma and psychological problems, and dealing with the ever-increasing problems of their children and their education.

Children and education

The government of Syria has had, for several decades, a clear policy of allowing all children from Arab countries living in Syria to enrol in Syrian schools and this policy obviously was applied to children of Iraqi refugees.

According to the Syrian Ministry of Education, 32,000 Iraqi children were attending Syrian state schools at the end of the 2006–07 school year. There were, in addition, 1,000 children enrolled in private schools.[51] If we accept the estimate of 1–1.2 million refugees and that children aged 5–18 usually represent close to 35 per cent of the population, this means there are, at a minimum, 350,000 children of school-age. This implies that less than 10 per cent of Iraqi children attend school, a much lower percentage than the Ipsos estimate due to the previously discussed problems with surveys. This is despite the fact that Syrian schools are accessible, and here there was no ambiguity about the admission policy unlike Jordan. Thus the question that begs itself is: why? To understand the answer, we have to look at the difficulties facing those children:

1) Some were turned away due to lack of space. Amnesty International had reports of many schools already overcrowded with up to 50 pupils in a classroom.[52] The problem lies in the fact that the educational infrastructure, even before the influx of refugees, was barely meeting the needs of the Syrian inhabitants. In certain schools, the number of Iraqi children began to outnumber the Syrian pupils which obviously created pressure on teachers, pupils and the community at large. Although UNHCR is helping with the construction of six schools, this will not resolve the fundamental problem of lack of schools and classrooms. UNHCR and UNICEF estimate the budgetary requirements to expand schools' capacity in Syria to accommodate a much larger number of Iraqi children at $88 million.[53]

2) Lack of correct documentation, such as school reports and certificates, which led to schools refusing to enrol the children. Sometimes, they were assigned to lower classes and as a result the children refuse to attend. (The same issue exists among Iraqis in Jordan.) In certain cases where the families do not have the visas to stay in Syria, they (again like in Jordan) are extremely reluctant to register their children for fear of being discovered and expelled from the country.

3) Some families are under the illusion that they are in a transitory state, and believing that within a few months they will return to Iraq or be resettled, end up not sending their children to school.

4) Cost of books and uniforms which are estimated at about 5,000 Syrian Pounds per year, or $100 (private schools cost about $500 a year). Only children enrolled at the beginning of the school year receive free books, otherwise they have to purchase them.[54] Given that the average Iraqi family has three to four children, the cost of education becomes a real burden for thousands of refugee families and the choice becomes between paying these costs or sending the children to work to earn some money rather than being a financial burden.

The Ipsos survey reported a high percentage (46 per cent) of children surveyed dropping out of school. Again, lack of documents was the most common reason, followed by lack of resources.[55] A major reason both for giving up school, and in some cases for not enrolling, is the psychological trauma that many children suffer from. The anxieties connected to being forcibly uprooted from their homes and neighbourhoods, and the trauma of witnessing or experiencing horrific acts of violence, diminish children's ability to learn and adjust to their new environment. A further reason for dropping out, as reported by Amnesty International, is the difficulty Iraqi pupils face in adapting to the Syrian school curriculum which differs from that in Iraq. For example, both French and English are taught from an early age in Syria but not in Iraq.[56] Some children also found adjusting to the local dialect hard.

The net result of the low numbers of children enrolling and the high percentage of dropouts is that illiteracy is spreading rapidly among refugee children. Aid workers are alarmed by the growing number of children who cannot read or write.[57] UNICEF and UNHCR have launched a joint appeal to provide education opportunities to Iraqi children in the host Arab countries, but it will take at least one to two years before results can be achieved.[58] It should be pointed out that Syria lags behind Jordan in terms of schooling and education. In 2003, illiteracy in Syria was 20.4 per cent of the population aged 15 and over (compared with 9.7 per cent in Jordan), and the gross enrolment rate for secondary education in that year was 63 per cent in Syria compared with more than 87 per cent in Jordan.[59]

The number of Iraqis in higher education in Syria is small and estimated in 2007 at only 470 students. In addition, about 300 were studying in private universities. Similar to attending schools, university education in Syria is open to Arab nationals and the cost is relatively low. Iraqis interviewed by Amnesty International described the Syrian universities 'as too few and overcrowded and alleged that Syrian applicants generally were given priority for enrolment'.[60] Private universities, on the other hand, are expensive and their fees range from $2,500 to $4,000 a year, depending on the faculty.[61] One such private university is the Syrian International University which is, for all practical purposes, an 'Iraqi University'; its dean and a high percentage of its professors and students are Iraqis. (Iraqis in Jordan always point to this university as proof that Iraqis are treated better in Syria.) As one fortunate student who can afford the fees of $4,000 told the BBC, he had to quit his studies in Iraq as he was targeted but that the International University in Damascus is 'a great opportunity' for him as the system is the same as in Baghdad University.[62]

One issue that was mentioned before and needs elaborating is child labour. The widespread poverty and the inability of many families to pay the rent led to an increase in child labour which is perceived as a means of increasing the family income. As the UN agencies reported in their assessment of Iraqi refugees in Syria:

> Iraqi children, both girls and boys, from poor families are prone to get involved in labour to supplement family income. They typically work long hours for little pay as 50 SYP [$1] a day with boys working in market places and girls as house maids. This correlates with the high proportions of children out of schools. Some instances of illness and injuries have been noticed as a result of the hard works that they perform.[63]

Poverty and hard economic conditions also led to the increase of physical and psychological illnesses among the refugees.

Health

Until the end of 2005, all Iraqis living in Syria received free health care in government hospitals. By 2006, with almost 2,000 refugees arriving daily, the Syrian authorities introduced a number of restrictions due to rising costs. Iraqi refugees still had access to hospitals in emergency cases but had to pay for treatment for serious illnesses, such as cancer or heart ailments.[64] As a result, many Iraqis use private clinics and hospitals. Private hospitals cost about $40 a day and an appointment at a private clinic costs about $10 to $20.[65] For those registered with UNHCR, patients with serious illnesses can receive a subsidized price at clinics run by the Syrian Red Crescent (where the patient still pays but only about 25 per cent of the cost).[66] Some of the poor Iraqis visit charitable clinics, in particular those run by churches (Deir Ibrahim Khalil in the Christian area of Jarmana is one example). According to the Brookings' field-report, religious affiliation does not have an impact on the quality of care Iraqi refugees receive and the determinant is the wealth of the patient.[67] In its assessment of the situation of Iraqi refugees in 2006, the UN agencies mentioned that 73 per cent of all families were paying for their health care.[68]

The health conditions of Iraqi refugees in Syria were indeed precarious. In their survey, Ipsos indicated that 17 per cent of those interviewed were diagnosed with a chronic disease; with the highest number of patients suffering from high blood pressure, diabetes or asthma. One of the most disturbing aspects is the state of health of refugee children. It was discovered that 23 per cent of children included in the Ipsos survey had had some kind of illness in the two weeks prior to the interview. But what is even more worrisome is the fact that 22 per cent of parents who had sick children did not seek medical advice, with almost half of them citing the cost of treatment as the main reason for not visiting a clinic.[69] Another troubling issue is the low coverage of vaccinations and high prevalence of diarrhoea; only 65 per cent of children under five were vaccinated against measles and only 75 per cent were adequately protected from polio.[70] Some international organizations have raised the alarm about malnutrition and UN agencies reported 2 per cent of children are malnourished and a further 3.5 per cent have the potential to become malnourished.[71] This serious issue seems to exist in Syria on a wider scale than in Jordan due to the deteriorating economic conditions of Iraqis in Syria. Thus the health sector appeal put together by UN agencies allocated more than two million dollars to deal with malnutrition and micronutrient deficiencies in Syria (with zero allocation to Jordan and just $58,000 to Egypt).[72] Of the total appeal budget of $84.8 million, Syria would receive about 60 per cent ($43.5 million), while Jordan would receive 34 per cent and Egypt about 6 per cent.[73]

Mental and psychological illnesses are prevalent among Iraqi refugees in general, and in Syria in particular. Data collected by Ipsos and analysed by the US Centers for Disease Control and Prevention highlight the fact that many Iraqi refugees are suffering from depression, anxiety and post-traumatic stress disorder. As one UNHCR official dealing with the refugees described it:

> …this [trauma] affects every aspect of their lives. We [UNHCR] have seen countless marriages that have not survived this stress, children that no longer attend school and people that find it increasingly difficult to cope with life.[74]

Some of the findings of the trauma are shocking: 77 per cent of refugees interviewed reported being affected by air bombardments and shelling or rocket attacks; 68 per cent said they experienced interrogation or harassment by militias or other groups; 16 per cent had been tortured; 72 per cent were eyewitnesses to a car bombing; and 75 per cent knew someone who had been killed.[75] Many Iraqis, whether in Syria or Jordan, continued to fear those who persecuted them in Iraq and, in many cases, they believed they actually have seen those who harassed them in their new refuge.

A serious gap in the health services in Syria (similar to Jordan) is the lack of psychological counselling and the proper structures for helping traumatized refugees. Another hurdle is the 'stigma of talking to a psychologist in many parts of Iraqi society' which blocks people using those services even when they exist.[76] Sister Malekeh, a Greek Catholic nun, told a journalist about the clinic at her convent of Deir Ibrahim Khalil and described the problems the clinic is dealing with:

> Depression, depression, depression. . . . Now we have a psychiatrist who started two months ago. Before they [refugees] didn't accept it and wouldn't come to the clinic, but now they have started to come.[77]

Another issue facing Iraqi refugees is disabilities. Ipsos found that 4 per cent of Iraqis who were interviewed said they have a disabled family member or are disabled themselves. Injuries are the cause of disability in 49 per cent of those who are disabled, with almost half being injured after the 2003 invasion.[78]

An NGO based in the Middle East and working with Iraqi refugees in Syria told me that for the Syrian government, apart from security, health is a very sensitive issue surrounding the hosting of Iraqi refugees. This is the reason that the Syrian Red Crescent has almost a monopoly to distribute the health services to Iraqis.[79] The explanation lies in the fact that the burden of those refugees, not only in magnitude but also due to their health conditions even before their arrival, is huge, and Syrian officials are wary of potential problems emanating from the health sector which could have an impact on the whole population. Syrian officials are worried, for example, about the low-level of immunization and the possible spread of communicable diseases across the borders. They keep stressing to WHO and the Iraqi government that while Syria is doing its utmost to offer health (and education) services to Iraqis, the health system is overwhelmed and unable to cope with such large numbers of patients.[80]

Minorities

The number of Iraq's non-Muslim minorities, such as Christians and Sabean-Mandeans, continues to be disproportionately high among the refugee population in Syria. As these communities found themselves in an increasingly vulnerable situation in Iraq, and given Syria's open borders policy, many exited Iraq for Syria. No accurate statistics exist of the numbers of non-Muslim minorities. The UNHCR categorization, discussed earlier in this chapter, might be an indication of the over-representation of minorities, but it would be difficult to accept that there are 60,000 Mandeans in Syria (among those registered with UNHCR, there were 5 per cent Mandeans, which, among the Iraqi refugee population of 1.2 million at the end of 2007, translates into 60,000 individuals). Mandeans interviewed say there are probably 10,000 to 15,000 living in Syria.[81] Before the influx of refugees began in earnest in 2005, UNHCR estimated that Iraqi Christians made up 20 per cent of the total refugee flow into Syria, although their overall percentage in the Iraqi population is less than 5 per cent. The reasons, as discussed in Chapter 1, are that they were among the first victims of ethnic cleansing and the violence in Iraq.[82] The existence of a large community of Syrian Christians attracted Iraqi Christians to come to Syria. The Christian community played a strong role in organizing humanitarian response to needy Iraqis by distributing aid and medical care: 'The religious sector has provided a sustained, life-saving response to Iraqis.'[83] Another important factor leading those minorities to head to Syria was the strength and efficiency of their migratory networks, and the presence of a sizeable community in Europe, North America and Australia that support and sustain these emigrants through remittances: 'Access to social networks and mobility can be among refugees' most important assets.'[84] The economic lives of these families centre on their extended families whether in Syria, Iraq or third countries; they receive or give help according to their situations and adjust their resettlement plans by the success or failure of other members of the family.[85]

As is the case in Jordan, most Iraqis who reach Syria seem to shed sectarian bitterness. Time and again, the message that comes across is simple: outside Iraq they have to coexist: 'The situation is different when you are out, because people see things differently. But inside Iraq, people are still blinded by hatred and grudges they carry against one another.'[86] As one Mandean living in Damascus told me: 'In exile, everyone is a brother. We are now Iraqis and not Sunnis, Shia or Mandeans.'[87] Along the same lines, an Iraqi told a journalist that 'being strangers in other countries has taught us to be more tolerant of one another'.[88] It should be noted that this phenomenon of coexistence is not unique to Iraqis. Balkans, Serbs and Muslims, who fought and massacred each other's community, lived together in exile in Germany or Austria – far from the sectarian hatred that dominated back at home. Thus non-Muslim minorities' lives are similar to those of other Iraqis. Depending on their socio-economic conditions, they have to cope with the same basic issues: employment, housing, securing income for an undefined period, health, education, visas and building a new life in Syria or waiting to be resettled.

As mentioned in Chapter 1, although Palestinians in Iraq are not a religious minority, they ended up having the same fate as minorities who lack protection. As the violence against them grew, Palestinian families attempted to flee to Syria. However, the Syrian government refused to allow a few hundred

Palestinians entry into Syria. HRW, together with other NGOs, tried to pressure Syria into taking those refugees but to no avail: 'It is hard to understand why Syria has provided refuge to nearly a million Iraqi refugees but is shutting the door on hundreds of Palestinians also fleeing Iraq.'[89] In a no-man's-land, 1,400 Palestinians live in Al-Tanf camp on the Iraqi–Syria border where the conditions are appalling.[90] By the end of 2007, the number of refugees in this camp rose to 2,000. Another camp, on the Iraqi side of the border, contains another 1,500 Palestinians and again the conditions of living are harsh during the hot summer and the cold winter. UNHCR continues its efforts to find a solution by resettling the Palestinians in third countries around the world.[91] In spite of these settings, UNHCR reported that 30–40 Palestinians per day continue to escape violence by leaving Baghdad to join those camps. By the end of 2007, it is estimated that 13,000 Palestinians still lived in Baghdad.[92]

Economic situation of Iraqis and their impact on Syria's economy

Syria is a middle-income, developing country and its economy is predominantly state controlled. The two main pillars of the economy are agriculture and oil. In 2006, its GDP was roughly $35 billion compared with Jordan's $14.2 billion, and its GDP per capita was only $1,464 compared with Jordan's $2,533.[93]

Unemployment is a sensitive issue in Syria and some believe that 'the government manipulates the figures to lower the rate of unemployment'.[94] The International Labour Organization (ILO) has estimated unemployment in 2003 at 11.2 per cent (23 per cent among women and 8 per cent among men),[95] and the unemployment rate was higher in rural than in urban areas.[96] Many Syrians adapt by holding multiple jobs and by participating in the informal economy. The arrival of so many Iraqis, particularly after 2005, who were desperate for work undermined the informal economy, with reports of Iraqi labourers willing to work for lower daily wages than Syrian labourers.[97] For unemployed rural Syrians emigrating to cities after 2006, the influx of Iraqis meant two things: fewer opportunities in the informal economy (and if they did find jobs then possibly at lower wages) and higher rents as will be discussed.[98]

Officially Iraqis are not allowed to work in Syria and for most, Syria's large informal economy is the only outlet. No accurate statistics of the size of this economy exists but UNDP estimated that the informal economy employed 48 per cent of the poor.[99] The UN agencies estimated unemployment levels for Iraqis in Syria at 80.7 per cent for women and 53 per cent for men; and men over 50 years of age make up only 11 per cent of the workforce, while children and adolescents between the ages of 13 and 22 make up 18 per cent of the Iraqi workforce.[100] (These statistics relate to early 2006 before the huge waves of Iraqis arrived in Syria.) 'Employed Iraqi refugees are extremely vulnerable due to the limited legal protection'[101] and to the nature of the informal economy. Thus Iraqi workers are highly susceptible to exploitation whether in terms of wages or conditions of work. In 2006, two-thirds of working Iraqis were in service-providing occupations, although many of them had held managerial and professional positions in Iraq.[102] Others have opened commercial businesses, often serving the local Iraqi community, though these ventures require a Syrian partner in whose name the business is registered. Again these small businesses are vulnerable to blackmail from Syrian security officials and unscrupulous business partners given that they tend to operate in a quasi-legal way. 'Squeezing' the Iraqis is a way of collecting bribes as part of the corrupt bureaucratic system that exists. In March 2007, it was reported that businesses with 'ostentatiously Iraqi names' such as Kebab Baghdad in Jarmana were forced to remove explicit Iraqi names from their signs and advertising.[103] Local business owners told journalists that Syrian security officials had informally told them that this measure was to remind them that they were not a permanent 'colony' in Damascus.[104]

One aspect of the economic impact of the refugees on Syria's economy is dissimilar from Jordan: the Iraqis did not commit large capital to investments in industry and the stock market (which in any case does not exist in Syria). Many of the businessmen who came to Syria already had ties in the country, but those who did not have large investments pre-2003 chose to move to Jordan where the business environment is more attractive.[105]

As discussed earlier in this chapter, many Iraqis survive by relying on savings and remittances from Iraq. Thus, the level of poverty among Iraqis in Syria, given the scarcity of employment in Syria and dwindling savings, continues to increase. Towards the end of 2007, UNHCR issued ATM (automated teller machine) cards to 7,000 needy Iraqi families in Syria given that an 'increasing number of refugees are finding it difficult to make ends meet'.[106] Each eligible family can withdraw $100 a month in financial assistance, plus $10 for each dependent from these machines, rather than queue outside the UNHCR office in Damascus to receive their financial assistance.[107] By the end of 2007, free food was being distributed to 51,000 refugees by WFP, UNHCR and the Syrian Red Crescent. According to WFP in January 2008, the number of Iraqi refugees relying on food aid was expected to reach 115,000 by the middle of the year.[108] However, by late April, the number had already risen to 150,000 and WFP aimed to provide assistance to 360,000 refugees in Syria.[109] One UNHCR official described the state of poverty among Iraqis:

People are finding themselves in extreme conditions and at the worst end
we're seeing child labour, early marriage and survival sex. . . . This is
something that these families would never have resorted to in Iraq. They're
facing drastic measures in order to keep some semblance of quality of
life.[110]

In spite of these conditions, Iraqis are habitually blamed by Syrians – just as
the Iraqis in Jordan are blamed by Jordanians – for price hikes in groceries and
property, and hence it is important to look at the refugees' impact on Syria's
economy.

There is no doubt that due to the influx of Iraqis, demand for housing, particularly in the rental market, has escalated and with it came significant
increases in prices. However, given the lack of official statistics, it is hard to
gauge how much of the increase in prices was due to Iraqis or expansion in economic growth accompanied by inflation. Real GDP growth increased from 1.1
per cent in 2003 to 3.3 per cent by 2005 and reached 4.4 per cent in 2006, while
the Consumer Price Index (CPI) rose from 5.8 per cent in 2003 to 10 per cent
in 2006.[111] 'What is certain is that the issue of rent prices is an emotional issue
for Iraqis and Syrians alike', as the Iraqis complain of exorbitant charges while
the Syrians blame the Iraqis for lack of housing and their need to pay higher
rents.[112] Syrian officials have said that their population of 18 million swelled by
7 per cent in one year and 'no economy can simply absorb so many'.[113]

The second issue blamed on the Iraqis is the rise in price of most staples.
Many Syrians also claim that the influx of refugees has dramatically pushed the
demand for state-subsidized goods and services, which in turn placed pressure
on the country's finances. Again, as in Jordan, this is true but it is only part of
the picture. In fact, Syria's economy grew at a slow pace between 1998 and
2003, but began to recover from 2004 as it benefited from Iraqi refugees'
income and abundant liquidity in the Gulf region. Inflows related to Iraqi
immigrants increased from $450 million in 2004 to roughly $1.3 billion by
2006, thus improving Syria's balance of payments.[114] The IMF (International
Monetary Fund) clearly considers that Syria's economic recovery and
increased momentum was partly thanks to Iraqi refugees.[115] As for the pressure on Syria's public services, one cannot overlook the fact that Syria had
mediocre public services in the first place. The country is not taking advantage
of Iraqi talents. For example, while the refugee crisis is pushing the limits of the
Syrian health system, many Iraqi doctors living in Syria are unemployed and
are desperate to practise their profession.[116] Akin to Jordan, Syria was struggling with many of these issues (public service, unemployment, inflation)
beforehand, but it is true also that after 2003, the stress on services such as education and health expanded and the dramatic increase in rental prices put
pressure on the Syrian government, whose response will be discussed below.

It is necessary to consider the influx of Iraqis into Syria in the context of Syria's economic condition and the problems the country is facing. Syria is undergoing economic changes and the IMF praised the Syrian government for its reforms and liberalization of the investment regime, and applauded the containment of inflationary pressures by the economy's supply responsiveness and timely fiscal adjustment.[117] However, Syria's struggles to reform the subsidies system, in its path to change the economy from a centralized-control economy to open and free markets, increases the likelihood of drastic economic shocks and possible social unrest. Meanwhile, the gap between rich and poor is widening, and a 2008 survey of Syrians in Damascus indicated that the financial situation of 70 per cent of the respondents has 'deteriorated seriously' in the last two years.[118] A UNDP report in 2005 found that 11.4 per cent of the population, or almost two million individuals, did not have the means to obtain their basic food and non-food needs and that poverty was more prevalent in rural areas.[119] It is plausible that the combination of economic modernization on one hand, and inflationary and system stress caused by the Iraqi influx on the other hand, 'has shifted the equation' of Syria having a socialist ideology 'with an economically more homogeneous population'.[120]

Another important economic element in understanding Syria's policies towards the Iraqi refugees is that 'Syria's public finances are headed for challenging times in the coming 10–15 years', given the fact that oil revenues, on which the budget relies to the tune of 25 per cent of GDP, are expected to decline rapidly over the next few years due to lower production.[121] Fortunately for Syria, the boost in oil prices since summer 2007 has helped its finances. Thus, when Syria claims that the Iraqi refugees have already cost $1.6 billion, and it would need about $1 billion to 'deal with the inflation caused by the arrival of refugees', this has to be put within the context of its economic challenges.[122]

Overall, from an economic point of view, the benefits of the influx of Iraqi refugees outweigh the negatives. Their arrival ignited the machine of economic recovery and might lead in the future to improvements in public services, particularly health and education. In many facets of the economic benefits of the refugees, Syria resembles Jordan. Obviously, the arrival of more than one million refugees over a short period 'stressed the system' and created resentment among the local population, which forced the Syrian government to take these aspects into account in responding to the refugee crisis.

Syria's, Iraq's and international responses

Syria's response

Syria's response to Iraqi refugees and its relationship with Iraq following the 2003 invasion is somewhat more complicated than in Jordan's case. The Syrian government, as the Jordanian government, is guided by two principles: security and economy. While the Palestinian issue is also important for Syria, it is a higher priority in Jordan given the vast differences in demographics between the two countries. Interestingly, neither country allowed a few thousand Iraqi Palestinians to enter, and instead both kept them in camps on their borders. The security issue is more complicated for Syria than for Jordan due to two factors: the historical animosity between Syria and Iraq until 2003, followed by the invasion of Iraq by a superpower that has placed Syria among the countries supporting terrorism. Unlike Jordan, Syria has been accused by the USA and Iraq of funnelling insurgents and arms across its border with Iraq. An Iraqi government spokesman claimed 'that 50 per cent of murders and bombings are by Arab extremists coming from Syria'.[123] Similarly, a Pentagon report was critical of Syria's role:

> Although Iraq resumed diplomatic relations with Syria in November 2006, Damascus appears unwilling to cooperate fully. . . . Syria continues to provide safe haven, border transit and limited logistical supports to some Iraqi insurgents, especially former Saddam-era Iraqi Ba'ath [sic] Party elements. . . , Syria remains the primary foreign fighter gateway into Iraq.[124]

Thus distrust prevails between Syria and the West, particularly the USA, and this has affected Syria's relationships with international organizations. Syria's close relationship with Iran is seen by the USA as another obstacle to good relations. Syria feels that it is paying a high cost for the American adventure in Iraq that went wrong:

> It was the Bush administration that promoted the war on Iraq and invented the excuses for it. . . . It waged the war without obtaining permission from the United Nations and without listening to the sincere and knowledgeable voices – headed by the voice of Syria – that warned against the dangers of the war and stressed that it would result in mass killings, destruction, looting and violation of all human sanctities.[125]

As we saw in the last chapter, the major security factor for the Jordanians is the Palestinian issue, while Syria sees its relationship with the Arab and western world through the Lebanese prism. Iraq is another card in the international game that is played to secure Syria's interests in Lebanon. Another important element for security is the same fear that Jordan has: Iraqi refugees might bring their sectarian rivalries with them. Indications are that the majority of refugees are actually running away from sectarianism and 'consciously trying to distance themselves from overtly sectarian groups'.[126] As noted before, the Shi'i 'factor' in Syria is not to be underestimated given the role that religious Shi'i institutions play in Syria, while the Sunnis lack such organizations. There is also a potential threat that extreme Sunni Iraqis could radicalize Syria's Sunni community against domination by the Alawite minority.[127] Both these threats have not materialized either due to lack of interest by the Iraqis or fear of the all-powerful Syrian security services. Iraqis, whether in Jordan or Syria, continue to fear these governments not because of their policies, but due to an attitude that they bring with them: the fear of authority.

The Syrian government strictly limits freedom of expression, association and assembly based on an emergency rule, imposed in 1963, and which remains in effect. According to HRW, 'state security services subject human rights activists to intrusive scrutiny and harassment that includes travel bans, arrest and trial'.[128] As in Jordan, Iraqis in Syria are not allowed to have their associations and in any case, under Syrian law the government has extensive jurisdiction to control the day-to-day operations of any association.

As for the economic pillar of Syrian policy, the basics, as we saw previously, are the impact on Syria's finances, and the pressure on the already stretched education system, health and public services. The Deputy Foreign Minister of Syria argued that the country's 'economy and infrastructure are buckling under the great weight of the [refugee] burden'.[129] He claimed that the sudden increase in the population led to 'a rise in costs in all areas of life'. According to him, prices of basic goods have gone up by 30 per cent, property prices by 40 per cent and rentals by 150 per cent. In addition, water consumption has increased by 21 per cent.[130] As a result, the government is worried by the increased resentment of the Syrian population (and this is interconnected to the security factor in the sense that anti-regime elements might capitalize on this resentment). Meanwhile, Syrian media insisted that the overall situation of the Iraqis in Syria is 'not bad'.[131]

Syria's policy towards the Iraqi refugees in part reflects political and economic calculations. The presence of a high number of Iraqis helps to 'deter the U.S. from destabilising the regime; force it to engage with Damascus on other political issues; attract international funds; deepen its influence in Iraq; or even expose the Syrian people to the heavy costs of the Iraqi model'.[132]

The Brookings' fieldwork concluded that relations between Syrians and Iraqi refugees and mutual perceptions between them are deteriorating. Syrians see Iraqis as 'arrogant, rough, ill-mannered and hold them responsible for the "perceived" increase in crime', while Iraqis see Syrians as 'greedy and corrupt'.[133] In an extensive investigative article by the Syrian *Al-Thawrah* newspaper, some Syrians in Jarmana expressed their anger: the Iraqis made the town crowded, pushed up the prices of everything and brought with them their social problems which are leading to theft and prostitution.[134] Needless to say, the increasing strain on the economy, coupled with the worsening mutual perception of Iraqis and Syrians, suggests that tensions between the Iraqi refugees and their Syrian hosts may become more problematic in the future, particularly if there is a significant slowdown in economic growth.

Until October 2007, Syrian policy towards accepting Iraqi refugees was generally welcoming. The Syrian authorities tolerated the fact that many Iraqis were working illegally and for some professionals such as doctors and engineers, work permits were issued. But in September 2007, in an attempt to stem the tide of refugees which was then estimated at 2,000 per day, the Syrian authorities introduced a visa requirement for Iraqis. Until that time, Iraqis could enter on a valid passport and were allowed to stay for three months, which was renewable. One Syrian minister explained the reasons behind the restrictions by saying that his countrymen 'are no longer able to offer the new arrivals a good hosting', as the number of refugees 'exceeded the reasonable number'.[135] A Syrian newspaper argued that these measures are not directed against the 'Iraqi brothers' but are simply to reduce the burdens carried by Syrian citizens.[136] In reality, months before the Syrian decision took effect, international organizations were warning of a looming crisis as the influx of Iraqi refugees was becoming almost out of control (some reports suggested 4,000 to 6,000 refugees per day), but unfortunately no action was taken by any country to help.[137]

The introduction by Syria of visa requirements for Iraqis signified a shift away from the previous open-door policy. Iraqis must first obtain a three-month single entry visa from the Syrian embassy in Baghdad before entering Syria, and visas are usually granted within 10–14 days. Tighter visa rules led to a dramatic drop in the number of Iraqis entering Syria, but still it is estimated that 400–500 were managing to enter the country daily by the end of 2007. In addition, Syria is not automatically deporting those that overstay their 'visits' in Syria unless they have entered illegally or committed criminal acts.[138]

Iraq's response

As discussed in the chapter on refugees in Jordan, Iraq's response to the refugee crisis was feeble at best. The impression in Syria is much like that in Jordan: the Iraqi government does not want to help the refugees nor does it feel responsible for them. In fact, when Syria imposed new visa rules, Syrian officials told journalists that 'they were responding to a longstanding request

from the Iraqi government to close their border'. According to these reports
the Iraqi Prime Minister Nouri Al-Maliki told Syrian leaders that 'the constant
flow of refugees undermined the Iraqi government's efforts to bring greater
security to the country'.[139] Iraqis living in Syria are astonished at the manoeu-
vres of Al-Maliki 's government to restrict the movement of Iraqis in Syria.
One media report suggested that Al-Maliki presented to Syrian officials a list
of the names of 91 politicians and 67 artists asking that they be handed over to
Iraq due to their opposition to his government.[140] Therefore the Iraqis in
Syria, like those in Jordan, worry each time an Iraqi official visits Damascus.
As one Iraqi family living in Damascus told me:

> Iraqi politicians do not seem to care [about us]. Although there is no
> solution in sight and stability for Iraq and for us [living in exile] seems far
> away, no one is doing anything. They [Iraqi politicians and officials] are not
> up to it.[141]

Another Iraqi commenting on Al-Maliki 's visit to Syria noted:

> His visit will not help any refugees. . . . Honestly, I don't think he can do
> anything for us. He has to give some money to the Syrians but it won't
> make a difference to us.[142]

One Iraqi politician, the speaker of Iraq's House of Representatives, admitted that 'the Iraqis in Syria receive more care from the Syrians than from the
Iraqis'.[143] However, it took a long time before the Iraqis contributed $15 mil-
lion (roughly $10 to $12 per refugee) to Syria towards the cost of hosting the
refugees,[144] which is indeed a pitiful amount. There were reports that Iraq
offered, at the request of Syria, subsidized prices for oil products, but the Iraqi
government quickly denied those reports and continued to pay only lip service
in helping the refugees without incurring any real cost.[145] The Syrian Deputy
Foreign Minister justifiably called for Iraq to help its refugees because
'assistance from the Iraqi government would reflect positively on the refugees,
especially when they return to their country', but unfortunately 'Syria is still
waiting for these obligations to be fulfilled'.[146]

In spite of Syria's generosity towards the refugees, the opinion of Syria by
Iraqis still living in Iraq is divided along sectarian lines, with 81 per cent of Shia
having a negative view of Syria and only 2 per cent seeing Syria's role as positive. This compared with 14 per cent of Sunnis having a positive view and 58
per cent having a neutral view.[147]

International response

Syria's view of the international response to the Iraqi refugees is clear: all countries and international organizations have a duty to help both the refugees and Syria, as the main host. Syria's policy is focused on receiving international recognition for its efforts, and thus, unlike Jordan, it accepts direct aid to the refugees. The Syrians felt bitter and frustrated: 'No one in the international community is helping us.'[148] Sharp criticism was directed at European countries when the European Union announced a donation of €18 million. A Syrian paper mocked the size of donation and blasted the EU for not intervening to help the refugees given that some European states, together with the USA, contributed to creating the problem and exacerbating it.[149] But the sharpest attacks are aimed at the USA. One Syrian official asserted that 'the American administration neither feels the humanitarian dimension nor does it respect conventions and human rights'.[150] Syrian media and officials speculate whether the 'failure of the world to provide sufficient assistance is a result of an American pressure' and constantly 'express surprise' about the US position.[151]

There is little doubt that 'the continued embargo by the United States of the Syrian government is severely hampering the humanitarian response'.[152] As Refugees International summed up the American role:

> United States political support and diplomatic initiative in responding to
> the assistance needs of Iraqi refugees remains conspicuously absent.[153]

Syria, for its part, refused for months to grant visas to officials from the US Department of Homeland Security in order to screen Iraqis in person for admission to the US Refugee Resettlement Program.[154] Only in November 2007 was the ban lifted, and then American officials headed to Damascus to interview Iraqis referred by UNHCR for resettlement.[155]

The Arab response to the plight of refugees in Syria is no different from the response to those in Jordan: a lot of talk about support with little action. UNHCR received a contribution of $10 million dedicated to Iraqi refugees in Syria from the United Arab Emirates,[156] and other countries in the area donate from time to time but nothing close to reflecting their wealth and economic power.

As we saw before, Syria is distrustful of international organizations and both Jordan and Syria followed a 'cautious approach to international involvement' as they were both wary of the consequences for their own population.[157] While the churches have been involved and effective within their humanitarian mandate, international NGOs in Syria do not have the same flexibility to work as in Jordan, and all their efforts have to be coordinated via the Syrian Red

Crescent. Similar to other Syrian governmental and semi-governmental institutions, the Syrian Red Crescent lacks the capacity to 'cope with the colossal
change' as its budget, derived mostly from UNHCR funding, grew from
$250,000 in 2006 to $10 million by 2008.[158]

In spring 2008, three NGOs – Première Urgence, the International Medical
Corps and the Danish Refuge Council – have signed a Memorandum of
Understanding (MOU) with the Syrian Red Crescent whereby they are
exempted from the 2 per cent 'overhead charges'. A total of 14 NGOs have
received their MOUs although some still view the conditions of the agreement
as 'restrictive'.[159] UN agencies operate from Syria and work with the refugees.
UNHCR is the most active of those organizations and has the important task
of registering and referring refugees for settlement. By June 2008, UNHCR had
registered 203,982 Iraqi refugees (13 to 16 per cent of the Iraqi population in
Syria). It is interesting to note that about 23,000 were classified as victims of
torture/violence; roughly 30,000 have serious medical conditions and almost
5,000 are considered women at risk.[160] The percentages by ethnicity – as presented earlier in this chapter – are not widely different from those registered in
Jordan with the exception of Mandeans (4 per cent in Syria versus
1 per cent in Jordan).[161]

As mentioned, with the increase in the level of poverty among the Iraqis,
UNHCR instituted a cash assistance programme through ATMs in Damascus
to help the most vulnerable 13,000 families.

There has been, however, criticism of these UN organizations. Refugees
International argued that given the deteriorating state of education among the
refugees, 'UNICEF's response has been late and insufficient'.[162] There were
complaints that some of these organizations are too bureaucratic and are not
coordinating their efforts whether in Syria or Jordan.[163] A report by the
International Catholic Migration Commission indicated that while Syria has
had a good relationship with the UN agencies, UNHCR in Jordan has 'not
been able to be as effective as needed in coordination and planning'.[164] Iraqis
bemoan the 'red tape obstacles' in dealing with these agencies which only add
to their suffering and cost them more money.[165]

One of the issues that UNHCR faces in Syria (and to a much lesser extent in
Jordan) is the question of returnees to Iraq. This will be dealt with in Chapter
7, but it is important to point out with regard to Syria that the main factors
leading Iraqis to return are the illegal status of most refugees, which prevents
them, inter alia, from obtaining work permits, and the continuing deterioration of their financial situation. Poor and struggling to survive, some have
resorted to desperate measures such as child labour and prostitution, while
others felt that their situation would be somewhat ameliorated if they
returned to Iraq. Thus it is likely that, if the situation were to improve
dramatically in Iraq, and given the poor conditions of most Iraqis living in

Syria, there would be a high number of returnees. One Iraqi returnee summed up the situation well:

> I know that I'm jeopardising my life with this return, but I've had enough and my savings are gone and I couldn't get official residency and I had to live as a fugitive fearing the authorities.[166]

By March 2008, it was estimated that 55,000 refugees had returned to Iraq from Syria. As will be discussed later, those returnees faced new obstacles and problems.

Chapter 4

Iraqi refugees in the rest of the world

Give me your tired, your poor,
Your huddled masses yearning to breathe free,
The wretched refuse of your teeming shore.
Send these, the homeless, tempest-tost to me,
I lift my lamp beside the golden door![1]

Following the 2003 invasion, the exodus from Iraq was not only to Jordan and Syria but also to many other countries worldwide: Arab countries, neighbouring Iran, Sweden, other European countries and North America. Iraqis who fled prior to 2003 were also dispersed with large concentrations in the neighbouring countries. By the time the 2003 war began, an estimated one million had found refuge outside the Middle East, with large clusters settling in Western Europe, North America and Australia.

This chapter will focus on the important aspects of this dispersal by looking at the main hosts: Egypt, Lebanon and Sweden. Other host countries such as Iran will be discussed briefly. Given the role of the USA and Britain in the 2003 war, this chapter will also address the policies of those two countries towards the resettlement of Iraqi refugees in their own territories.

Egypt

Egypt has historically been a place of refuge for various groups, including Armenians who fled the 1915 massacre under the Ottomans, Palestinians after 1948 and Sudanese after 1983. Nowadays, refugees residing in Egypt come from 36 countries with most being from Africa. The Sudanese are the largest contingent with estimates ranging from two to four million.[2]

Egypt is one of three countries in the Middle East that has ratified the 1951 Geneva Convention (the other two are Yemen and Israel). Egypt, however, had numerous reservations regarding the Convention and hence, 'the rights of refugees are significantly constrained', and refugees have no right to acquire citizenship. As a result, 'the possibility of full integration in Egypt for refugees is effectively ruled out'.[3]

A trickle of Iraqis relocated to Egypt during the decade of sanctions in the 1990s and, by 2003, their number was just a few thousand. The trickle turned into a flood after 2003 and particularly after February 2006. Once again, estimates of the number of Iraqi refugees in Egypt vary significantly from 40,000 to 150,000, with most being around 80,000 to 100,000.[4] Overall, three main reasons for choosing Egypt could be underlined:

1) Economic reasons. Egypt is perceived to be a much cheaper place to live and access essential services than Jordan and Syria.

2) Safety and distance from the locus of violence and sectarianism. Egypt has a population of about 75 million and some refugees felt that a relatively small number of Iraqis could easily assimilate in a vast city such as Cairo. As one Iraqi woman described it:

> Living in safety is the main source of happiness for Iraqi women in Egypt. Just to go out alone shopping is a luxury they could not afford back home.[5]

3) Many Iraqis saw Egypt as a transit point given the high number of non-Iraqi refugees who have been resettled from Egypt to third countries since the end of the 1990s. In fact, international organizations expressed their fears that 'the existence of generous resettlement opportunities might be acting as a pull factor and draw asylum seekers to Egypt in increasing numbers'.[6] One refugee described his feelings:

> We don't want to live in Egypt . . . Egypt has its own problems with too many people here. We're just hoping someone from another country with an embassy here will take us.[7]

Iraqi refugees in Egypt live predominantly in Cairo and the overwhelming majority are from Baghdad. The majority are Sunnis, which is unsurprising given the fact that the Egyptian government has made anti-Shi'i statements in the past.[8]

The average Iraqi family size in Egypt is four persons and 26 per cent of households are headed by women. A high percentage are middle-class professionals but only a few have managed to find appropriate jobs for their qualifications. Some 40 per cent are children under 18 years of age.[9]

Economically, a considerable number of Iraqis in Egypt rely on remittances from Iraq. Refugees in Egypt are not allowed to work and can only secure an income through illegal employment in the informal economy. Thus the main problem for Iraqis is looking for a job in such a tenuous legal situation. The situation is exacerbated by the fact that Egypt faces enormous development challenges and struggles with a number of socio-economic problems. Per capita GDP stood at about $1,500 in 2006 and while the economy managed to grow at about 7 per cent in 2007, the immense challenge continues to be creating jobs. The growth spurt helped in creating about 2.5 million jobs between the end of 2004 and March 2007,[10] but given the population growth, official unemployment statistics still indicate 9 to 12 per cent.

Those Iraqis with insufficient resources to open their own business, which by law needs an Egyptian partner, are left with no alternative but to seek work in the informal economy along with thousands of Sudanese and other refugees. Competition for (both legal and illegal) employment in Egypt is tough for Iraqis and many are heavily reliant on savings and remittances from Iraq. For example, many Iraqi doctors who came to Egypt discovered that even when they found jobs, obtaining the necessary Egyptian medical licence is expensive and difficult. This is not helped by the fact that Egypt is experiencing a 'glut' of doctors who also cannot find jobs in their own country.[11] Life in Egypt is much more expensive than many Iraqis had expected. As in Jordan and Syria, savings dwindle as time goes by and pressure on Iraqis mounts. One refugee described the situation:

> Life here is very tiring. There are no schools, no money, no home and no help from Egypt. We came on [sic] our savings, but they're almost gone now.[12]

Housing is one of the most pressing needs and rents continue to rise. Egyptians, like Jordanians and Syrians, blame the Iraqis for the rise in property prices. Given the small numbers of Iraqis in large cities such as Cairo and Alexandria, this is hard to justify. Inflation in Egypt hovered around 11 per cent in 2006–07 due to higher world commodity prices and an increase in demand stemming from the high growth in economy.[13] Year-on-year inflation hit more than 12 per cent in February 2008, leading to growing fears about social displacement in a country where it is estimated that one in every five people cannot meet basic needs.[14] In fact, in April 2008, a general strike paralysed Cairo, underscoring the discontent arising from food prices, depressed salaries and an unprecedented gap between rich and poor.[15]

Egypt has restricted the access of refugees to public education and public health. As a result most Iraqi refugees are generally barred from government education. Those children that attend pay higher fees than Egyptian children: roughly $44 compared to $7 to $9 by Egyptians.[16] Private education is expensive and can range from $140 to $1,140 per year.[17] Some private schools expelled Iraqi refugee children when their visas expired.[18] According to Egyptian officials, 4,209 Iraqi children attended schools in 2007, mostly at private schools.[19] In addition, there were some 2,600 children attending local schools with the support of UNHCR.[20] Assuming the number of school-aged Iraqi children to be around 25,000 to 35,000, attendance is 19 per cent to 25 per cent. Again, as in Syria, these numbers are shockingly low and will have severe consequences in the future. The cost of education and fear of 'official' registration are, as in Jordan and Syria, the main drivers behind the low numbers. There is also another element in Egypt: Iraqis believe that they will be resettled quickly and thus enrolling children in school is deemed unnecessary.

The health conditions, physical and psychological, of Iraqi refugees are in a precarious state along the lines previously discussed in Jordan and Syria. Among the Iraqi population in Egypt, many have developed serious psychological and stress-related illnesses, including cardiac problems. A medical doctor working with the refugees ascribed the increase in cases of heart disease and diabetes to the relentless stress surrounding all aspects of life for these refugees. Poverty and the endless stream of bad news from Iraq, coupled with the realization that swift resettlement is unlikely, are creating this damaging stress:[21] 'With children out of school, parents unable to find jobs and support families and memories of violence experienced in Iraq so powerful, mental health problems are growing.'[22]

Access to health services is limited to emergency cases. The main problems, according to WHO, are lack of 'decentralized access to the subsidized health care system and affordability of health care'.[23] An increasing number of Iraqi refugees are not able to afford to pay for treatment costs, including medication. The UN agencies, in their appeal to improve the health needs of Iraqis in host countries, allocated $5.5 million out of $84.8 million to Egypt, mostly to improve access to health services.[24]

Egypt's policy towards the Iraqi refugees changed in late 2006. Until then, Iraqis were granted tourist visas renewable after three months. By early January 2007, the Egyptian authorities began imposing restrictive procedures, and at least one member of each family seeking entry to Egypt was required to undergo a face-to-face interview in the Egyptian consulates in Damascus or Amman.[25] Shia reported to international organizations that they were being harassed, and the main reason for the change in attitude towards the Iraqis, according to Egyptian officials, was 'concern over security'.[26] Given this 'concern', Egyptian authorities deemed 'inappropriate the "doors wide open" policy for indefinite numbers of Iraqis to come and live in Egypt'.[27] In fact, Egypt has, in the past, also changed its policy towards the Sudanese based on security grounds; the authorities limited the rights of the Sudanese refugees for work, education and residency following an alleged assassination attempt on President Mubarak during his visit to Addis Ababa in June 1995.[28]

Overall, the Egyptian population has responded positively towards the Iraqis who have managed to blend in with the local population. But, as discussed earlier, the Egyptians perceive the Iraqis as well-off and blame them for an increase in rents. Iraqis on the other hand, while grateful for Egypt taking them in, are frustrated that they are not allowed to work legally and remind the Egyptians that Iraq has hosted more than one million Egyptians and provided jobs for them.[29] Iraqis in Cairo and Alexandria socialize mostly with Iraqis whom they knew in Iraq and feel they can trust. Again, akin to Jordan and Syria, Egypt does not allow the creation of societies or clubs for Iraqis which means that they lack organized support networks.[30] Interestingly, other refugee groups (Sudanese, Ethiopians and Somalis) have been allowed to form their local associations. Shia have also been restricted from forming their own houses of worship.[31]

The Iraqi government's response to the refugees in Egypt is consistent with its policy towards other refugees in the area: apathy and lack of assistance. The Iraqis in Egypt react in exactly the same way as their brethren in Jordan and Syria when an Iraqi official visits Cairo. When Iraq's Prime Minister Nouri Al-Maliki visited Cairo in April 2007, an Iraqi refugee described his response:

> What are we supposed to make of this visit by Maliki? Nothing. Maliki and people like him are a major part of the problem in Iraq. They are not the government of the Iraqi people. They are not Iraqis – not real Iraqis. They are power groups that are only after their interests. They do not care for the Iraqis.[32]

UNHCR and, particularly, NGOs were ill-prepared for the unexpected influx of Iraqis,[33] and the current political climate in Egypt makes it difficult to establish an NGO.[34] As mentioned before, Iraqis arrived in Egypt with high expectations for resettlement but, by April 2008, less than 11,000 were registered with UNHCR, which means a much smaller number were referred for resettlement and even fewer were granted visas by third countries. Among those registered, 62 per cent were Sunnis, 18 per cent Shia, 2 per cent Christians and 16 per cent under the category 'Islam unspecified'.[35] Registration with UNHCR grants the refugees legal residence which needs to be renewed every six months, and similar to Jordan and Syria, UNHCR refers some of those registered to Caritas Internationalis and Catholic Relief Services for limited medical and educational support.

In conclusion, Iraqis in Egypt face the same problems as refugees in Syria and Jordan: lack of legal employment, low enrolment in schools and rising costs for health services. Being a smaller number in a much larger country, Iraqis in Egypt blended in more easily than the Iraqis in Syria and Jordan.

Lebanon

Lebanon has hosted Iraqis since the 1990s – mostly Shia fleeing Saddam's regime. Christians fleeing the regime also preferred to head to Lebanon because of its large Christian minority. Prior to 2003, estimates of Iraqis in Lebanon were put at 10,000.[36] Following the invasion, Iraqis began arriving in Lebanon and by mid-2005, a survey by the Danish Refugee Council estimated their number at about 20,000 persons.[37] The survey found that of the 590 respondents, 63 per cent were Shia, 21 per cent Christians and only 7 per cent Sunnis.[38]

The Samarra bombing of February 2006 led to an influx of refugees as referred to in Chapter 1. A second and more comprehensive survey, also by the Danish Refugee Council, published in November 2007, came to the conclusion that the number of Iraqis is about 50,000 based on data provided by the Lebanese General Security Office. However, given the complexity of the survey, the Danish Council asserts that the 50,000 is an estimate for a range of 26,000 to 100,000.[39] Surveying refugees, mostly illegal, in urban areas is a complex project on its own even before political interests enter the equation, as was underscored with Fafo's survey in Jordan. Interestingly, this survey indicated that about 15 per cent refused to participate in the survey. These refugees felt that 'such studies are useless' and 'a waste of time', and more importantly they are 'illegal and fear being arrested'.[40] Also these surveys tend to be skewed due to 'the time element' as time of arrival obviously impacts on all the answers. Surveys of Iraqi refugees were influenced by the fact that there was a flood of refugees exiting Iraq in a relatively short period of six to nine months (peaking between the end of 2006 and mid-2007).

Most Iraqis have entered Lebanon via Syria and they found it impossible to obtain an entry visa. According to the Danish survey, 71 per cent of the respondents had illegal status (77.5 per cent of the households in the survey).[41] The overwhelming majority of Iraqi refugees – 95 per cent according to UNHCR figures – are smuggled into Lebanon across the porous border with Syria.[42] Once inside Lebanon, they have no legal status and lack protection which, needless to say, had a tremendous impact on Iraqis residing there.

The average household of Iraqis in the 2007 survey is 2.86, and 51 per cent of respondents were Shia, 25 per cent Christians, around 12 per cent Sunnis and 10 per cent under 'other'. Unlike Iraqis in Jordan, Syria and Egypt who mostly opted for the capital and are concentrated in particular city neighbourhoods, Iraqis in Lebanon were scattered with 79 per cent in the Mount Lebanon area, 9 per cent in Nabatiyeh and 6 per cent in southern Lebanon.[43]

One major reason that led Iraqis to seek refuge in Lebanon was the economic circumstances in Syria from where most came. One Iraqi described his choices:

...stay in Syria, where Iraqis need not fear arrest, but where there are very limited opportunities, wages are low, and prices high; or go to Lebanon where they [Iraqis] risk arrest for being in the country illegally, but where it is easier to earn enough money to survive.[44]

A second reason is that some felt 'unsafe' in Syria because those who threatened them in Iraq could also threaten them in Syria. A third reason, analogous to Egypt, is that refugees believed it is easier to be resettled from Lebanon as they heard that UNHCR in Beirut deals with registration faster than in Damascus. Finally, and similar to other countries, family and affiliation played an important role, particularly for Christians from Iraq.[45]

As in other host countries, educational enrolment levels are low. Interestingly, however, among those surveyed by the Danish Refugee Council, enrolment rates were higher among females (64 per cent) than males (54 per cent), as boys were expected to join the workforce. Iraqi children are sent to work in menial jobs by their parents who believe 'children are less likely than adults to get caught without official papers'.[46] Among the reasons given by respondents for why the children are out of school (and this is also applicable to other countries) were: cost (41 per cent); the need to generate income for the family (10 per cent); lack of proper documentation and fear of being 'exposed' (7 per cent); language difficulties due to a different dialect and curriculum (9 per cent); and 'other', which probably includes economic and fear factors (29 per cent).[47]

The health situation of Iraqis in Lebanon is deteriorating as in other host countries. Among those surveyed, 10 per cent suffered chronic problems, with diabetes and hypertension being the most common diseases. During the three months preceding the 2007 survey, 14 per cent of the 2,471 respondents had sought health care due to acute health problems. Again, akin to refugees in other host countries, the cost of treating acute conditions and chronic illnesses was borne mainly by the refugees themselves. NGOs and religious charities covered the cost of 24 per cent of cases of acute illnesses and injuries.[48] This obviously put even more economic pressure on Iraqi households as most medical services in Lebanon are private and refugees are treated on the same basis as Lebanese regardless of their legal status, provided they can pay for their treatment.

Psychologically, Iraqis are suffering in Lebanon because of anguish about their condition and their lack of hope for the future. People feel dejected and despondent as they live on the margins of Lebanese society. One woman explained: 'There is no stability. . . . There is no future for us here.'[49] There are reports of increasing incidence of alcoholism and drug addiction as well as an increase in domestic violence.[50]

With regard to employment, the survey found that a higher proportion of men with illegal status were working compared with men with legal status, but the survey does not explain the reasons behind this finding. Most males work as labourers, employees in shops and other manual labour, and 83 per cent said they rely on employment for income. Interestingly, 74 per cent of the respondents indicated they do not have properties in Iraq, but even for those who do, more than half cannot access their properties due to either damage or occupation.[51]

Economic difficulties in Lebanon, particularly after the war in summer 2006, exacerbated the overall situation for the Lebanese and the Iraqis. Real GDP was flat in 2006 and inflation accelerated in the second half of that year, reflecting supply shortages during the conflict and the ensuing blockade by Israel. Inflation reached 7 per cent from a low of 0.5 per cent in 2005 and it stabilized in 2007 back to roughly 2 per cent.[52] The political tensions that erupted between the government and the opposition affected economic activity and new investments.[53] Iraqi refugees have had to accept jobs for lower wages than the Lebanese as it is very hard for them to get proper work permits. According to HRW, some Lebanese employers (similar to what we saw in other host countries) 'take advantage of the Iraqis' lack of legal status and their lack of recourse to the Lebanese authorities when their rights are violated'.[54] Iraqis are also forced by some landlords to pay higher rents. They are at the mercy of landlords and employers due to their illegal status, and this is pushing many to live on the edge with reports of prostitution coming from several communities.

The Lebanese, constantly focused on the religious 'balance' between the different communities, did not integrate the Palestinians to the same extent as Syria or Jordan did. Thus Lebanon's response to the Iraqi refugees is dominated by the presence of about 400,000 Palestinians in a country with a population of about 4–4.5 million people. Having gone from one political crisis to another during the past 30 years, the Lebanese are wary of hosting another refugee population whose prospects of returning home in the near future are remote. Furthermore, the sectarian tensions in Iraq also plague the Lebanese society and there are fears that the presence of large numbers of Iraqis might exacerbate those tensions. Lebanon has repeatedly announced that 'it is not a country of asylum due to its demographic and social composition'.[55]

Lebanon is not party to the 1951 Geneva Convention and thus it treats people who enter the country illegally to seek asylum, or overstay their visas, as illegal immigrants who are subject to imprisonment, fines and deportation. Despite the existence of an MOU between UNHCR and the Lebanese authorities since the end of 2003, the treatment of refugees continued to be regulated by laws from 1962 relating to the entry and stay of foreigners. The authorities justified detaining refugees by 'the need to assure their removal'.[56] By early November 2006, there were 500 Iraqis in detention,[57] and UNHCR reported 600 being incarcerated by early 2008.[58]

Among the respondents to the Danish survey, 12 per cent of the 1,019 households reported that one member of their family had been detained; half of whom were released and a quarter of whom were returned to Iraq.[59] Some refugees believed that agreeing to repatriate was the only way to negotiate their release from prison.[60] While HRW is very critical of the Lebanese government for its official policy towards the refugees, it argues that in practice:

> ...the Lebanese authorities have shown a remarkable tolerance of the Iraqi presence in Lebanon. The police and the Internal Security Forces (ISF) do not systematically arrest Iraqis who do not have valid visas or residence permits.[61]

Following a visit by the UN's High Commissioner for Refugees, António Guterres, to Beirut in February 2008, the Lebanese government announced that it will give Iraqis who have entered the country illegally or overstayed their visas three months to regularize their stay. The UNHCR praised the decision and called it 'a very important and positive development'.[62]

The Lebanese, as discussed, are themselves going through difficult times; the combination of war and destruction in 2006 followed by internal political tensions which are affecting the economy negatively. While some landlords and employers take advantage of the Iraqi refugees, the majority have welcomed them: 'The Lebanese are respecting us, they are friendly and helpful.'[63] As for the Iraqis, living in Lebanon, for most, means still living in fear. As one Iraqi said:

> When we go out, we don't know whether we will return. When I see a policeman or a member of the authorities, I am very afraid, despite the fact that I am old and sick. Any time there is a checkpoint, we can get caught.[64]

Because of this risk, many men stay home and women and children are sent out to work instead. In the Danish Refugee Council survey of July 2005, 60 per cent of respondents rated security in Lebanon as bad or very bad and in the November 2007 survey, 52 per cent said they 'never feel safe'.[65]

Iraq's response to the Iraqi refugees in Lebanon is not dissimilar from its policy vis-à-vis refugees in the other countries discussed so far. In November 2007 the Iraqi government agreed to extend $2 million to Lebanon to 'ameliorate the living conditions' of the Iraqis, and 'soothe the burden' for Lebanon.[66] Iraqi embassy officials insisted that they 'do not encourage anyone to go back to Iraq', but facilitating the return of detainees is part of their job.[67]

With regard to UNHCR in Lebanon, in practice it had limited success in obtaining the release of Iraqi detainees,[68] and the Iraqis, as in other host countries, were disillusioned with the resettlement plans. UNHCR registered about

11,000 individuals by April 2008, 57 per cent of whom are Shia, 30 per cent Sunnis and 12 per cent Christians.[69] Lebanon is the only Arab country where UNHCR registered more Shia than Sunnis.

Rest of the Arab world

In this section, we will briefly look at Iraqi refugees in four Arab countries and the role of the Arab League.

Kuwait

Having been invaded and occupied in 1990–91, Kuwait has a unique historical relationship with Iraq and Iraqis. In the early 1960s, Abd Al-Karim Kassem declared that Kuwait is part and parcel of Iraq and although there were periods of excellent relations, tension between the two countries rose frequently. Following the Gulf War of 1991 and the expulsion of Iraqi troops from Kuwait, the Kuwaiti government expelled large numbers of Iraqi and Palestinian residents accusing them of being traitors. They joined the ranks of the increasing number of stateless Arabs (*Bidun*) to whom Kuwait refuses to grant any rights.[70] Once the invasion of Iraq began in 2003, Kuwait announced that it would not permit Iraqis to enter its territories. This policy has not changed since then and there are no official figures for the number of Iraqis still living in Kuwait, but rough estimates suggest 10,000 to 50,000.[71]

Saudi Arabia

Saudi Arabia was no more hospitable than Kuwait. After the 1991 Gulf War ended, about 30,000 of the 90,000 Iraqis who had arrived with Coalition forces stayed behind. Saudi Arabia held them in two closed camps under very harsh conditions.[72] Over the years, the refugees were resettled outside the region or returned to Iraq. By the start of the 2003 war, there were about 5,200 refugees left in Rafha camp,[73] and by the end of 2006 less than 100 Iraqis, remained in the camp.[74] As the sectarian violence spread throughout Iraq, the Saudis began building a security fence on the borders with Iraq, to be finished by the end of 2009, to 'stop infiltration operations'.[75] Saudi fears about Iran and the domination of the Shia over the Iraqi government are behind the building of the fence. In addition, the Saudi Shia make up about 10 per cent of the population, but they are heavily concentrated in the oil-rich Eastern province. The fence will be 896 kilometres (560 miles) long, using state-of-the-art technology to detect people crossing the border, and will cost more than $1.1 billion.[76]

Despite the tremendous wealth of the country with oil prices above $100, Saudi Arabia has not contributed directly to help the Iraqi refugees except for its indirect contributions to UNHCR and other UN agencies. UNHCR estimates 5,000 Iraqis living in Saudi Arabia[77] (probably the vast majority on work contracts).

Yemen

Although Yemen does not share a border with Iraq, it has been host to a large number of Iraqis both before and after 2003. Since the first arrivals of Iraqi refugees during the Iraq–Iran war, the Yemeni authorities applied 'the principles of Arab unity'. This meant that Iraqis are residents with the right to work, education and social benefit on the basis of being Arabs. While Iraqis could claim asylum in Yemen, 'they opt not to because they get better legal stability and rights as Arab aliens'.[78] It is thought that many Ba'thists moved to Yemen after the fall of Saddam and UNHCR estimated that 100,000 Iraqis were living in Yemen in 2004.[79] Many of those Iraqis use Yemen as a base and there has been active movement of Iraqis in and out of Yemen, particularly after Yemen shifted its policy to a more restrictive one, purportedly 'an anti-trafficking in women' measure.[80] It is very difficult to find official or updated estimates relating to the Iraqi population in Yemen, although *IRIN*, put the number in July 2007 at 70,000.[81]

Gulf States

For many years, Iraqis have lived and worked in the United Arab Emirates (UAE), Qatar and Oman. They helped set up universities and hospitals and some worked as advisors to the royal families in those emirates. However, after the 2003 war, only very skilled or well-connected Iraqis managed to get to those countries. UNHCR estimated in 2008 the Iraqi population at 100,000 in UAE and 50,000 in Oman, Qatar and Bahrain. Combined with Saudi Arabia and Kuwait, UNHCR registered 1,816 Iraqis in the area.[82] All those countries do not have an open policy to welcome refugees and only Iraqis with visas obtained before their arrival can enter those countries. Of all the Gulf States, UAE has been the most generous with its donation of $10 million to UNHCR.

The Arab League

It is remarkable that the Arab world represented in the Arab League has not marshalled its resources to help the Iraqis in any significant and meaningful way. In spite of repeatedly bombastic declarations about the 'suffering of the Iraqi brothers', no real action to remedy the situation has been taken. At the beginning of 2008, almost five years after the war, the Arab League launched a 'fund raising and public awareness campaign to help hundreds of thousands of Iraqi refugees'.[83] Under the slogan '*Yad Al-Arab bi-Yad Al-Iraqiyin*' (Arabs Hand-in-Hand with the Iraqis), artists and celebrities were recruited to raise the Arab public's awareness of the tragedy. Interestingly, upon visiting a refugee registration centre, one such artist was shocked by the condition of the Iraqis:

> I did not know before today that there are many layers [of Iraqi refugees] under the poverty line. . . . It is time now for the Arab people to do their share and support Iraqi refugees.[84]

The lack of generosity on the part of Arab countries can be attributed to a combination of the belief that Iraq is a US problem, fear of bolstering the Shi'i government in Iraq by having more Sunnis fleeing Iraq, and finally the strained relations between the Gulf States and Syria due to the latter's close ties with Iran.

Iran and Turkey

Iran

Since the 1979 revolution, the Islamic Republic of Iran has hosted some of the largest refugee populations in the world. Following the Soviet invasion of Afghanistan in 1979, 2.6 million Afghans flooded Iran and probably more than 1.2 million Iraqis sought refuge first during the Iraq–Iran war (1980–88) and then following the Gulf War of 1991.[85]

Most Iraqi migrants to Iran were forcibly displaced people. During the 1980s and 1990s, between 200,000 and 300,000 Faili Kurds (Shi'i Kurds) and many Iraqis of alleged Iranian origin were absorbed in Iran. After 1991, Marsh Arabs (*Ma'dan*) found refuge in Iran. For those politically motivated – sympathizers of political Shi'i – Iran was the natural place. But even for those not ideologically motivated, Iran was simply the easiest destination, the cheapest in terms of travel costs to be paid to cross the border without documents, and the one that offered the most secure refuge, with no risk of expulsion.[86]

Before the 2003 war, Iran announced that if the USA attacks Iraq 'we will not authorize any Iraqi refugee to enter Iranian territory'.[87] Iran assumed that there would be an influx of refugees in the aftermath of the war. (Interestingly, the Americans had the same assumption and the two main assignments for General Jay Garner, who was in charge of the Office of Reconstruction and Humanitarian Assistance (ORHA), were to deal with refugee problems and oilfield fires.)[88] Not only did the anticipated flow not occur (and neither the oilfield fires) but no Iraqi sought asylum in Iran. In fact, between 2003 and 2005, more than 100,000 refugees returned to Iraq from Iran.[89]

In April 2008, UNHCR estimated the Iraqi population in Iran at 57,000, with the large majority living outside camps in urban areas. About 300 ethnic Arab Iraqi refugees have been held up near the border since mid-2007 waiting for security clearances from Iraq before they can return home.[90] Only 3,673 Iraqis were registered with the agency,[91] and although there is no breakdown of the overall population by religion, one can safely assume that the vast majority are Shia. For Iraqis living there, Iran has become a 'home'. Many pilgrims, after 2003, came to visit Qom, the holy city, and some stayed for respite from the violence and for the free medical care that the Iranians provide.[92]

Iran plays today a major role in Iraqi political and economic life. Tensions between the USA and the UK on one side, and the Iranians on the other side, rise frequently. The USA accuses Iran of training and financing Shi'i extremists and believes that 'Iran's interests are a weak government of Iraq'.[93] Whether for this reason or not, Iran (like Saudi Arabia) has built a security barrier seven metres high along its border with the southern city of Basra.[94]

Turkey

Turkey was a reluctant host to about 500,000 Iraqis, mostly Kurds, in the aftermath of the 1991 Gulf War. Those refugees were kept in camps on the border until a 'safe area' was created by the Coalition forces and then they returned to the Kurdish autonomous zone (1991–2003).

As the 2003 invasion approached, Turkey also anticipated a large influx of refugees and tightened its security on the border, particularly in light of its conflicts with the Kurdistan Workers' Party (PKK) based in northern Iraq.[95] Iraqis are not allowed to enter Turkey overland without a prior visa which has to be obtained from a Turkish embassy or consulate abroad, although those arriving by air may obtain a visa at the airport.[96] Turkey also announced in late 2007, in keeping with other countries in the Middle East, that it intends to erect a 473-kilometre (295-mile) fence, part concrete and part electronic monitoring, to stop infiltration of the PKK rebels.[97]

UNHCR estimated that in 2008, 6,000 to 10,000 Iraqis were living in Turkey, of whom about 5,400 were registered. Of those registered, 39 per cent are Sunnis, 28 per cent Christians, 21 per cent 'Islam unspecified' which probably means Turkoman, and 11 per cent Shia.[98] As the violence intensified in Iraq and the economic conditions deteriorated in Syria, many refugees tried to reach Turkey in transit to Europe. The Turkish government was worried that if Syria were to seal its border, following the initial restrictions it imposed in autumn 2007, more refugees would find their way to Turkey.[99]

Sweden

> Most societies are wary of strangers, especially those who, forced to flee, threaten to be dependent on others for their care and succour. Even those nations that pride themselves on their diversity frequently erect barriers to prevent the influx of those fleeing persecution.[100]

The western world prides itself on liberalism and diversity, yet Sweden has been the only country to open its doors to the Iraqi exodus. Sweden has had a liberal immigration policy for decades. Political refugees from Chile to Kurdistan found refuge in Sweden where the laws of family reunification are easier than in most other western countries.

Although there are no official statistics, estimates put the Iraqi population in Sweden at 130,000 to 150,000. It is thought that about 90,000 to 100,000 were already there by April 2003, and about 40,000 have arrived in Sweden since the collapse of Saddam's regime.[101] Sweden has a population of about nine million, of which about 12 to 13 per cent were born outside the country, a high number considering that Sweden is not an immigration country.

Iraqi emigration to Sweden began in the mid-1970s and until 1982 almost all the Iraqis in Sweden were Kurds. After 1982, others, such as Assyrians, began to arrive but Kurds were still about two-thirds of the Iraqis. Following the 1991 Gulf War, the Shia sought asylum in Sweden due to Saddam's persecution. This was also the first time that Sweden received Iraqis who were not, as before, mostly educated and political activists. After the 2003 invasion of Iraq, there were three waves of Iraqis who came to Sweden. The first, in 2003–04, were mostly those affiliated in one way or another with Saddam's regime, many of whom came via Syria. After 2005, the majority of the second wave of arrivals was minorities: Chaldeans, Mandeans and Assyrians. But there was also a third category of refugees post-2005: educated middle class. As many as 300 Iraqi doctors are believed to have settled in Sweden, thus contributing to the ongoing Iraqi brain drain.[102]

In 2006, Iraqis topped the list of asylum seekers in Sweden with 8,951, followed by Serbia/Montenegro with 2,001 refugees (the total for that year was 24,322),[103] while in 2007, about 18,600 Iraqis sought asylum in Sweden.

Most of the Iraqis arriving in Sweden had to take the arduous and risky trip across Europe until they reached Sweden. Some of the stories are hair-raising: the cost, the risk to their lives, and the strain of moving illegally from one place to another. One woman told me that when she realized she couldn't renew her visa in Syria, she decided to escape. From the day she left Damascus until she arrived in Sweden, it took her a whole month of being hidden in trucks and a ship, staying in 'safe houses' and paying a large sum to the smugglers without having any real guarantees.[104] Depending on the route, it costs between

$10,000 and $25,000 to be smuggled into Sweden. Some began their journeys in Turkey and were driven through Greece, then a boat to Italy, driven through Austria, Germany, Denmark and finally into Sweden.[105] Other journeys were shorter but the danger and cost were the same. One Iraqi living now in Södertälje in Sweden told me his story:

> As a medical professional from a minority I was targeted in Iraq, mainly for religious reasons. I left Iraq in August 2006 when I realized that my family and I were in constant danger having received many threats. Syria was the first stop, but from the beginning I saw it as a transit. After four months in Damascus, I was introduced to an Iraqi smuggler who came with high recommendations. The night before departure he came and took my Iraqi passport. He told me that there would be four other Iraqis, one Muslim and three from my community. The next day, the four of us in addition to the smuggler took a night flight from Damascus to Madrid. He warned us to restrict ourselves to minimum conversation during the journey, and we were told to dress as businessmen and take one piece of luggage. The smuggler came with us and we were ushered through passport control easily, obviously using forged passports. In Madrid, we stayed at the airport for two hours and got on a flight to Bulgaria. Again after a few hours in transit, we caught a flight to Germany. From there the smuggler rented a car and drove us to Sweden via Denmark. In Malmö, he received the balance of the money. Each has paid $15,000: $5,000 in Damascus and the balance in Malmö. The next day we all went to the Swedish Migration Board to ask for asylum.[106]

Interestingly the Iraqi interviewed had no idea what the smuggler would have done with their passports. Trade in Swedish passports is also booming; reporters from a Swedish radio station were offered $10,000 for their Swedish passports.[107]

Why do Iraqis take this gargantuan risk to reach Sweden? First and foremost, safety. 'They came here to survive' is a sentence one hears repeatedly. One man told the BBC:

> We wanted to get as far away from Iraq as possible. . . . Everyone wants to go to Sweden, it has always been good to Iraqis. They respect human rights here. I wanted my children to grow up in a safe country, that's why we chose Sweden.[108]

For Christians and other religious minorities, living in Sweden means being able to practise their religion in a safe environment: 'In Iraq, we were deprived of even the simple right to go to church, and we want to hold on to our religion.'[109] Unlike host countries in the Arab world, Sweden gives Iraqis residence permits and helps them medically and educationally. This is a critical point because as we saw so far, the threat of being expelled or having the visa not renewed hangs constantly over the majority of Iraqi refugees.

As highlighted in previous chapters, the presence of family and friends is an important driver for all refugees in choosing where to seek asylum and settle. Since more than 100,000 Iraqis live in Sweden, this has been an important factor: Kurds, Assyrians, Chaldeans and other Iraqis had already found refuge there during Saddam's era. The Federation of Iraqi Associations in Sweden (FIAS) was founded in 1995 in Stockholm by 13 Iraqi associations from eight Swedish towns. Since then, the number of member associations had risen to 58 by 2008. FIAS is recognized by the Swedish government as the official representative of the Iraqi minority in Sweden. According to the FIAS website, the organization represents 'directly over 13,000 Iraqis and indirectly over 60,000 Iraqis (both members and non-members)'.[110] The Federation works with the government and humanitarian organizations in their activities with children, women and migration issues. Easy access to medical, social and educational services in Sweden is another factor for choosing Sweden, particularly for families and elderly people.

Most of the Iraqis live in Stockholm and its sprawling suburbs. Some live in the south, mainly in Malmö or in its surrounding towns. Others chose Södertälje, a small industrial town (Saab, Scania and Astra Zeneca have bases there) about 30 kilometres (18 miles) south-west of Stockholm. Södertälje is the antithesis of the mayhem of Iraq; it is nestled among lakes and steep pine- and birch-covered hills. When the Iraqis could no longer afford the rental prices in the centre of the town, they began moving to nearby towns connected to Södertälje such as Ronna and Hovjö.

This town of 60,000 people has about 6,000 Iraqis, 2,500 of whom arrived in the last two years. The majority, according to an interview with an official in the municipality, are Christians and Mandeans (official statistics in Sweden do not indicate the respondents' ethnicity or religion). Of the 1,300 that came in 2006, 39 per cent have an academic background; among them are 11 dentists, six doctors and a few nurses. Södertälje took 1,268 refugees in 2007 of whom 96 per cent were Iraqis; 850 of those were between the ages of 20 and 55 which augers well for their integration. The town, as part of the national policy to integrate refugees, provides an introductory programme lasting 18 months whereby courses are taught in Swedish language, introduction to Swedish society and practice jobs to help the newcomers adjust to Swedish life.[111] Incredibly Södertälje accepted, in 2006 and 2007, almost twice as many Iraqi refugees as the whole of the USA. In Södertälje and in other areas of Sweden, issues relating to housing, education and integration within society are surfacing. Unlike the Iraqis who went to Arab countries, those in Sweden encounter language difficulties in their attempts to become integrated with, and accepted by, the Swedes. Throughout the history of exiles, language has been a crucial instrument with which refugees can overcome marginalization and assimilate with their hosts:

> Cushioned by social security but imprisoned by linguistic inadequacy, many of the unemployed [refugees] hardly go out. The migrants are here physically but many have not made the mental leap.[112]

Many of the Iraqis are not well-integrated; Sweden is not a melting pot for immigrants like Canada and the USA. Sweden, unlike other immigration countries, does not choose its immigrants; the main criterion for admission has been simply making it to Sweden. In addition to language, another factor hindering integration is Swedish labour laws by which all workers are to be paid at a minimum wage. While this is progressive, it prevents Iraqis (and for that matter other immigrants) who do not know the language or system from competing as business concerns see no advantage in hiring people from outside their education and cultural systems. It is also far more difficult for older people (in their fifties and higher) to be integrated into the workforce as there is a need to invest two to three years in learning the language and skills of the job, something which not many employers are willing to do for people in their fifties. In fact, a few hundred Iraqis of age 55 and plus were told in Södertälje to stay on the welfare system (rather than be trained for jobs) until they reach pensionable age of 65. In other words, these people, unless they find employment in the black market, are blocked from pursuing their careers.[113]

Iraqi children, given Sweden's generous system of education, will probably have far better chances than their parents of integrating successfully. Children attend preparatory classes at the Ronna school in Södertälje aimed at integrating them.[114] Most endured the horrendous journeys with their parents and many suffer from trauma. Some of the teenage boys came alone without their families as Sweden was the only sanctuary for them.[115] Having no guardian or family, stories of abuse and beating by different smugglers and gangs abound, and these boys arrived in Sweden in a state of shock and trauma.[116] The desire to be with family and community is leading many Iraqis to want to live only in Södertälje in spite of housing problems, crowded schools and the problem of finding professional jobs without full command of the Swedish language. The local authority and the national government 'are desperate to get them to live somewhere else in Sweden', because every language class in town contains about 98 per cent Iraqis which impedes integration and learning the language.[117] Iraqis balk at those offers to be dispersed around the country as they want to remain close to the Iraqi community. As one Iraqi told me, the Iraqis in Damascus, particularly the minorities, knew they needed to reach one destination in Sweden: Södertälje. For each family, the larger community is a strong magnet. Such is the fear of the unknown that Iraqis prefer to live in Södertälje with few job prospects than to move elsewhere in Sweden.

Within Sweden, there have been calls to reduce the influx of immigrants and some opposition political parties are warning of the implications of the 'Iraqi flood'. In the 2006 elections for the municipality parliament of Södertälje, two fringe parties (National Democrats and Swedish Democrats) won about 6 per cent of the seats. Their xenophobic policy aims to block more refugees from coming into the town and they tabled a proposal (that was rejected by other parties) to have a referendum in Södertälje on the number of immigrants the town should accept.

When the USA and Iraq announced that the 'surge' was leading to reduced violence in certain areas in Iraq, the Swedish Migration Court agreed with the Migration Board that 'asylum seekers can no longer claim that they are in danger in Iraq – particularly the southern part of the country and Baghdad, and that they must have a personal valid reason to obtain a residency permit to stay'.[118] Following a Superior Court of Migration decision in late 2007, Sweden's official position now is that all asylum seekers from Iraq must demonstrate that they personally risk persecution in order to be allowed to stay,[119] although the Secretary of State in the Ministry of Justice, Gustaf Lind, assured me 'that the demands to demonstrate personal persecution are not high'.[120] Another aspect in tightening the entrance of Iraqis is reunification of families. Until late 2007 once a refugee had received his permit he was allowed to ask for reunification of his immediate family. This has changed so that a successful applicant needs to prove that he or she has a job and an apartment before applying for reunification. On the other hand, in a conciliatory gesture, the Board of Migration was asked by the Swedish government to reduce the time it takes for the newcomers to get residency permits from the average of 9–12 months in early 2008 to six months by 2009. In fact, some Iraqis whom I met had not heard about their permits in 16 months.

In early 2008, Sweden signed a deal with Iraq that allowed some asylum seekers to be returned forcibly. Swedish immigration officials stated that there were 400 Iraqis whose requests for asylum had been rejected.[121] As the Swedes figured out that the international community is not willing to step up and share the burden, they decided to introduce some obstacles to reduce the number of Iraqi refugees and prevent masses flooding the country. It is important to point out that until summer 2007, the prevalent feeling among Iraqis was that Sweden had its doors totally open and that its welfare system was the most generous one in the world. Following these new rules and the new reunification measures, the number of Iraqis arriving in Sweden dropped substantially. This is a dramatic shift in Sweden's liberal policy. The Swedes feel frustrated; their country is neutral and it was the USA and the UK who invaded Iraq, but now Sweden is carrying the burden for the rest of Europe and for the USA. On a visit to Iraq in the autumn of 2007, the Swedish foreign minister expressed his worries of the implications for Europe of a further deterioration in the situation and emphasized the importance of having stability in Iraq.[122] Sweden made many efforts to convince other EU states of the need to deal with the refugee crisis but without success. Understandably, Sweden feels caught in a vicious circle: due to lack of assistance from other European states, it is becoming the destination of choice – a fact that obviously will have further repercussions for the Swedes in the longer term. When Sweden raises the issue with European partners about sharing the burden, the response it receives is that its open-door policy is causing the mayhem rather than the lack of European cooperation. Although the responsibility to share the financial or physical burden for global refugee protection is recognized in the Preamble to the 1951 Geneva Convention, '"burden-sharing" has not been formally recognized as an international legal obligation to the same extent as the principle of non-refoulement'.[123] Thus Sweden changed its policy in late 2007 as it stood alone to help the refugees while the rest of Europe, as will be discussed next, failed to reach the right humanitarian policy towards the Iraqi exodus.

Rest of Europe

With continued efforts by the EU to secure its external borders, access to European territories and thereafter to the asylum procedures has become extremely difficult. The principal route for Iraqis to enter the EU is via Turkey into Greece. We will look at the Iraqi refugees in Greece, Germany and the UK, and will then analyse the asylum applications and the EU policy towards Iraqi refugees since the 2003 invasion of Iraq.

Greece

A considerable number of Iraqis view Greece as a country of transit. For many, however, the transit country becomes the country where they decide to stay. There are no official statistics on the size of the Iraqi population in Greece, as there is reluctance among Iraqis to lodge their applications for asylum or even to register their presence in Greece, 'wishing to retain the right to apply for asylum elsewhere in Europe'.[124] Although Greek legislation states those seeking protection may not be deported until a final decision on their claims has been reached, there have been worrying reports that Greece is preventing Iraqis who enter the country illegally from making asylum claims. According to reliable information, in February 2007 a group of 54 Iraqis who crossed on a boat illegally from the Turkish coast to the Greek island of Chios were arrested and detained. A few days later, 13 of them who belonged to families with small children were released and ordered to leave the country, while the other 41 were kept in detention.[125] In August 2007, 16 NGOs issued a statement expressing their profound concern regarding the Greek government policy of refoulement of Iraqis back to Turkey, from where forcible returns to Iraq have occurred.[126] Even the fortunate Iraqi asylum seekers who managed to make an official claim saw their requests rejected; in 2006, Greece accepted zero out of 1,415 Iraqi applications for asylum. As Table 4 indicates, it was the only country in the EU, apart from Slovakia, with a zero overall protection rate.

As signatories to the 1951 Convention, all EU states have an asylum policy, but as one observer put it, the 'distinction between asylum policy and refugee policy has often been neglected by both the European press and policy makers alike'.[127] The fact that the EU has ignored dealing with this humanitarian crisis will be more evident in the next few pages.

Table 4: Recognition rates for Iraqis in the EU in 2006 (in %)

	Applied during year	Otherwise closed	Refugee status	Overall protection rate (refugee status + complementary protection)
Austria	380	40	48	74
Belgium	695	30	8	13
Cyprus	132	46	0	81
Denmark	507	0	0	2
Finland	225	15	6	63
France	116	0	10	23
Germany	2,117	24	7	11
Greece	1,415	11	0	0
Ireland	215	6	50	50
Netherlands	2,766	23	1	18
Slovakia	206	65	0	0
Sweden	8,951	12	3	90
United Kingdom	1,305	12	3	12

Sources: ECRE, *Guidelines of the Treatment of Iraqis*, Appendix III, p. 28; Sperl, *Fortress Europe and the Iraqi 'intruders'*, p. 18.

Germany

Germany was very generous towards Iraqi refugees during Saddam's regime and it is estimated that 53,000 Iraqis found a home in Germany.[128] This generosity ended abruptly with the 2003 war as the Germans believed that the threat of persecution from the Ba'th regime was no longer present. Since 2004, the German authorities have revoked the refugee status of around 20,000 Iraqis granted protection during Saddam's reign, thus placing them in a state of uncertainty and precariousness.[129] Germany's recognition rate for Iraqi refugees in 2006 was 11 per cent (see Table 4) compared with an average of 57 per cent between 1997 and 2001.[130] The Germans, like most other Europeans, have refused to take into consideration the pervasive violence and human rights violations that have been taking place in Iraq since its occupation. In April 2008, Germany appealed to other European countries to take in more Christians from Iraq. Christian churches in Germany applauded the move,[131] but the EU presidency rebuffed those calls, insisting that decisions on asylum could not be based on religion.[132]

United Kingdom

The UK, like Germany and several other EU states, ruled that the situation in Iraq post-2003 does not warrant providing protection for refugees. Between 1997 and 2001, the UK had an impressive 44 per cent rate of protection, but by 2006, it dropped to a mere 12 per cent (see Table 4), but still an improvement compared to 2005 when UK authorities rejected 1,675 out of 1,835 applications (granting asylum to only 8.7 per cent).[133] Britain is also the only country in Europe that forcibly repatriates Iraqis in significant numbers. In 2005, for example, 85 were involuntarily returned to north Iraq. For those whose claims have been rejected, they are able to stay in Britain but live on the margins of society unable to work and in a constant legal limbo.[134] By March 2008, however, leaked Home Office documents seen by *The Guardian* newspaper indicated that 1,400 rejected Iraqi asylum seekers must go back to Iraq as the British Government considered Iraq safe enough. Those Iraqis, according to the documents, were to be told that unless they sign up for a voluntary return programme to Iraq, they would face being made homeless and without state support.[135] The secretary general of the European Council on Refugees and Exiles (ECRE) explained the British view of the security situation in Iraq:

> The British government is insisting it is OK for people to go back to Iraq because recognising that it is not means acknowledging that the military operation there has failed.[136]

The UK authorities have rejected a number of important UNHCR recommendations in their handling of Iraqi asylum claims, on the premise that most Iraqis have fled the general violence and not as a result of state persecution.[137] It is an incredible interpretation of events particularly in light of the fact that

British forces participated in the invasion of Iraq which led to the ensuing mayhem and violence. In fact, an official of UNHCR asserted that the UN 'strongly advise against the return of anyone to central or southern Iraq' and that as things stand in April 2008, 'a sword of Damocles hangs over the head of every Iraqi in the UK'.[138]

British policy towards asylum seekers of all nationalities has come under criticism. The Independent Asylum Commission, led by an ex-senior judge, said the treatment of asylum seekers was a shameful blemish on the UK's international reputation. In its thorough report, the commissioners said policymakers were at times using 'indefensible' threats of destitution to force some asylum seekers to leave the UK (exactly as was shown above with regard to Iraqi asylum seekers). The co-chairman of the commission, Sir John Whaite, told the BBC:

> We are a country with a basic instinct of fair play – the system denies fair play to asylum seekers not out of malice but because of a lack of resources.[139]

The UK's stance is even more shocking when it comes to resettlement of Iraqi interpreters who risked their lives by working with the British Forces in southern Iraq. A letter sent to former Iraqi employees of the British Forces spelled out the hurdles to be overcome before they could be granted refugee status, and that they would, even if approved, be unable to enter the country before summer 2009. A number of applications were rejected on the grounds of 'absenteeism' as some of these interpreters did not show up for work following threats they and their families received from militia groups.[140] As one Member of Parliament put it:

> If those Iraqis who have helped us are now being told that they can't come here because their absence was regarded as a resignation, this is the world gone mad.[141]

Due to pressure in parliament and the media, the British government agreed in principle in March 2008 that Iraqis who risked their lives working for Britain can resettle in the UK. However, some interpreters working with the British army accused the government of making the procedures to apply overly complicated and slow and claimed that they were under pressure to accept a cash payment instead of moving to the UK. Out of a total of 775 Iraqis who applied for help, 360 were turned down as they had to prove they had worked for the British for at least 12 consecutive months; 160 of those approved took the one-off cash payment of £3,300, and the rest (around 255) will be given the right to settle in Britain.[142]

Iraqis whom I interviewed in Europe and the Middle East feel bitter and betrayed by the British government. They wonder why the UK, a country which always had a special relationship with Iraq and Iraqis, many of whom studied here and speak the language, is now rejecting Iraqis. Some estimates put the number of Iraqis in Britain at 70,000 to 80,000 back in 1991.[143]

Other European countries did not do much better than Greece, Germany and the UK. France made many compassionate pleas to the world to help the refugees but did little to back those pleas with money or hospitality. France had a higher rate of acceptance than Germany or the UK but it received only 116 applications, as Table 4 indicates. When France announced at the end of 2007 that it was studying the possibility of welcoming Iraqi refugees particularly Christians, some NGOs welcomed the move but expressed reservation about resettling refugees in France on the basis of religion.[144] Meanwhile hundreds of Iraqis are stuck on the French side of the English Channel trying daily to cross clandestinely to the UK. This led the deputy mayor of Cherbourg to demand the expulsion of those 'squatters'.[145]

Some countries such as Belgium and Switzerland (not an EU member) provide accommodation to asylum seekers who have been turned down for refugee status, but are still in the process of appealing against that decision. Other countries do not do that, forcing the asylum seekers into homelessness and destitution.[146] Denmark, which joined the war effort, took only 2 per cent (see Table 4) of Iraqi asylum applicants. (In early 2008, the Danish government announced that it will take all Iraqis who worked with the Danish forces in Iraq.)[147]

While Iraqis topped the list of applications for asylum in industrialized countries for 2006 and 2007 (Iraqis made 45,200 claims during 2007, a dramatic increase on the 22,900 claims in 2006),[148] the fact remains that the number of applications for 2006 or 2007 is still less than it was in 2002 (52,331).[149] The reasons are that restrictive policies in many of the industrialized countries have made it very difficult for refugees to get to those territories in the first place, and that enough legal hurdles have been erected to deter them from applying even if they do manage to reach those countries.[150] Out of the 45,200 Iraqi claims lodged in 2007, 18,600 were submitted in Sweden (41 per cent), which is more than double the claims of 2006 (8,951) and seven times higher than in 2005 (2,300). Greece received 5,500 Iraqi asylum claims, while Germany and Turkey recorded 4,200 and 3,500 applicants respectively. Britain received 2,100 claims and the Netherlands 2,000.[151] It is interesting to note that the rise, globally, of asylum claims in 2007 (338,300 versus 306,300 in 2006) can by and large be attributed to the sharp increase in Iraqi asylum seekers.[152]

Although UNHCR called on Europe to accept more asylum seekers from conflict-torn Iraq, the call fell on deaf ears. The EU cannot agree a common policy towards the Iraqis and the EU members' diverging policies towards the refugees clearly 'demonstrates that the first phase of harmonization has so far failed to lead to a convergence in national asylum practice or increase sharing of the responsibility to accept asylum seekers among EU states'.[153] The reality is that since the 1980s, there has been a growing unwillingness to provide shelter for refugees in Western Europe. Economic conditions might not have been most propitious for accepting refugees, but it is the political climate which has significantly changed with a strong bias against taking refugees.[154]

The USA

The US policy towards the exodus from Iraq was, until 2006, simplistic: pretend it is not there and hopefully the problem will go away. After the media started focusing on it, the Bush administration still would not make official statements about the fate of the refugees. Admitting that these people were fleeing Iraq because of the total chaos would be to admit failure of the US policy towards Iraq. Addressing the issue of refugees would also have required tackling the challenge that Iraq's most talented citizens are leaving their country, thereby compounding the problems that Iraq will face in the future.

While hundreds of thousands of Iraqis were fleeing to Syria and Jordan, the USA did not want to open its doors to refugees because of the two above factors and for security reasons. In January 2007, the US Senate Committee on the Judiciary met to discuss the plight of Iraqi refugees. The chairman of the committee introduced this discussion:

> It is perverse and it should be embarrassing to us as the stewards of a
> country that has been known throughout our history as a safe haven for
> refugees.[155]

Senator Edward Kennedy expressed his dismay that the USA admitted only 202 Iraqi refugees during 2006 and the immigrant visa programme for Iraqis (and Afghanis) working for the US military had a six-year waiting list. He urged the administration to spend more on refugees given that the USA was spending more than $8 billion a month to wage the war and only $20 million for the whole year (2006) to meet the needs of the refugees.[156] In fact, from the end of the war in April 2003 up until the end of 2006, the USA admitted only 466 Iraqi refugees. The administration explained that it was due to the fact that Congress had enacted significant changes in the law that created a need for much enhanced security testing.[157]

Following pressure from Congress and the media, the US government increased humanitarian assistance (directly and indirectly) from a total of $43 million in 2006 to just under $200 million in 2007. The budget allocated about $106 million to international organizations and roughly $76 million to NGOs. Only $10 million was targeted directly to the Jordanian government to support health and education programmes in communities affected by large numbers of Iraqi refugees.[158] Obviously Syria, which does not enjoy a good relationship with the USA, was not mentioned in the budget. In early 2008, however, the USA announced it will contribute $5 million to WFP for its emergency operation in Syria,[159] but still in the 2008 budget there was no direct assistance to Syria. There is no doubt that the USA has significantly stepped up its financial assistance to the international organizations and NGOs to help them address the humanitarian needs of the refugees. But as Senator Kennedy put it: 'Money is not everything, but is a pretty good indicator about where the administration is.'[160] The fact remains that while the USA has spent hundreds of billions between 2003 and 2008 on its war effort, at most only half a billion dollars, a trifling amount in comparison, were spent to aid Iraqi refugees. While humanitarian programmes have been largely neglected, billions of dollars in international funds have been allocated to reconstruction projects in Iraq, most of which cannot be implemented due to the spreading violence.

In April 2008, 89 members of Congress expressed their deep concern over the plight of displaced Iraqis. In a letter to President Bush, they stated:

> Rarely does confronting a crisis align our moral and national security interests as closely as does providing assistance to the Iraqis displaced by violence. There are few more important tests of our foreign policy than our leadership in response to the growing crisis confronting the displaced population of Iraq.[161]

A fundamental factor in US policy was the belief that the exodus is not a crisis and that anyway it was not triggered by American action. John Bolton, who was Undersecretary of State for Arms Control and International Security in the Bush administration, and later ambassador to the United Nations, told a journalist that the refugees have 'absolutely nothing to do with our overthrow of Saddam'. He elaborated further:

> Our obligation was to give them [the Iraqis] new institutions and provide security. We have fulfilled that obligation. I don't think we have an obligation to compensate for the hardships of war.[162]

As international and domestic political pressures mounted, the US administration announced that 12,000 Iraqis would be allowed into the country in fiscal 2008 (1 October 2007 to 30 September 2008). The USA admitted only 1,608 in fiscal 2007, 400 short of the 2,000 target, and already a big reduction from an initial target of 7,000.[163] Between October 2007 and August 2008, about 9,000 Iraqis were cleared to enter the country, with July having the highest number of Iraqis admitted in a single month.[164] It is interesting to note that while the media in the USA covers events in Iraq extensively, a Pew Research study shows that during the first ten months of 2007, coverage of Iraqi civilians made up only 3 per cent of stories and 5 per cent of overall news, while daily violence grabbed almost 47 per cent of the news.[165] Overall coverage of Iraq by the American media plummeted as public interest continued to wane since mid-2007.[166]

A case in point of the American attitude vis-à-vis the refugees are the Iraqis who worked for or helped the USA at all levels since its invasion of Iraq, from interpreters to labourers for US contractors. There are no official statistics of how many Iraqis worked for the US army or government but there are estimates of 100,000 Iraqis employed by US contractors – from office cleaners to managers – and they face similar dangers and all underwent rigorous background checks.[167] Iraqis desperate for work when jobs are extremely hard to come by, agree to work with the Americans, although that affiliation automatically makes them targets. Iraqis tell elaborate lies to conceal from other Iraqis their work for the Americans. Sometimes they even lie to their own families to protect them, and most pretend to have different jobs from what they are actually doing on a daily basis.[168] When they realize that danger is imminent, or in some cases belatedly after they lost a member of their families, they flee the country to Jordan or Syria in the hope of utilizing their ties with the Americans to gain an entry into the USA: 'But most languish for months in a bureaucratic and psychological limbo, their status as uncertain as their future.'[169]

As in the UK, the media and Congress began to call for action. The Senate heard statements by a US officer who stated that the US military needs 'the service of Iraqi translators who join our ranks at great risk to themselves and their families'.[170] Based on a long article written by George Packer for *The New Yorker*, a play called *Betrayed* depicted the suffering of Iraqis who risked everything to help the Americans in Iraq and all too often received insufficient protection in return.[171] In the play, one Iraqi translator says to another, 'sometimes I feel like we're standing in line for a ticket, waiting to die'.

In early 2008, a law was signed creating 5,000 special immigrant visas each year for the next five years for Iraqis who are US government employees or contractors. To qualify for these visas, Iraqis must have 'provided faithful and valuable service' for not less than a year, and have experienced 'an ongoing serious threat as a consequence of that employment'.[172]

As important as these measures are to help Iraqis, human rights groups and some members of Congress have criticized the overture as 'a token gesture'.[173] One commentator described showering financial aid and intending to process a few thousand refugees as 'velleities', given that these US concerns have been unmatched by results in comparison to countries like Sweden.[174] The USA took 157,000 refugees from Kosovo and Bosnia, and 600,000 from the former Soviet Union. The real comparison, however, is with Vietnam from where more than one million refugees were allowed to come to the USA, but some cynics say that was only after the USA accepted its defeat in the Vietnam War.

Finally, the reaction of other rich countries in the world to the crisis was diverse. Australia, which sent troops to Iraq, is credited with a decent record of accepting settlement referrals from UNHCR (1,871), and in early 2008, it announced that Iraqis employed with Australian troops (about 600) will be offered a permanent home if they pass the strict health and security checks.[175] Canada, which did not join the war, settled 1,521.[176] Another country that has been helpful is Brazil which agreed to settle 117 Palestinians who were stuck in a camp in the desert on the Jordan–Iraq border.[177] Almost every rich and developed country promised, in theory, to help the refugees, but so far this theoretical commitment has not been translated into practice.

Chapter 5

The role of humanitarian organizations

Exile is the emptiness – for however much you brought
with you, there's far more you've left behind.
Exile is the ego that shrinks, for how can you prove
what you were and what you did?
Exile is the erasure of pride.
Exile is the escape that is often worse than the prison.[1]

This chapter will deal with the role of international humanitarian organizations such as UNHCR on the one hand, and the miscellaneous NGOs
(international and local) on the other, towards Iraqi refugees since 2003. Their
policies, successes and failures, and the issues facing them mainly in the two
major host countries, Syria and Jordan, will be addressed. While this chapter,
as the whole book, is focused on Iraqi refugees outside their country, a brief
look at the humanitarian work in Iraq is deemed necessary to put the discussion in context.

Prior to the fall of Saddam, the main obstacle facing international
organizations in their efforts to help the displaced people within Iraq was the
regime, which was the party responsible for violence and displacement. UN
humanitarian agencies and the International Committee of the Red Cross
(ICRC) were active and participated in the Oil-for-Food programme. Among
the NGOs, the Middle East Council of Churches helped provide school
uniforms and blankets, while others such as CARE Australia and Première
Urgence helped repair damaged buildings such as community centres. Overall,
however, these activities were curtailed by the Iraqi government and it is hard
to gauge their impact.[2]

Some researchers have pointed out that the USA and its allies contributed
to 'humanitarian action becoming thoroughly and intensely politicized' in
Iraq before and after the war.[3]

After the 2003 invasion, humanitarian organizations entered Iraq en
masse and by July of that year, 200 international aid agencies were present.
Simultaneously, there was an exponential growth in the number of local

humanitarian actors.[4] These organizations failed to foresee the rapid deterioration of the security situation in Iraq and were confident that the insurgents would not target them. The UN was torn between turning to Coalition forces for protection and worrying that the presence of US forces near their offices might in itself provoke an attack. On 19 August 2003, a suicide bomber drove through the UN compound destroying the headquarters and leading to the deaths of 23 people, including Special Representative of the Secretary-General Sergio Vieira de Mello.[5] Two months later, suicide bombers slammed an ambulance packed with explosives into the compound of the ICRC, killing 18 civilian bystanders and wounding dozens more.[6] As one observer, bemoaning the impact of violence, wrote:

> A striking characteristic of the Iraq war and its aftermath is that at
> junctures when Iraqis have most needed humanitarian assistance, it has
> been both very difficult and dangerous for humanitarian organizations to
> provide.[7]

The attack on ICRC led many organizations to withdraw entirely from the country, while others scaled back their operations. Many experts believed that opting for 'a bunkerized approach to security' by some organizations has few benefits as the local population find it difficult to trust and be open with aid workers visiting them under escort from well-armed western security contractors.[8]

Within this context, these humanitarian actors moved to neighbouring countries, mainly Jordan, to serve the Iraqi population from afar, not realizing that within a couple of years, Iraqi refugees abroad would constitute a new crisis and test their abilities to cope with such a massive influx of people over such a short period.

As mentioned in the introduction to this book, HRW warned prior to the invasion that a massive flight of refugees might result not only from the direct effect of war, but also from a humanitarian crisis. It is worth emphasizing again how some organizations foresaw, to a large extent, the consequences of the invasion. In its briefing paper before the war began, HRW portrayed the following scenario:

> In the event of war, new refugee flows in the immediate vicinity of Iraq, . . .
> may overwhelm local authorities and agencies. The scale of flight is likely to
> be affected by the intensity of the conflict as well as by whether or not
> biological or chemical weapons are used.[9]

HRW's predication that 'a large number of refugees would seek to flee to Iran' did not materialize, neither its expectation that only 'a small number' will reach Jordan given the country's insistence at the time that it would only admit refugees who are in transit to a third country. However, it anticipated accurately that 'Sunni Muslim Arabs, might try to reach Syria, particularly if there are extended attacks on the Baghdad area and the predominantly Sunni Arab central provinces'.[10] The point is not to see whether these agencies forecasted correctly or not the events, but to ask a more pertinent question: if UN agencies expected large internal displacement and refugees fleeing to Iraq's neighbouring countries, then why were they not ready when the onslaught began?

There are, unfortunately, no definitive and conclusive answers. One explanation could be that the UN agencies expected a refugee camp situation rather than what actually happened: Iraqis were dispersed in the major cities of their host countries. The belief, at the time, was that the majority of Iraqis would be put in camps although some would reach the cities:

> Since many of the refugees hosted by Iraq's neighbours are already living in cities, and since new arrivals may also attempt to do so, particular attention must be paid to the human rights of these refugees.[11]

But here comes the real difference between expectations and planning, and what actually took place post-2003:

> During the emergency phase of a large refugee influx, governments may require newly arriving refugees to reside in camps located a safe distance from the border, where humanitarian relief may be more easily distributed and where security can be better guaranteed.[12]

Historically, the only time that Iraqi refugees were in camps was in the aftermath of the 1991 Gulf War, where thousands of Kurds were in camps near the Turkish–Iraqi border.

A second possible reason for the question raised before is that the UN humanitarian agencies might have predicted the event but 'have been very slow to respond to the building crisis',[13] possibly due to their bureaucratic structure. This is not the first time that UNHCR and other organizations were caught unprepared despite early warnings. During the Kosovo crisis, UNHCR was 'widely criticized for not being well prepared once the influx began and being unable to deliver emergency supplies or to build camps quickly enough'.[14] Not dissimilar from the Iraq crisis, in Kosovo, the UNHCR had few personnel and resources in the region and had 'inadequate senior staff' to lead its efforts.[15]

Another plausible explanation is that both the Coalition forces and humanitarian organizations expected a flood of refugees in the immediate aftermath of the war, but when that did not occur, their preparations for a dramatic surge in violence leading to displacement a few months after the invasion dropped precipitously.

Given the fact that it is difficult for international NGOs to operate freely and independently in assisting Iraqi refugees in Syria and Jordan, and because the UN agencies already had an established presence there, these organizations were in 'a unique position to offer assistance and technical expertise to host countries'.[16]

UNHCR and other UN agencies

There is no doubt that UNHCR plays a unique role in the life of Iraqi refugees in their host countries and in deciding, to a large extent, their destiny given the fact that UNHCR is the body that determines the categorization of these refugees.

UNHCR has to deal with certain important aspects of this Iraqi exodus which were previously discussed in detail: the refugees are primarily middle-class urban dwellers who have been categorized by the receiving countries as 'guests' or 'visitors' or 'illegal immigrants' (such as in Lebanon). Three out of the four main hosts (Syria, Jordan and Lebanon) are not signatories to the 1951 Convention. Thus the primary task for UNHCR was to provide protection to the arriving refugees by having 'access to safety and non-refoulement', and 'non-penalization for illegal entry'.[17]

The next critical issue that UNHCR had to deal with was the fact that the crisis was becoming highly political. On the one hand, donor countries, particularly the USA, were reluctant in the years 2004–06 to give significant aid to UNHCR as there was no acknowledgement that there was a crisis. By the end of 2007, when the security situation improved in Iraq, the US government (and the Iraqi government) were unhappy with the UNHCR advice that conditions in Iraq were not conducive for a massive return. On the other hand, the host countries, particularly Syria and Jordan, were worried, as we saw before, about the impact of the influx of refugees on their economies, the violence and sectarianism, and the possibility that the refugees would import those problems with them. UNHCR, while working with the governments of these countries, had to be sensitive to their specific concerns of hosting large numbers of Iraqis. Thus an important challenge for UNHCR was to strike the right balance between ensuring protection for the Iraqis while simultaneously 'meeting the concerns of Governments as regards issues of state security and sovereignty'.[18]

Sometimes striking the right balance becomes difficult when fundamental differences with governments arise. In April 2003, UNHCR declared a temporary protection regime (TPR) on behalf of Iraqi refugees in Jordan, Syria and

Lebanon in anticipation of an influx of refugees from Iraq. This is a temporary form of protection to prevent refugees from being forcibly returned to Iraq. Until the end of 2006, UNHCR maintained that Iraqi nationals in Jordan, Syria and Lebanon should be granted temporary protection status. As a result of this arrangement UNHCR decided not to proceed with interviewing refugees to determine their status, with the exception of extremely vulnerable individuals or people with special protection problems.[19] Both Jordan and Lebanon refused to give effect to the TPR and both governments insisted they never agreed to this arrangement and thus refused to acknowledge it. One Jordanian official told HRW that the TPR was 'a unilateral declaration that we did not recognize'.[20]

Relations between UNHCR and the Jordanian government began to deteriorate. UNHCR continued to issue asylum seeker cards to refugees who arrived after April 2003 as though the TPR was accepted. The Jordanian authorities, meanwhile, refused to recognize them and the holders of the cards did not gain a legal status or the right to work. Caught in the middle, the refugees had to face yet more disappointment and confusion. Iraqis, who anyway do not trust international organizations, found upon arriving in Amman that UNHCR was not easily accessible and some were suspicious that UNHCR would not protect their confidentiality. As a result, Iraqis in Jordan had, unsurprisingly, little understanding of what benefits these asylum seeker cards bestow on their holders. One Iraqi talked about his experience with the card:

> After I overstayed my visa, I went to UNHCR and got the [asylum seeker] paper from them. But when the police came to raid this area [Raghdan, Amman], they said to me that the UNHCR paper doesn't mean anything to them, that it is useless . . . [UNHCR] told me to come back in six-months to renew [the asylum seeker card]. But I didn't go back, as the document is useless.[21]

Jordanians and NGOs told me that relations had hit rock bottom in the second half of 2006 when the Jordanian government informed senior UNHCR officials in Geneva that they would not cooperate any longer with the organization until a change in policy and personnel in Amman took place. Meanwhile, the security situation was continuously deteriorating in Iraq, forcing thousands of Iraqis to leave their country and seek refuge in neighbouring countries. UNHCR was left with little choice as it realized that its TPR was not providing protection to the increasing masses of refugees. In January 2007, UNHCR decided to replace the TPR and announced that Iraqi nationals from central and southern Iraq will be recognized as refugees on a prima facie basis.[22] Later that year, UNHCR appointed a new senior representative to Amman, Imram Riza, thus turning a new page with the Jordanian government. UNHCR also acknowledged that Iraq's neighbours do not 'consider local integration of Iraqis to be a viable option' and that 'voluntary repatriation is considered the preferred solution' under safe circumstances.[23] UNHCR strengthened its resettlement staff in the region and began registering Iraqi refugees for third-country resettlement at a more intensive pace. By summer 2007, as Table 5 indicates, UNHCR had 365 staff in total dedicated to the 'Iraq operation'.

Table 5: UNHCR presence in relation to the Iraq operation

Location	Iraq	Syria	Jordan	Lebanon	Turkey	Egypt	HQ	Total
International staff	11	18	15	6	0	0	4	54
National staff	55	41	78	26	8	3	5	216
UN volunteers	7	48	33	7	0	0	0	95
Total Staff	**73**	**107**	**126**	**39**	**8**	**3**	**9**	**365**
Offices	9	2	2	1	1	1	1	17

Source: UNHCR, *Iraq Situation Response*, July 2007.

UNHCR has also to contend with the fact that different host countries, as previously mentioned, have variant policies towards humanitarian organizations. Jordan, for example, insists that aid to Iraqis comes within the national context and must not be to the detriment of Jordan's development programmes in the fields of education and health. Given the fact that the Jordanian government refused to frame the aid in refugee terms, UNHCR in Jordan was forced to become more of a development agency working with other UN agencies in education and health. Syria, on the other hand, accepts direct aid to refugees but has a clear agenda of getting international recognition (and thus aid) for its efforts in helping the Iraqis.

Aside from the political dimensions to the crisis, and once protection for the refugees is ensured, UNHCR's main objectives are to ensure that the Iraqi refugees can access essential services, particularly the vulnerable among them (their number, as we saw in the previous chapters, had a dramatic surge between the beginning of 2006 and summer 2007). Education, health, food, social, legal and psychological counselling are all critical for the two million Iraqis living in those Arab countries. UNHCR works closely on many projects with the other UN agencies such as UNICEF (education), WHO (health) and WFP (food). In addition, and throughout the region, UNHCR partners with ICRC, the national Red Crescent societies, the ministries of health, education and interior in the respective countries.[24] UNHCR also partners with NGOs (national and international), and by late 2007, it had signed 58 partnership agreements with governments and NGOs in the region to deliver protection and assistance to Iraqis throughout the region.[25] (In Syria and Jordan, UNHCR had 15 partners in each country.) Many of the major projects and activities of UNICEF, WHO and WFP were discussed in the respective country chapters. However, it is important to note here that their work has become increasingly critical over time given the tough economic conditions in the host countries, coupled with lack of legal employment for most refugees which are leading more and more Iraqis to turn to those organizations for help. In addition, UNHCR works closely on specific projects with the sister UN agencies such as UNFPA (in Syria, a programme was launched aiming to prevent and respond to sexual gender-based violence in the Iraqi community); and UNRWA (in Syria to support Palestinian refugees from Iraq who are stuck in refugee camps).[26]

Apart from providing basic services to Iraqi refugees, some UN organizations have other tasks. The IOM, for example, carries out many diverse activities, one of which is to help the Iraqi Ministry of Displacement and Migration (MoDM) in its task to deal with the consequences of mass displacement, and eventually to facilitate the return of Iraqis to their homes. Another objective of the IOM (in partnership with UNDP and Iraqi Ministry of Planning and Development Cooperation) is to encourage the return of educated Iraqis through a joint programme called 'Iraqis Rebuilding Iraq'. Although the IOM relocated its offices from Baghdad to Amman as the violence spread, it is helping the Iraqi government to 'recruit and place qualified nationals for the reconstruction and rehabilitation of the country'.[27] Both the issue of the exodus of skilled educated Iraqis and the question of their possible return are important for our understanding of how this crisis will develop in the future, and Chapters 6 and 7 will be devoted to those two subjects.

UN organizations have a huge bureaucratic structure and are under constant pressure to provide protection and basic services to displaced people worldwide. However, as problems and crises develop in those troubled regions, UNHCR and other UN organizations need financial donors to support their activities. Iraq's invasion was a politically loaded issue even before the first bullet was fired. In general, humanitarian agencies have a recurrent complaint about the extent of politicization in donor behaviour, and obviously in Iraq this behaviour was even more prevalent. Funding for humanitarian activities in Iraq went through many stages, and dropped to such a low level that it compelled some operational NGOs to withdraw from Iraq completely by the end of 2005, at a time when a humanitarian response was ever more needed. One senior UN manager described to Greg Hansen, a senior researcher for the Feinstein International Center at Tufts University, the reasons for the low level of funding:

> There is an environment of denial among donors that reconstruction has been less than successful. There is resistance against the idea that there is a humanitarian problem in Iraq because it's seen as an admission of failure.

Iraq has been sitting on a budget surplus, which is inevitable for a failing
state which donors still regard as a construction site. Couple that with a
die-hard assumption that Iraq is a developed, middle-income country that
is awash in fungible donor funding and oil wealth.[28]

The corruption that plagues the Iraqi government and its contractors,
which is frequently reported by the media and confirmed by reports from the
American Special Inspector General for Iraq Reconstruction (SIGIR), did not
raise confidence among international donors.

By the end of 2006, and despite the rapidly deteriorating humanitarian conditions inside Iraq and in neighbouring countries, donor support had declined
significantly. As a result, UNHCR was forced to suspend a number of activities
in the last quarter of 2006.[29] According to Hansen, 'donors have not calibrated
funding for humanitarian programs to needs and have been careless with
funding for reconstruction'.[30] Meanwhile, calls by UNHCR for donors to step
up and assist the two countries caring for the biggest proportion of Iraqi
refugees – Syria and Jordan – were not heeded: 'It is unconscionable that generous host countries be left on their own to deal with such a huge crisis.'[31]
UNHCR emphasized in 2007 that its programme to raise $100 million for
Iraqi refugees is 'just a drop in the ocean' compared to the huge needs in the
region.[32] As UNHCR has significantly expanded its operations in Syria and
Jordan, the funding for such programmes has been 'woefully inadequate'.[33] It
should be noted that UNHCR's budget requirements in 2007 for the Iraq operation stood at about $124 million distributed among all host countries in the
region, Iraq and administrative costs. The education and health and nutrition
budgets receive large percentages of the allocation.[34] For UNHCR's Iraq operation for 2008, only 53 per cent of the funding ($139.5 million out of $261
million) had been filled as at May 2008. In fact, UNHCR announced in mid-
2008 that it might be forced, due to lack of funding, to reduce and in certain
cases halt a number of assistance programmes.[35] As of May 2008, the largest
donor was the USA with $95.4 million followed by the UK with $6.25 million,
the EU $6.17 million, Sweden $5.97 million and Australia $5.52 million.[36]
Saudi Arabia and the Emirates were conspicuous in their absence, although
Kuwait donated one million dollars.

Some observers believe that the UN, member states and international leaders must achieve a 'better balance of funds for Iraqis displaced outside Iraq and
those inside in order to avoid the risk of creating a pull factor (i.e. incentives
to leave Iraq)'.[37]

Following criticism by donors that UNHCR was launching multiple
appeals for its different programmes related to the Iraq operation, UNHCR
combined its three budgets for its three main activities: protection, assistance
and resettlement. UNHCR was hoping to avoid confusion and 'demonstrate

UNHCR's overall engagement in response to the Iraqi displacement crisis; and simplify procedures'.[38] Thus the total budget for 2008 for those three programmes stood at $261 million, with education and health again receiving the largest allocations across the region.[39]

UN and non-UN humanitarian agencies are concerned that although the level of commitment by donors increased in 2007 (the USA, as we saw, increased its allocation dramatically), the pace of reaction to the Iraqi crisis is far too slow. Syria and Jordan, the two main hosts, complain that UNHCR has not secured financial assistance from Iraq for either state, short of the Iraqi promise to allocate $25 million to both countries to help the needs of the 1.75–2 million refugees residing there. Some observers of humanitarian aid policies have, justifiably, looked down upon the small size of this offer considering the number of refugees and others noted 'the irony of the Iraqi government paying foreign states to house Iraqi citizens, especially given the existence of widespread suspicions of the sectarian bias of the current Iraqi government'.[40]

It is also plausible that because there is a widespread sense among some donors that 'humanitarian organizations have lost their proclaimed neutrality' in Iraq,[41] it made it 'easier' for them not to provide as much assistance to the Iraqis outside Iraq:

> The perceived neutrality, impartiality of genuine humanitarian action is
> threatened in Iraq by blurred distinctions between military, political,
> commercial and humanitarian roles.[42]

In fact, one year after the end of the war, aid agencies that went to Iraq came to the conclusion that their decision to deploy was driven more by politics than local needs:

> The driving consideration about the allocation of resources to Iraq was not
> a first-class humanitarian crisis but rather a high profile political
> imperative.[43]

Politics and ideology played a critical role in the decision by a number of humanitarian organizations not to accept money from governments that have troops in Iraq, as this could 'jeopardise their own security and independence'.[44]

Some Arab commentators felt that the 'Western agencies' may not be able to help with the crisis without 'Iraqi and regional grassroots engagement', and called on Arab groups to 'offer ideas that reflect the region's culture and contribute to, rather than exacerbate, the Iraq problem'.[45] It might be a sound idea, but unfortunately as previously discussed the contribution of the wealthy Arab countries is negligible, and while Syria and Jordan carry most of the burden, the rest of the Arab world have, on the whole, offered a plethora of advice and a paucity of action.

On a historical level, it is interesting to compare the contributions to the Iraqi crisis versus other major events such as Kosovo. Unlike Iraq (and Iraqi refugees), UN appeals for assistance to deal with the emergencies of the Kosovo crisis were met quickly by governments. Within one month (April 1999), a total of $475 million was raised to help about two million refugees (almost an identical number to the estimate of Iraqi refugees): 'It was one of the highest per capita levels of international relief for a refugee population ever provided.'[46] One cannot but wonder whether the politicization of the 2003 war to such an extent has curtailed contributions to help the internally and externally displaced Iraqis. On the other hand, humanitarian workers and ICRC are currently complaining of inadequate humanitarian assistance to unprotected civilians in Darfur and Somalia due to the fact that funding is not keeping pace with the humanitarian tragedy that is taking place in Africa.[47] One observer, Alexander Betts, pointed out:

> Although states' voluntary contributions to UNHCR are intended to provide a form of north–south burden-sharing, they generally amount to a combined sum of less than USD 1 billion per year [this is correct for 2003] and are largely earmarked in accordance with state-specific interests.[48]

Betts believes that the northern states, by allocating over $10 billion per year to their asylum systems and less than $1 billion to UNHCR, 'chose to prioritize unilateral border control above comprehensive refugee protection'.[49]

Despite the potential blurring and intensity of political feelings, it is hard to justify the low level of financial help provided to those refugees. There is no doubt that some countries in the region, and outside, are using this crisis of the exodus to exert indirect pressure on the USA, the Iraqi government and to a certain extent on Syria and Jordan. Thus it is not surprising that the UN organizations are finding it difficult to be fully effective.

NGOs

The Iraqi refugees, scattered in the major urban centres of their host countries, reluctant to come forward and be assisted by the major UN and international organizations, unable to form societies or clubs to help each other, turned to the NGOs (local and international) for help. Iraqis, usually relying on family and community networks to cope with their basic needs, found to their dismay that some of these networks were ruptured in exile and not functioning properly. As we saw before, for those urban refugees, access to resources and to information about them were the main hurdles they faced. Whether inside Iraq or outside Iraq, religious organizations began to fill the void:

> Faith as a motivation for relief operations as a form of solidarity provides Muslim faith-based NGOs with an advantage over other HAs [Humanitarian Actors] in terms of building trust with local actors, and therefore enhances their access to vulnerable populations.[50]

But it is not just Muslim faith-based NGOs; Christian faith-based charities and churches play an important role in helping Christians throughout the region and in countries such as Jordan, and even more in Syria, they have played a critical role.

In Jordan, there are about 40 international and local NGOs operating; some work as national partners to UNHCR while others run their activities independently. Certain organizations, such as CARE International, have extensive networks while others are active in specific areas (women, children, nutrition, shelter, etc.). Broadly speaking, services are provided in five different categories: legal aid and shelter; housing and food; income and cash assistance; health and psychological problems; and education (including informal education).[51] We will review some of the major actors (and by no means the full list) in those areas to provide an overall picture of the local NGOs.

In legal aid, Mizan, a law group for human rights and a partner of UNHCR, provides legal counselling and representation, training on human rights issues and awareness of the legal rights of refugees. Mizan also deals with the legal problems Iraqis face as a result of working illegally.[52] According to Mizan, lawyers in Jordan usually charge between $375 and $625 per case, which means in practice that women (and poor people) are often deprived of legal aid.[53] It has three main projects funded by the EU, UNHCR and other organizations and these projects are: Himaya (legal aid through mobile clinics), Juveniles (provides legal aid in eight juvenile centres) and Women at Risk (assistance to women).[54]

The Jordanian Hashemite Charity Organization, which supports the Jordanian Alliance Against Hunger, is the main distributor of food and hygiene kits. Some NGOs were assigned to distribute food in certain governorates such as Terre des Hommes (an international federation working for the rights of children worldwide[55]) and a local NGO called Tikeyet Um Ali. With regard to housing, Caritas Internationalis offers home visits to vulnerable individuals (such as female heads of households or single parents, elderly people and children, and women victims of violence) and provides house repairs (broken windows, installing door locks), and supplies heaters, mattresses and other necessities.[56]

For income and cash assistance, CARE International is the main organization in the Amman area, helped by Mercy Corps in certain neighbourhoods and a couple of governorates outside Amman, while the Jordanian Alliance Against Hunger is responsible for most governorates of the Kingdom.

In the health arena, there are a number of providers. Caritas Internationalis offers subsidies for doctors' fees and medication and it has established strong links with clinics located in areas with high concentrations of refugees.[57] CARE International, another partner of UNHCR, has a number of activities in the realm of psychological counselling and therapy programmes. The International Catholic Migration Commission also provides psychological assistance to refugees.[58] Mercy Corps and International Relief and Development are involved in basic health education and raising awareness about health issues. Médecins Sans Frontières brings Iraqis injured in suicide bomb attacks for surgery, mainly plastic and reconstructive, to Amman. The waiting list for this specialized surgery is about one to two years.

In the field of education, there are again a number of providers. In addition to UNICEF (which is the focal point for educational issues and for coordinating with the Jordanian Ministry of Education), the International Catholic Migration Commission, operating through Caritas Internationalis and Terre des Hommes, has been instrumental in helping Iraqi children acquire books and uniforms. These organizations are also involved in non-formal education, whereby students acquire vocational training.[59] Mercy Corps is another NGO helping with vocational and life-skills training, library services and home schooling. The Jordanian Ministry of Education officially adopted in summer 2007 the non-formal education curriculum which runs for two years and comprises Arabic, mathematics and life-skill components.[60] These NGOs are also targeting the large numbers of Iraqi youth who are dropping out of school by providing them with recreational and educational activities to stem the rising delinquency rate among them. Save the Children helps with kindergartens and pre-school day care, and has established a project to assist Iraqi families in registering their children in schools after the announcement in summer 2007 that all Iraqi students would be accepted to schools regardless of their residential status (a topic discussed in the chapter on Jordan). The Chaldean Church also provides support by sponsoring Iraqi Christians at private schools which provide Christian religious classes.[61]

In Syria, as discussed in Chapter 3, international NGOs were initially not allowed to operate. But as the scale of the Iraqi exodus widened, and international pressure mounted, the Syrian authorities signed MOUs with 14 international NGOs. In addition, many faith-based organizations are involved. Overall there are four areas of services:

1) Distribution of non-food items: the British Islamic Relief, Caritas Syria, Terre des Hommes Syria and Greek Orthodox Charities provide this service.

2) Organization of community centres: the Danish Refugee Council is involved.
3) In the field of education: there are a wide range of NGOs such as French Première Urgence, the Norwegian Refugee Council, the Greek Orthodox Charities and the British Save the Children.
4) In the health sector: again there are numerous players with different responsibilities. These include, inter alia, the American International Medical Corp., Médecins du Monde, Terre des Hommes, Caritas Syria and the national Red Cross, or Red Crescent societies of a number of countries such as Qatar, Turkey, the Netherlands, the UK and France.[62]

Several Catholic religious groups who provide these services do not need to be registered as they benefit from the direct patronage of the Syrian First Lady, Asma Assad. Muslim charities are also active particularly in the Shi'i neighbourhood of Sayyidah Zainab, where they run more than 12 health centres and other social services. Although UNHCR is not supposed to work with local NGOs in Syria according to regulations by the Ministry for Social Affairs, in reality it does work with a few local NGOs (or charities as they call themselves). These 'charities' tend to be Catholic and include convents, Caritas Internationalis and Terre des Hommes, and UNHCR keeps its involvement with them low-key.[63]

As national NGOs in Syria do not have the right to work with refugees, UNHCR's official and main implementing partner is the Syrian Arab Red Crescent. By early 2008, the Red Crescent had opened nine clinics and one dispensary in areas of high concentration of refugees. These clinics provide subsidized health services for refugees that have either registered or applied for an appointment to register with UNHCR. Many Iraqi patients have received medical treatment through the Ibrahim Khalil Convent, and the Syrian NGO Terre des Hommes helps with rehabilitation and health care for children in need of surgery.[64]

Our focus so far has been on the humanitarian organizations and their effectiveness in providing the services to the refugees, but it is important to look at the difficulties of the humanitarian actors as individuals and not just organizations.

There is no doubt that these service providers are under tremendous pressure in dealing with the refugees, the local authorities and their headquarters. UN staff relive daily the horror stories of the Iraqi refugees and many of them are deeply affected by what they hear and see during the interview process. Some refugees remove some of their clothes to show the interviewers scars from beatings or shrapnel wounds. As a result many suffer from anxiety and depression because of the intensity of their work.[65] These humanitarian actors, whether employees of a large international organization or a small NGO, have to contend with the resentment and the occasional hostility of the local population towards the refugees who are competing for the same jobs and homes, and accessing the same basic services of education and health. As we saw before, some of the local press add fuel to the fire by underlining the burdens carried by the local population as a result of giving refuge to the Iraqis. Indeed, it becomes a delicate balancing act between helping the refugees, satisfying the national government's rules and regulations and dealing with the local popular reaction. The one advantage they have in comparison with their colleagues in Iraq is the lack of violence. The host countries might not be entirely free and democratic but NGO staff do not face death everyday as those in Iraq do.[66]

One important element that surely affects the quality and effectiveness of these NGOs is the high level of staff turnover. A large number of those humanitarian actors do not speak the language or understand the Iraqi/Arab culture. Sometimes they get transferred to the Middle East from another continent for a period of one to two years and are expected to work miracles in a relatively short time. Not only is it almost impossible to achieve those targets in such difficult circumstances as described above, but the reality is that the lack of continuity, cultural and linguistic understanding negatively affects the recipients of aid.

Finally, it should be emphasized that all those organizations and NGOs have to deal with the refugees' deep feelings of disappointment which emanate from high expectations of these organizations: the refugees believed that international organizations and NGOs had the power to resettle them in a third country swiftly and smoothly or at least to ameliorate their conditions considerably. NGOs, on the other hand, had to deal with government restrictions on their activities in countries such as Syria, while in other cases, as in Egypt, NGOs were not ready for the large numbers of Iraqi refugees given that their attention was focused on the much larger population of Sudanese refugees. As we saw, neither resettlement nor dramatic change in the conditions of the refugees took place, and thus the sense of the 'uselessness' of these organizations prevails among the Iraqi refugees, a factor which might become critical if ever those refugees were to return to Iraq in significant numbers.

Chapter 6

Iraq's economy and its brain drain

I live now, torn away from my life's work,
a nameless shadow life I never knew,
in which there is no struggle and no striving.
And no one cares to know what work I do.[1]

In Chapter 1, we saw that the pervasive violence was the main impetus for hundreds of thousands of Iraqi refugees to flee their country. But violence was not the sole reason: Iraq's economy was mismanaged pre- and post-Saddam, inducing many people, particularly the skilled and educated, to leave Iraq to escape violence and to look for better opportunities for themselves and their families. This chapter will discuss the management of Iraq's economy and in particular the two main economic causes of the brain drain – unemployment and inflation; the prospects for the country's reconstruction following the invasion; the degradation of the country's bureaucratic machine and the overwhelming corruption in all facets of Iraq's economy;[2] and finally, the characteristics of the brain drain and its effect on some vital sectors such as the health sector.

Iraq's economy

By 2003, after two wars, many years of sanctions and the increasing economic autonomy of Kurdistan, Iraq's economy was highly fragmented and there was little in the way of a national macroeconomic policy. Since 1980, Iraq had faced one economic and political crisis after another, and 'normal' circumstances did not exist. The country's dependence on its relatively huge oil revenues since the early 1950s culminating in the late 1970s and early 1980s turned Iraq into a classic case of rentierism.[3] A system of economic patronage was established reporting to Saddam himself and his close entourage.[4] Decisions were not made on economic grounds but to reward or punish certain groups.

Two wars and more than a decade of sanctions did not lead to reform or internal collapse. By 2003, however, Iraq's economy was severely weakened in every area; foreign reserves were depleted, development planning had virtually ceased, the infrastructure was severely damaged and a vast majority of the population was impoverished.[5] In spite of the shattered economy and the weak institutional organization, Iraq as a state functioned and essential services were provided to the population. However, after the fall of Baghdad, the Iraqi state collapsed, its power structures disintegrated and there was nothing to replace them. Essential services were halted, and the looting which followed spared no bank, hospital, power station or government office. It was estimated that the cost to the economy was $12 billion.[6]

The CPA, under Ambassador L. Paul Bremer III, issued within a week of his arrival in Baghdad the decree of de-Ba'thification. Overnight almost 30,000 Iraqis – including middle management in economic ministries, teachers and doctors – were dismissed from their jobs.[7] The senior management of the country had already fled or been arrested and now middle management were kicked out. The result was a huge vacuum which the Americans could not fill.

Bremer believed that Iraq needed 'a vibrant private sector to succeed'.[8] He imagined Iraq as a post-war Germany or post-communist Europe and believed things could turn around fast: 'The biggest influence on Coalition economic policy was the experience of the transition economies of eastern Europe and central Asia during the 1990s.'[9]

The American belief that mass privatization at a fast pace would work in Iraq naively ignored the fact that Iraq is not Russia or Poland as it lacked the industry and level of organization in these countries. But even in countries such as Russia, the experience was not straightforward and smooth.[10]

Meanwhile, the CPA was dealing with one crisis after another (political and economic) and was trying to cope with a crippled economy plagued by price distortions and inefficiencies. The Americans were under pressure to show progress. This led to an emphasis on headline projects to deliver the essential requirements such as oil, electricity and potable water to the population, while long-term projects to improve agriculture and industry were pushed aside.[11] Although Congress had allocated, by the end of 2005, aid totalling about $21 billion, more than a third remained unspent. In fact, the failure to spend Iraq's reconstruction money, particularly in the first year of the war, was a contributing factor to the increased violence and high unemployment.[12]

Since the CPA was dissolved on 28 June 2004, 'militias appear to have carried out or co-opted their own areas of economic control and regulation'.[13] Corruption and trade in smuggled oil became the cornerstones of the new economy of Iraq. It is essential to look at Iraq's economy and its major problems to understand fully the reasons that people fled Iraq.

The first economic issue facing Iraq which has had an impact on many refugees is inflation, a recurrent problem for Iraq. As a result of the invasion of

Kuwait and the subsequent sanctions, hyperinflation became a structural problem.[14] Consequently, people were forced to liquidate their assets and huge disparities in income between the rich and the poor were created.[15] This signalled the weakening of the middle class in Iraq which gathered momentum after the 2003 invasion.

After the collapse of Saddam's regime, inflation stabilized at around 32 per cent to 34 per cent per annum. However, in late 2005 inflation began to rise sharply due to increased violence, the fallout from state control, corruption, increasing wages, increasing cost of house rentals and the rise of fuel prices.[16] By January 2007, inflation reached 66.5 per cent reflecting shortages of key commodities, primarily fuel. Following an intensified policy effort by the Iraqi government to bring inflation under control, the annual inflation rate declined to 38 per cent in May 2007,[17] and to 15 per cent by the end of that year.[18] The Iraq Central Bank has played an important role in combating inflation and, in fact, the establishment of a relatively independent Central Bank has been one of the major achievements in post-war Iraq. By raising interest rates, the Central Bank forced the Iraqi dinar (ID) exchange rates to appreciate, thus reducing the imported inflation. (The ID which, after its introduction in 2004, initially traded at around 1,450 to the US dollar, reached 1,225 to the US dollar by the end of 2007, and further strengthened to 1,196 to the US dollar in June 2008 with the increase in oil prices.)

Inflation continues to be an issue facing Iraq and during the peak period of emigration (especially in the second half of 2006), hyperinflation was definitely an economic push factor encouraging middle-class professionals to flee the country. Violence and dysfunctional government did not just lead to the brain drain; it led many wealthy Iraqis to flee with their capital, dealing a heavy blow to the country's war-torn economy. Among the Iraqis who fled were business people, entrepreneurs that the Americans wanted to encourage to help build a new economy in Iraq.

The second issue facing Iraq from an economic point of view, and which had more severe consequences for those who fled the country, was unemployment. Estimates for unemployment range from 25 per cent to 40 per cent, which even at the lower rate is socially and economically destabilizing.[19] A UNDP survey in 2004 indicated that the labour force participation rate in Iraq is 40.9 per cent, which is comparable to that in neighbouring countries of 37 per cent to 43 per cent (Iran, Jordan), while Syria had a somewhat higher activity level of 53 per cent. The main reason for the low participation rate is that most women are not economically active.[20]

Employment (or lack of it) is a serious problem for Iraq. Under Saddam's regime, employment was a political tool and after 2003 continued to be so as Herring and Rangwalla referred to 'employment brokerage' by the different political parties.[21]

The dissolution by Bremer of the Iraqi Army which had employed between 400,000 and 500,000 people (estimated at 7 per cent of the labour force), coupled with de-Ba'thification, added something like 8 per cent to 10 per cent to unemployment, especially among the Sunnis. High rates of unemployment tear at the fabric of society by depriving families of economic security. The unemployment crisis also threatens the gains that had been made by women in Iraq during the 1960s and the following two decades. Unemployment among women was estimated at 70 per cent in 2004, and has forced professional females to seek employment as housekeepers and other domestic work.[22]

In spite of the high unemployment among Iraqis, US subcontractors have been attempting to rebuild the infrastructure in Iraq with cheap migrant labour from South Asia.[23]

The statistics in the UNDP survey of 2004 showed that unemployment reached an astonishing 37.2 per cent among young men with secondary or higher education.[24] The implications of this high level of unemployment are explored further in the section on the brain drain. The combination of high inflation and unemployment has led to a severe increase in poverty, forcing people to engage in murky businesses to make a quick buck (crime, arms sales and prostitution are all dramatically on the increase), and corruption, as will be discussed later, became the norm in every facet of life.

For various reasons, American officials and commentators called for efforts to reduce unemployment. The US Ambassador to Iraq between 2005 and 2007, Zalmay Khalilzad, believed that job creation would reduce violence by providing job opportunities for members of the different armed groups in the country.[25] One American commentator felt that a 'job surge, not a military surge, remains Iraq's best hope'.[26] Interestingly, four years after the big privatization efforts of the CPA, American and Iraqi officials began advocating restarting some of the old factories (considered after the war to be 'inefficient, government-subsidized behemoths') as they could represent a good chance to push reconstruction forward and increase employment.[27]

Small businesses have also suffered as a result of violence, fear and the deterioration in the economy. The Americans, after their invasion, rarely focused on small family businesses, as they were keener to focus on the enormous state-owned enterprises given the ideological aspect of those 'Soviet-style factories'.[28]

Iraqi economists have been warning that unemployment is a time bomb and that the major reason for its spread is the 'impairment to the economic basis' of the country following the invasion.[29] Whatever the reasons and however strong the efforts were to resolve this crisis, the results were poor. Even three years after the UNDP survey, a poll by an independent opinion research company of 2,000 Iraqis across all 18 provinces clearly indicated that the quality of life in Iraq has further deteriorated in 2005 and 2006. More than three-quarters of respondents to the poll said that jobs were hard to find and that the availability of clean water, medical care and basic goods and services have, after some improvement in 2005, all deteriorated.[30]

An important contributor to quality of life is electricity. The CPA and later Iraqi governments realized not only the economic importance of the sector but also its psychological effect on the population. In spite of the fact that electricity has received about 23 per cent of the allocation for reconstruction ($4.2 billion out of a total of $18.3 billion),[31] the outcome is still far from satisfactory, particularly for the Baghdad population. The pre-war average of 4,075 megawatts has been barely exceeded in spite of the dramatic increase in demand.[32] While average hours of electricity per day improved nationwide compared to the pre-war level (about 10 hours per day versus 4–8 hours before the invasion), in Baghdad, average hours per day dropped dramatically from 16–24 hours during Saddam's era to 7–9 hours per day in the years 2005–07.[33] Some in the Iraqi media believe that even those numbers are exaggerated as the Ministry of Electricity is 'doctoring' the statistics about the output, and that the bombastic statements made by the minister about production surpassing 6,000 megawatts is nothing but a 'lie, lie, lie'.[34]

The question that begs itself given what was discussed above is: what is happening to Iraq's reconstruction and what are the prospects from an economic point of view for the Iraqis in Iraq and in exile?

Iraq's reconstruction

Since 2003, US taxpayers have spent about $40 billion to $50 billion to rebuild Iraq's infrastructure and pave the way for its reconstruction. In addition, Iraq with its oil wealth (especially when oil is trading at over $100 a barrel) has accumulated by 2008 large reserves of $50 billion to $60 billion. Although US agencies have undertaken a variety of programmes to help Iraq execute its capital projects budget, the impact has been feeble. A report by the US Government Accountability Office (GAO) concluded that 'the central ministries had spent only 4.4 per cent of their investment budget, as of August 2007'.[35] This is scandalous considering the hardship the Iraqi people are living under, and the number of refugees leaving their country due in part to lack of employment opportunities and essential services. GAO pointed out a number of factors that limit the Iraqi government's ability to spend its capital project budget: (1) violence and sectarian strife delay capital budget execution by increasing the time and cost to award and monitor contracts, and by reducing the number of contractors willing to bid for project contracts; (2) recent refugee outflows and de-Ba'thification have reduced the number of skilled workers available and contributed to their exodus from Iraq; (3) weakness in Iraqi procurement, budgeting and accounting procedures impedes the completion of those capital projects that are initiated.[36] No wonder then that Iraq's failure to devote its own resources to rebuild the country's infrastructure has brought severe criticism from Western governments and technical organizations.

One American expert felt that there had been a big improvement in Iraq's infrastructure from hospitals and electricity to water plants, but that the 'striking, and lamentable, fact about our economic efforts in Iraq is that for the most part we don't have the foggiest idea how well they are working'.[37] The problem with Iraq's reconstruction is that it was initially imposed with ideas and ideology that were not applicable to Iraq given its past. The combination of 35 years of dictatorship with a rigorous sanctions regime led to the economic and administrative decline of the country. Thus the gap between Saddam's era, characterized by 'a clannish and personalized system of favouritism in which ruthlessness and corruption played a major part',[38] and the liberal ideas of swift privatization and a market-based economy, was absolutely huge. Rory Stewart, who served as the CPA deputy Governorate Coordinator of the southern provinces of Maysan and later Dhi-Qar, aptly summed up the differences:

> The CPA in the Green Zone wanted to build the new state in a single frenzy.
> Instead of beginning with security and basic needs and attempting the
> more complex things later, we implemented simultaneously programmes
> on human rights, the free market, feminism, federalism and constitutional
> reform. We acted as though there could be no tensions between the
> different programmes, no necessity to think about sequence or timing. But
> people in Maysan talked about almost none of these things. They talked
> about security.[39]

Some academics, such as Sultan Barakat, believe the fact 'that the vision for the "New Iraq" was not developed within Iraq or by Iraqis made it inherently unworkable, however it was conceived'.[40]

The effectiveness of federal economic management in Iraq is constrained due to the lack of security and the polarization stemming from sectarianism. Thus the reconstruction process 'is wrapped in uncertainties: political, economic, institutional and security'.[41] This uncertainty and increased sectarianism has created a corruption-based patronage and this does not augur well for those in exile. Jobs and opportunities are not given on merit, but due to affiliation to the right party and clan. Corruption in Iraq has, unfortunately, become a central feature of the post-2003 economy and deserves attention given its implications for the brain drain and the refugees.

Corruption in Iraq

Corruption was already prevalent during Saddam's regime but the Oil-for-Food programme which accompanied the sanctions in the 1990s almost institutionalized corruption. Different estimates of illicit Iraqi income from surcharges on oil sales ranged from $300 million to $7.5 billion. Saddam created a true patronage and reward system not only internally but also with foreign companies and influential individuals outside Iraq.[42] Unfortunately, corruption and the patronage system continued after the 2003 invasion. Philippe Le Billon describes dramatic transitions similar to what happened after the fall of Saddam:

> Political and economic transitions are particularly prone to corruption and transitions in conflict-affected areas are no exception. Corruption is often one of the key concerns of local population in conflict-affected [areas] during reconstruction, along with insecurity and unemployment.[43]

Indeed, this general description fits Iraq: transition, reconstruction, insecurity and high unemployment.

Ali Allawi, who served in the Iraqi government from the end of 2003 to mid-2006, described 'the explosion in corruption' that took place in different ministries and the shocking methods of embezzlement by so many ministers and senior officials.[44] He succinctly described the country and its bureaucracy following the invasion:

> ...the Iraqi state combined the worst features of a centralised bureaucracy with vestiges of the occupation, and a near collapse of the information, reporting and control mechanisms that underpin any functioning government authority. The legacy of corrupt practices, outdated management systems, incompetence and nepotism was neither seriously challenged nor bypassed.[45]

SIGIR devotes a large part of most of his quarterly reports to Congress to corruption and graft. In a testimony to the House of Representatives, Stuart Bowen, the SIGIR, warned that the 'rising tide of corruption in Iraq' is 'a second insurgency' that:

> ...stymies the construction and maintenance of Iraq's infrastructure, deprives people of goods and services, reduces confidence in public institutions, and potentially aids insurgent groups reportedly funded by graft derived from oil smuggling or embezzlement.[46]

One of the characteristics of Iraq's corruption is that insurgents, smugglers and corrupt officials collaborate at different levels, weaving an intricate web that makes it difficult to distinguish amongst them. The US embassy in Baghdad has argued that the Iraqi government 'is not capable of even rudimentary enforcement of anti-corruption laws' and the prime minister's office is openly hostile to the idea of an independent anti-corruption agency.[47] A report by the Brookings Institution affirmed that 'corruption is probably the single greatest factor inhibiting the creation of a credible Iraqi political institution. Like the problem of insecurity, with which it is intertwined, corruption undermines nearly every aspect of reconstruction.'[48]

One-third, and possibly more, of the fuel from Iraq's largest refinery in Bayji, 208 kilometres (130 miles) north of Baghdad, on the main road to Mosul and in a Sunni Arab-dominated region, is diverted to the black market. 'Tankers are hijacked, drivers are bribed, papers are forged and meters are manipulated'[49] to finance the insurgency, pay corrupt officials and reward the smugglers. Gas stations are often built to get fuel at subsidized government rates to be resold later onto the black market at higher prices. The police chief of a town near Bayji told *The New York Times* reporter that owners of bogus gas stations pay $20,000 in bribes to an oil ministry official in Baghdad to get their paperwork approved: 'In each station you'll find high Iraqi officials who have shares.'[50]

Estimates for smuggling range from $2.5 billion to $4 billion per year,[51] and there are indications that 100,000 barrels of oil are being smuggled from Iraq on a daily basis.[52] The smuggling stems from a number of factors: first, the lack of metering of Iraq's oil exports;[53] second, subsidies set up under Saddam and still continuing have led to a huge differential between Iraqi product prices and those of nearby countries;[54] and finally, the lack of proper control systems due to the degradation of the bureaucracy after 2003.

With oil prices reaching more than $130 a barrel, Iraq's oil revenues in 2008 could reach $60 billion. US senators are furious at the amount their government has spent and continues to spend on Iraq 'despite Iraq earning billions of dollars in oil revenue over that time period (2003–08) that have ended up in non-Iraqi banks'.[55]

The corruption was in most ministries and sectors. A newspaper investigation highlighted the shadowy arms deals which sidestepped anti-corruption safeguards, including the approval of senior uniformed Iraqi Army officers and an Iraqi contract approval committee. Indeed, at the urging of the Defence Minister, Abdul Qadir, the Prime Minister Nouri Al-Maliki abolished the national contracts committee, a mandatory review agency for all government purchases of more than $50 million.[56] The former commissioner of the Iraqi Commission on Public Integrity told a Congress committee that the Iraqi government, led by Al-Maliki, has thwarted investigations into corruption at the top levels of the administration, including probes of Al-Maliki's relatives, while nearly four dozen anti-corruption employees or their family members have been murdered.[57] Meanwhile, Al-Maliki announces, time and again, that this year or next year will be the year of 'fight against administrative corruption'.[58]

Thus corruption and wasteful reconstruction efforts have dominated Iraq's economy, but this is, unfortunately, not limited to the central and southern governorates of Iraq. Kurdistan, which has enjoyed relative stability and safety and whose economy has prospered, is also suffering from wastefulness and corruption. When Kurdish villages suffered flooding in December 2006, the Kurdish authorities had no capacity to assist the villagers despite years of development assistance and economic boom.[59] Again, and in spite of the lack of violence, cronyism and corruption have become integral to Kurdistan's economy.

Kurdistan, with a population of about four million, has become an oasis in violent Iraq and is enjoying an economic boom. It has two international airports (Arbil and Sulaymaniya) and five universities operate in the area, which has received many displaced academics and professionals from central and southern Iraq. The Kurdish government has promulgated a liberal investment law allowing foreign investors to own 100 per cent of the investment project capital, while giving them a ten-year tax holiday and a five-year exemption from customs and duties on the import. However, Kurdistan's economy is also suffering from unemployment and inflation. School and university graduates clamour for jobs in the government ministries and one report suggested excess positions are created in the public sector, in order to reduce unemployment and provide jobs to these young people.[60] Meanwhile, due to the construction boom, Asian and African labour is imported to do the manual work.[61] Kurdistan is flourishing but 'beneath the façade, ordinary Kurds are struggling to survive, while state money gets siphoned off into private pockets'.[62]

Two families control the political and economic activity of Kurdistan. The Kurdish Democratic Party (KDP), which controls Arbil and the surrounding cities, is headed by Masoud Barzani, while the Patriotic Union of Kurdistan (PUK), which controls Sulaymaniya and surrounding cities, is headed by Iraq's President, Jalal Talabani. Each party has its local government but more importantly each has its own economic arm.[63] The Zagros group of companies is the KDP's economic arm in Arbil, and the Nokan group is the PUK's economic arm in Sulaymaniya. These two families have direct control over, and involvement in, their two respective companies. Every member of the two families has a senior job either in the government, the security services or the economic conglomerates which they control.[64]

Kurdistan sits on large oil reserves, explored and unexplored, and while there is still wrangling between the Kurdistan and Baghdad governments

about an oil law that would define Kurdistan's oil rights and resolve the
conflicting interests among the Kurds, Shia and Sunnis, the Kurds receive 17
per cent of Iraq's oil revenues (in 2007 estimated to have been $6.1 billion)
from the central government in Baghdad.[65]

The lack of transparency is remarkable. The budget of the Kurdish government based on the allocation from Baghdad is divided between the two parties
– 52 per cent to KDP and 48 per cent to PUK – but no fiscal data are published
by the Kurdish Regional government. One Kurdish commentator summed up
the situation:

> The Kurdish leadership has been running the country without any
> accountability and bookkeeping. This is a grave failure with serious
> implications and raises questions as to why there were not any data
> available for the last few years. The first thing [that] comes to mind when
> looking at the status quo is abuse of power and corruption.[66]

In spite of the corruption, cronyism and nepotism, there were some
achievements in Iraq's economy. Can these achievements pave the way in the
future for a new economy with plentiful opportunities for its people and its
exiles abroad?

Setting up an independent central bank and issuing the new dinar currency
were both success stories in Iraq's economic management after the invasion.
Reducing the external debt was another. In 2004, Iraq's external debt stood at
about $132 billion (500 per cent of GDP) to countries and commercial
creditors worldwide, but by 2008, the country's debt had dropped to about $33
billion, representing only about 46 per cent of GDP.[67] It is interesting to note
that Saudi Arabia and Kuwait, countries that benefited from the toppling of
Saddam, refused to reduce or forgive the debt. With regard to Kuwait, Iraq
claims that the $16 billion 'debt' to Kuwait was actually grants given to support
Iraq in its war with Iran.[68] An Iraqi government spokesman said his government should not have to pay off the debts incurred by Saddam Hussein's
regime: 'Russia forgave 12 billion dollars of Iraqi debt. We have not seen
similar moves from our neighbours.'[69] In July 2008, however, UAE agreed to
forgive Iraq of $7 billion of debt and bank interest.[70]

A balanced assessment of progress in Iraq was provided by a US National
Intelligence report:

> There have been modest improvements in economic output, budget
> execution, and government finances but fundamental structural problems
> continue to prevent sustained progress in economic growth and living
> conditions.[71]

A senior Iraqi diplomat based in Europe explained to me that the main reason for lack of progress, apart from violence, is that many of Iraq's economic managers post-2003 are not equipped to run large concerns as they lack the ability to plan on a long-term basis; their focus is on short-term gains. He assured me, however, that Iraq is rich and everything has to change. He described Iraq as 'Le Grand Chantier' (big construction site) for the next 20 to 25 years whereby everything will be replaced.[72]

In my interviews with Iraqis in the Middle East and Europe, I found that the only ones who were optimistic were young entrepreneurs who left Iraq because of the violence but are still doing business there. They saw tremendous business opportunities in Iraq and believed that once the violence comes to a halt or ebbs, Iraq will become a successful and prosperous country. Interestingly, a recent economic study indicated that even though civil war has devastating consequences, and its aftermath can be immensely difficult, if there is a real lasting peace, recovery and improvement are achieved.[73]

Unfortunately, violence has not come to a halt, although it has abated from its peak. The 'aftermath' in the theoretical study mentioned above is defined hypothetically as a seven-year period; an 'eternity' for the Iraqi refugees living abroad. During the Ba'th regime, Iraqis, particularly middle-class professionals, chose to flee because as Charles Tripp put it:

> These twin, interlinked features – the restricted circles of the rulers and the primacy of military force – have combined with the massive financial power granted to successive Iraqi governments by oil revenues to create dominant narratives marked by powerful, authoritarian leadership. The ideas of politics as discipline and of participation as conformity have figured prominently, facing many Iraqis with a choice between submission and flight.[74]

After the invasion, many Iraqis fled their country because by 2006 the situation, as summed up by Ali Merza, was:

i. Insecurity, violence and sectarian strife.
ii. Low level of services; mainly power, fuel, water, sewerage and waste disposal.
iii. High levels of unemployment . . . and inflation.
iv. Persistent, and potentially growing, poverty (around 10 per cent of Iraqis are below the poverty line).
v. Corruption in the civil service.
vi. Smuggling of and profiteering in energy and subsidized goods. . . . [75]

As a result of the above factors, Iraq witnessed a massive brain drain at all levels and in all sectors.

Brain drain

In the aftermath of the 1968 coup d'état that brought Saddam and the Ba'th party to power, a first wave of brain drain began. Some of the best physicians left in 1969 and many of the teaching faculty of the Baghdad Medical School emigrated to the West.[76] During the 1970s and 1980s, the government began focusing on attracting Iraqis back, and many incentives were introduced as part of reviving the private economy. Emphasis was put on education and laws were passed to enhance women's rights and encourage them to study. The urban middle class of professionals, high-level civil servants and businessmen was growing until 1991. Phebe Marr described this class as 'the backbone of modern, developed Iraq' and estimated it to be 22 per cent of the total population at the end of the 1970s.[77] Even before the Gulf War, estimates put the Iraqi exile community at 1.5 million. But after the 1991 war, a second wave of Iraqis began to leave as they realized that with two wars, almost back-to-back, the opportunities for professional careers would dwindle dramatically. 'The fabric of Iraq's society seriously began to unravel during the 1990s' and the changes affected the middle class more than any other group.[78] As we saw before, this decade witnessed hyperinflation and the Iraqi dinar collapsed (from ID 1 equalling $3 in the 1980s to $1 being worth ID 2,000 in the 1990s).[79] This was truly the beginning of the demise of the middle class.

By 2003, estimates of Iraqi exiles ranged from two to four million people. Whatever the statistics are, there is no doubt that Iraq suffered an enormous brain drain with many settling in the West or in Arab countries such as Jordan and Yemen, while others found jobs in the Gulf States.

The end of Saddam's regime brought optimism to the well-educated professionals abroad who believed a new era had opened. This optimism was short-lived. Those academics and doctors who were, even remotely, associated with the Ba'th party were targeted after they lost their jobs. The targeting soon extended beyond those affiliated with the previous regime and a combination of militias and criminal gangs began killing or kidnapping professionals (in particular doctors, lawyers and academics) or their families. Educational institutions were also singled out.[80] In a report by *The New York Times* during the graduation ceremony at Al-Mustansiriya University in Baghdad in 2007, students interviewed talked about their lives being shattered by daily violence, and 26 out of the 30 students interviewed were planning to flee their country as their dreams of having a brilliant career and studying for more advanced degrees in a stable Iraq 'have evaporated'.[81]

Before we look in detail at the impact of the brain drain, in particular on the health sector and to a certain extent on education, it is important to point out that in spite of the high numbers of professionals who left Iraq, the opportunities for those who stayed behind were rather slim, forcing many to move to the north looking for better opportunities.

As was mentioned earlier, unemployment among the young and educated was high in the 2004 survey. Many professionals and artists were forced to take any job to make ends meet. One artist, who carries a bag with his paint-brushes and colours and goes from door-to-door searching for work, told a journalist:

> I have been searching for a permanent job for four years but in vain.
> Because of nepotism or corruption or because I am not a member of the right party, I am still unemployed.[82]

Some of those who could not leave the country moved to the calmer Kurdistan to find jobs and sanctuary from the debilitating violence in Baghdad and central Iraq. Kurdish universities have integrated some of the academics, mostly Sunnis, who left central Iraq. However, given the history between Kurdistan and the previous Iraqi governments, many Kurds are nervous about the arrival of so many Arabs (who are required to register with the Kurdish security services) and hence the number of Arab academics in Kurdistan is restricted.[83] There are no accurate statistics about the number of academics and professionals who moved there, but Kurdistan's health minister claimed that about 1,000 Iraqi doctors emigrated to Arbil from Baghdad, Basra and Mosul.[84] Kurdish officials from the Ministry of Higher Education & Scientific Research whom I interviewed in northern Iraq in September 2008, talked of about 700 Iraqi Arab academics obtaining jobs in Kurdish universities.

The targeted attacks on academics gathered momentum in 2006 with the spread of violence. The dividing lines between insurgency and mafia-style gangs became blurred. Some kidnappings, for example, were connected to the sectarian strife, but others were carried out purely for ransom. The gangs believed professionals were an excellent target due to their position in society and their theoretical earning power. In January 2004, there were about two kidnappings per day in Baghdad, but by mid-2006, there were 30 daily kidnappings in the capital.[85] Iraq became the 'killing fields' for academics. The BRussells Tribunal website compiled a list of academics murdered, stating their names, their profession, qualifications and their university affiliations if they had ones. As of April 2008, there were 353 names, with the vast majority being PhD holders. The crème de la crème of society has been wiped out.[86] Another list comprises the names of 74 academics threatened or kidnapped. Interestingly, while there were entries of murdered academics in 2008, the last entry of kidnapping was October 2007.[87] The same website also carries a list of 247 Iraqi media professionals murdered by mid-2007. In addition, according to the Iraqi Lawyers Association, 210 lawyers and judges have been killed since the invasion, and dozens injured in attacks against them. The Association said the number of lawyers offering services in Iraq had decreased by about 40 per cent from April 2006 to April 2007 and hundreds of cases had been shelved awaiting lawyers to take them on.[88] Not all killings were by militias or gangs; with violence spreading and life becoming cheap, people began settling scores. In April 2007, for example, two lawyers were killed after winning a case for a family who had lost their house and belongings when they were taken over by another family. The losers shot dead the lawyers while leaving the court, in the middle of the street.[89]

Thus, faced with threats of murder or kidnapping, many professionals voted with their feet and left the country. It should be pointed out that in my interviews with Iraqi exiles, another reason, in addition to violence, for leaving the country was given to me: the encroachment of religion and the Shi'i militias over the day-to-day academic life which makes it impossible to write or express freely secular or opposing views.

Thus hundreds of Iraq's finest minds were left with no option but to flee the engulfing flames of sectarian hatred and pervasive violence that dominated every aspect of life and threatened their whole families. As we saw in the previous chapter, they found refuge in Syria, Jordan, Sweden and other countries. As the Iraqi veteran politician Dr Adnan Pachachi put it:

> Hundreds of thousands of Iraqis, among them highly qualified
> professionals, have been forced to leave their homes and some have
> emigrated to neighbouring countries. The Iraq brain drain which began in
> Saddam's time has now reached alarming proportions.[90]

We will look now at the impact of the brain drain on the health sector. Doctors and medical workers at hospitals were specifically targeted. Armed gangs infiltrated not just the hospitals, but the Health Ministry itself. As was discussed in Chapter 1, the Ministry of Health became, from the end of 2004, a base for Shi'i militias; one deputy minister was arrested for being in charge of the kidnapping and torturing of opponents inside the ministry's building. Unlike Saddam's era when doctors left Iraq because they were individual victims of the regime, in the Iraq of post-2003, they became a target as a group. They were kidnapped for ransom and were tortured and killed to disrupt the basics of civil society. As they had to move around in public in and out of clinics and hospitals, they became an easy and soft target for their attackers. Nurses were also a target: between 2003 and the end of 2006, it was estimated that 160 were murdered and more than 400 wounded.[91] For the nurses fleeing the country, a secondary factor was the relatively poor pay (roughly $150 per month), and some hoped of getting better paid jobs in safe countries.

According to an estimate by Dr Ismail Jalili, 23 per cent of all academics murdered in Iraq were doctors, 90 per cent of whom were medical doctors, 6 per cent veterinary surgeons, 2 per cent dentists and 2 per cent pharmacists. Almost 50 per cent of those murdered were specialists, with 14 per cent being surgeons. The vast majority (98 per cent) were Muslims (no identification of Sunni or Shi'i but one could assume a high percentage of the former) from the Baghdad region.[92]

The government was helpless in stopping the haemorrhaging of doctors fleeing the country. In late 2006, it took a cue from Saddam's regime in order to stem the flow and announced that medical schools were forbidden to issue diplomas and transcripts to new graduates. One of the senior doctors in the Iraqi Medical Association described this decision as a 'scandal'.[93] The Association was issuing 30 to 50 'certificates of good standing' to Iraqi physicians every day. Unable to protect medical workers, the government decided to simplify gun license procedures for doctors, allowing them to get licensed weapons faster than other Iraqis.[94]

By October 2007, with the improvement of security on one hand and the restrictions imposed by Syria and Jordan on the other hand, the number of doctors leaving the country began to dwindle. The Health Ministry, according to the Minister of Displacement and Migration, is building ten hospitals and intends to prepare varied and diverse programmes to bring those doctors back to Iraq.[95] It is too early to tell what success these programmes will have in the future and this topic will be further discussed in Chapter 7.

How many physicians have left Iraq after the invasion? The statistics vary widely. Many newspapers have reported that 12,000 to 18,000 doctors out of 34,000 have fled the country. The head of Iraqi Red Crescent believes there were 34,000 doctors in 2003: overall 50 per cent had left by the end of 2007 but among the specialists 70 per cent fled the country.[96] The problem with these statistics is that no one really knows how many doctors were in Iraq in 2003, as there was no official register. The Medical Association and the Ministry of Health compiled a list of physicians working but it was not updated regularly. Estimates, however, by the Ministry of Health in early 2004, based on statistics collected in 2003, indicated that there were about 17,200 physicians: 14,500 in the central and southern governorates and about 2,700 in the northern governorates. This number represented about 6.3 physicians per 10,000 population, and this varied from one area to another with Baghdad having 9.3 per 10,000 population.[97] In addition, according to the same report, there were 3,000 dentists and 1,634 pharmacists. Thus it is possible to estimate that there were 22,000 doctors and pharmacists at that time. WHO, in its country profile, does not present a total number of physicians but indicated there were 6.6 per 10,000 population in 2005 (which was equivalent to roughly 17,000 doctors).[98] Medact, the global health charity, estimated that 25 per cent of

Iraq's 18,000 physicians had emigrated by 2006,[99] which seems a reasonable figure. There are no official or accurate statistics about the number of doctors who left the country. What is clear, based on many knowledgeable sources within the health sector, is that a high percentage of specialists are no longer in Iraq.

Whatever the number of those who left and those who are still working, there are two definite observations. First, Iraq lost thousands of its physicians and with them the country lost a wealth of experience. Second, Iraq's health system has crumbled and, as shown in Chapter 1, the health conditions (physical and mental) of Iraqis have deteriorated dramatically in the five-year period following the invasion. There are endless media stories describing the conditions in hospitals. For example, at Ibn Al-Betar Cardiac Hospital in central Baghdad, surgeons were performing 60 to 80 operations a week. As a result of the departure of 15 of its surgeons, the number of operations dropped by half.[100] In Diyala, a province in eastern-central Iraq, shortages of doctors led nurses to take on tasks and procedures for which they are not qualified. Diyala's health department said that at least 80 per cent of the doctors who used to work in the province have fled due to violence.[101]

It was not only a lack of surgeons and specialists that affected hospitals. Medical supplies in many hospitals have been low since the end of 2003, and whenever there are major incidents or battles, such as the fight that took place between the government's army and Sadr's militias in Basra in March 2008, stocks have dropped to a critically low level.[102] Even without major fighting, the situation was not much better. One neurologist who fled to Amman told the BBC:

> By the time I left the hospital, there was a great shortage of medicines.
> Nursing staff was zero.

And before he left Iraq, the professor told his resident staff while on a tour of the ward:

> This hospital is not good even for pets. No medicines, no bed linens, the smell is very bad. Sewage is out on the floor.[103]

Certain areas of specialized medicine, such as radiology and anaesthetics, had to shut down due to lack of specialists.[104] One psychiatrist estimated the number of psychiatrists in Iraq pre-2003 at 80 and said that only 20 to 25 were left by spring 2007.[105] Another psychiatrist now living in London told me that there were around 150 psychiatrists after the war, but the number dropped to 65 as the majority have managed to get jobs in the Gulf States or Jordan.[106]

The implications of this brain drain for all patients in Iraq were severe. Two Iraqi doctors from Diwaniya and Kufa colleges of medicine wrote in the *British Medical Journal* (*BMJ*) that:

> Medical staff working in emergency departments admit that more than half of those killed could have been saved if trained and experienced staff were available. Our experience has taught us that poor emergency medicine services are more disastrous than the disaster itself.[107]

The Iraqi health system was no longer able to give proper care for victims of violence, particularly those with severe burns or in need of prosthetics surgery. Dr Alwan, a former minister of health in Iraq after 2003, told the *BMJ* that a substantial proportion of critically injured people – almost 70 per cent – die in casualty departments because of shortages of medical staff, supplies and equipment.[108]

There is another serious consequence of the brain drain which is the fact that access to proper health care is being impeded for a large sector of the Iraqi population. Iraqis I interviewed told of how many patients die due to complications from simple procedures or operations because hospitals are overcrowded and understaffed. It is important to point out that statistics of casualties of war and violence rarely take into account these 'accidental' deaths stemming from the crumbling of the system.

Immediately after the fall of Saddam, training in certain medical areas, such as psychiatry, began in earnest. Also, there were hopes of receiving new equipment from the West and adopting new technologies into the health system. US assistance was aimed at providing vaccines and improving maternal and child health, health infrastructure, health policy and management.[109] These hopes, however, were dashed, as the exit of the experienced physicians commenced in 2004, and then came the violence which triggered the brain drain, leaving the health system in a shabby state.

Can Iraq replenish the drain? Obviously not with regard to the years of experience, but can the physicians who have left the country at least be replaced with junior doctors? To start with, it makes sense to compare the number of medical students with the number of physicians who fled the country.

UNESCO's report of 2004 on education in Iraq carried statistics on the number of students in each of the 20 universities then operating in Iraq. From a compilation of the 12 universities that had medical schools at the time, the total number of medical students was 18,018 (out of a total number of 250,000 university students).[110] That means roughly 2,000–3,000 graduated every year, which indicated that Iraq has lost the equivalent of two years to five years (depending on which statistics of doctors one uses) of graduates but hundreds of years of experience.

What is striking is that while the brain drain was going on, Iraq was adding medical schools and universities as though it had an excess capacity of teachers and facilities. Before 2003, there were seven medical schools; by 2004 the number rose to 12, and by the end of 2007 it mushroomed to 20. The proliferation of medical schools in such a short period was driven more by political than educational objectives. Sectarian provincial factors were the driving forces behind their creation; each party and sect wanted the prestige of having a medical school in its territory regardless of whether it had experienced faculty members or not. Some of these schools do not even have a medical library or a proper laboratory,[111] so although they might turn out the necessary quantity of doctors to replenish the brain drain, it is unlikely that the quality of their education will be of an acceptable level.

It was not just medical schools that were being added. In December 2007, the Ministry of Higher Education & Scientific Research announced that it had approved the establishment of seven new universities in several Iraqi provinces. The plan for the new universities called for adding two more to the large existing one in Baghdad, one in Najaf, and others in different provinces of the country.[112]

Given this proliferation of educational establishments, the question that begs itself is: what happened to the level of higher education since 2003? The quality of higher education and research has been steadily deteriorating since the late 1980s. The real drop in the level was in the 1990s as a wave of brain drain took place and the research community suffered from total isolation from the international academic community. No research journals were allowed to arrive in Iraq once the sanctions took effect. Also, there was a total embargo on Iraqis participating in international conferences. At that time, the internet was not prevalent and so research journals and conferences were the main channels for learning and development, particularly with regard to scientific research. Interestingly, Saddam reacted to this by expanding the number of universities in an attempt to prove to the world that the sanctions and wars were not affecting Iraq. Thus it is important to keep in mind that Iraq's higher education has been on a slippery slope since the early 1990s.

In the immediate aftermath of the 2003 invasion, universities were among the first institutions to face looting. By summer 2003, almost no institution had escaped: from the veterinary college in Abu Ghraib that lost all its equipment to the faculty of education in Waziriya, a suburb of Baghdad, which was raided daily for two weeks.[113] Two years after the end of Saddam's regime, a report by the United Nations University stated that 84 per cent of Iraq's higher education institutions had been burnt, looted or destroyed. According to the report, the infrastructure that survived mostly had unreliable water or electricity supplies, was badly equipped and lacked computer facilities. Overall, the teaching staff was under qualified; 33 per cent held only bachelors degrees despite rules requiring a minimum of a masters degree, 30 per cent held masters degrees and only 28 per cent of the teaching staff had PhDs.[114] Students complained that Iraq's university system had significantly declined, dragged down by chronically cancelled lectures and decrepit equipment.[115]

At the same time, the atmosphere of terror and violence began dominating the campuses and the day-to-day lives of all academics. Similar to the doctors, lecturers and university staff were being targeted. No one could explain the motives for these assassinations as there was no pattern to the killings. The assassinations, compounded by the dismissal of academics with Ba'th affiliation, led to disruption in the curriculum and if classes took place, many students opted to stay away out of fear. Among many Iraqi academics, there was a widespread feeling that they were witnessing a deliberate attempt to destroy intellectual life in Iraq. Conspiracy theorists blamed the Americans, the Israelis or the Iranians.[116]

As the violence intensified, a reign of terror ruled in those institutions. According to Dr Jalili, out of the 307 academics murdered by April 2006, 80 per cent belonged to universities, with Baghdad and Al-Mustansiriya universities bearing the brunt, followed by Basra and Mosul. Iraq's Minister of Higher Education confirmed that over 200 professors had been killed by summer 2007.[117] The violence against education and academia reached a new high in November 2006, with the brazen kidnapping of up to 150 employees and visitors at a Ministry of Higher Education building. The daylight attack was carried out by gangs wearing police uniforms. Some of these hostages were killed and others were tortured before being released. The Prime Minister tried to minimize the importance of the kidnapping, saying that 'what is happening is not terrorism, but the result of disagreements and conflict between militias'.[118]

A Council for Assisting Refugee Academics (CARA) report indicated that, by 2008, 1,500 Iraqi academics were living in Syria, Jordan and Egypt since the 2003 exodus began.[119] Scores of Iraq's best minds were exiting the country, running away not just from the violence but from the creeping control of the religious parties, through their militias, over the lives of the universities. In Basra, the militias forced segregation between males and females in classes. One graduate medical student now living in Jordan told me that in the last two years women at Baghdad University are not allowed to do autopsies on male bodies. Militias gather in the courtyard of universities to make sure that men and women do not leave the building together. Lecturers in class are not allowed to express any opinion which could be interpreted as anti-religious (anti-Shi'i to be specific). A professor of literature from Al-Mustansiriya University in Baghdad blamed the Shi'i militias for the threats and harassment that drove him from Iraq because, as he put it:

> This is the rule of the militias, the mob, the rifraf [sic] of people. They
> don't like education, they don't like intellectuals, and now the campuses are
> overruled by the firebrand clerics.[120]

One Iraqi writer said that despite the absence of official censorship, 'new censors from within' have sprung up, restricting to a great extent what a writer would produce. He described the current environment for writers and artists:

> The Iraqi writer is now besieged by many Nos . . . there is now what is
> described by writers as the banned trinity that includes sex, religion and
> politics, and such a prohibition means empty [sic] the writer's mind of
> tools.[121]

The level of education dropped precipitously. First, the academic institutions faced international isolation for more than a decade, and then came the violence post-2003, and during both periods, the country witnessed two waves of brain drain. Finally, after all this, religion is creeping into these institutions, creating a system where women's rights are restricted and secular views are not tolerated. An ex-dean of the Engineering School in one of the universities, who fled in 2007 to Jordan, told me that subjects such as thermo-dynamics, an essential subject, are not being taught anymore for lack of professors. Surveying is not done as part of a civil engineering course for a different reason: it is too risky to send students on fieldwork.[122]

The Iraqi government is helpless to tackle this crisis. It has raised the salaries of university professors to a respectable level (particularly in comparison with the real value of their earnings by the end of the 1990s).[123] While this is an important step, violence has to stop and universities have to regain the ability to decide on the curriculum in an objective and scientific way without pressure from militias. Many of the Iraqi academics living abroad whom I met feel that the Iraqi government does not want them back as anyone with a senior position in the university was seen as having connections to the old regime. They pointed out that the government's decision to grant pension rights to many of those academics carried a message that their days of running education institutions or being active senior academics are over.

As mentioned before, many academics fled to northern Iraq, and Kurdistan is providing a haven for them. Unfortunately, the Kurdish authorities are also pushing to open more and more universities; currently there are five universities and 15 higher education institutes employing a total of 3,000 staff. An American university has been granted permission to operate in Sulaymaniya to attract students and teachers worldwide.[124] Officials from the Ministry of Higher Education & Scientific Research attributed this phenomenon to the explosion in demand for higher education in Kurdistan: in 2008 there were about 33,000 high school graduates but the current capacity at Kurdish universities is around 50 per cent (16,000 new students). Thus private education institutions are mushrooming and universities are expanding without too much emphasis on the level of the curriculum. International conferences are being held in Kurdistan and many representatives from international universities are attending.[125]

Can Iraq's brain drain be reversed, how does it compare with the experiences of other countries and what are the long-term implications for the country?

The brain drain in Iraq, as was discussed, is not a new phenomenon for the country. It also happens all over the world. In Iraq, this wave took place over a short period of time (2006–07) and, unlike in other countries, Iraq is not being compensated for the loss of its human capital by the exiles' remittances. This is a critical point when one looks, for example, at the brain drain in Lebanon, Egypt or India. Remittances are, in many countries, an important source of foreign exchange for the country and income to their families at home.[126] Very few Iraqis are working abroad and earning enough to remit back a portion of their income. On the contrary, there is a reverse remittance whereby, as we saw in the previous chapters, refugees are reliant on their own savings in Iraq or remittances from their families to support them given the lack of employment opportunities in the host countries.

The cost of a brain drain for any country is huge. One study indicated that the loss from the brain drain for Arab countries is estimated at $200 billion[127] and for Iran about $40 billion.[128] The fact that Iraqis who fled their country took with them large amounts of capital (and since then have made very little, if any, new investments in Iraq) further extended the loss. One could justifiably argue that for wealthy countries, such as Iraq or Iran, remittances are not as important as they are for poor countries such as Egypt or Pakistan.[129] That might be true to a certain extent, but the loss of human capital, in the long run, is far more important for a country than the monetary loss. Developed wealthy nations such as Taiwan understood the importance of its human capital loss and made enormous efforts to attract people back, particularly scientists and engineers. In Taiwan's case, the brain drain was subsequently reversed and became a source of technological dynamism.[130] Arab countries, especially those whose economies are reliant on oil exports, have not been able to create the technological stimulus to reverse the brain drain.[131]

With its loss of human capital, Iraq lost its middle class. Two economists who researched the middle class reached the conclusion that the middle class is the driver of democratization and has a crucial role in consolidating democracy. In fact, their research indicated that countries like Costa Rica and Colombia, with comparatively large middle classes, have also had relatively stable democracies in comparison to El Salvador and Guatemala, both of which lack a strong middle class.[132]

The USA, which invaded Iraq to create democracy, did not take enough steps to protect and expand the middle class, thus losing the major contributor and beneficiary of having a democratic state. Whether in the reconstruction of Iraq, creating democratic institutions or changing the economy into a free market one, the American administration forgot an important aspect of human behaviour: one cannot build social capital from above. One US Army major succinctly said that 'we usually are only able to point to schools opened, or clinics refurbished, or businesses started. But is that really building social capital or just moving boxes?'[133] The lack of a core middle class of professionals implies a number of things for Iraq:

1) Given its role in building democratic civil society, the absence of a strong middle class could make Iraq more vulnerable to falling victim to authoritarian rule.
2) Lacking the human capital with the necessary skills to keep Iraq's institutions, bureaucracy and economy running efficiently, Iraq might become even more dependent on the USA and the international community for assistance.
3) Iraq will need to train and teach a new generation to replenish the loss of skilled professionals and academics.

The indications, five years after the end of the war, are that the Iraqi government is attempting to train a new generation as it is doing little to get back those it lost. However, as was seen previously, the level of higher education has dropped dramatically and it will take years to regain the lost skills and experience. On the one hand, foundations such as the Bill and Melinda Gates Foundation are helping to relocate persecuted Iraqi scholars to other countries through a donation of $5 million to the Scholar Rescue Fund. The US Congress has also approved $5 million to rescue Iraqi scholars.[134] On the other hand, the Iraqi government has done very little to attract those scholars back or to provide them with the right incentives to secure their return. It was rumoured that Prime Minister Al-Maliki told the UNHCR commissioner, on his visit to Baghdad in early 2008, that he does not want those professionals and academics back as they are all Ba'thists. Whether this is true or not, one cannot say for sure, but unfortunately the evidence so far suggests that it may be.

Research on the brain drain has indicated that the longer the professionals and skilled labour stay abroad, the lower the probability that they will return home even when political and economic conditions improve.[135] The difference in Iraq's case is that some of the academics and doctors could not find suitable jobs in their host countries (a situation defined by economists as brain waste),[136] particularly in Syria and Jordan. This point, however, will be discussed in detail in Chapter 7.

The best way to sum up this chapter is to quote from the testimony given by Robert Malley, of the International Crisis Group, to the Senate Armed Service Committee in April 2008. Malley talked about three pillars to the strategy to create a local and regional environment that minimizes the damage flowing from the departure of US troops from Iraq which, in his opinion, must occur sooner rather than later. The third pillar is:

> A long-term commitment to invest in and replenish Iraqi human resources. Our obligations and responsibility will not end after our troops have left. Iraq's human resources have been sapped by years of sanctions, warfare and post-war mismanagement. Much of the qualified middle class lives in exile or is stuck in professional stagnation. The educational system is eviscerated. Universities are dysfunctional, children barely learn how to read and girls have been particularly victimised. Blanket de-Baathification [sic] removed experienced managers. Civil war dynamics in urban centres purged them of less sectarian and more open-minded professionals. Oil-rich, Iraq today is also humanly bankrupt. It will take decades to recover and rebuild.
>
> To this end, Iraqis need training of civil servants, scholarships and agreements with foreign universities. Refugees also must be tended to. Many belonged to Iraq's middle class and fled precisely because they were non-sectarian, were unaffiliated with any given militia, and therefore lacked the necessary protection. They should not be abandoned, left to stagnate and languish but rather be prepared for their return. Exile should be used to hone new skills that will facilitate their eventual social reintegration. There is every reason to assist host countries – Syria included – in that endeavour.[137]

Chapter 7

Return and returnees

Nahr: But the place that you are going back to is no longer yours.
Rabah: Nor is this my place. I no longer feel that there is a place for me.
    Why are you associating the idea of place with houses, streets
    and gardens? Nahr, place is something else.[1]

This chapter explores the possibility of return to their homeland for Iraqi
refugees and examines the issues that face the returnees. The first part of the
chapter looks at the 'myth of return' and presents historical comparisons. The
second part looks at the main host countries in the Arab world and the West
and discusses the reasons and potential for return. The third part analyses one
of the major obstacles to return: property rights and restitution.

The myth of return

For refugees, Iraqi or not, the possibility of return to their country is a powerful force that gives them the necessary hope in order to be able to cope with
being in exile. In his work on Pakistani immigrants in Britain, Dahya describes
this factor:

> ...the migrant continues to re-affirm his adherence to the myth of return
> because for him to do otherwise would be tantamount to renouncing his
> membership of the village community.[2]

Refugees, and to a certain extent migrants more generally, cling to this
notion. As we saw previously, many families in Syria and Jordan felt that it was
unnecessary to send their children to school as they would be returning 'soon'
to Iraq:

> The myth is, therefore, a pragmatic solution to the dilemma of being part
> of two contexts, two countries and two sets of norms and values.[3]

Many studies have pointed out that one of the ways refugees address this dilemma of being between two worlds is by turning to religion. Although most Iraqis have historically been secular, many of the refugees are turning to religious associations for daily help (particularly among the Iraqi Shia in Syria) and it is too early to tell whether non-Shi'i Iraqis will also become more religious as the span of their exile prolongs. A study among Iraqi refugees in Michigan who left their country between 1990 and 2003 showed the importance of Islamic faith for these refugees in dealing with their traumas.[4]

Protracted exile creates a dynamic context in which the lives of refugees are continually changed and reshaped socially, economically and politically. As time goes by, refugees balancing between adaptation to their new homes and the concept of return begin to tilt to the former but rarely give up totally on the latter. Zetter indicates in his research that 'the myth of return is in some respects a misconceived shorthand. More accurately, what is mythologized is not return per se, but home.'[5] This is a critical point for many Iraqi refugees who lost their homes, as will be discussed later. Thus home becomes the symbol of return as Zetter described:

> Home is frequently reconstructed in an idealized form and is mythologized
> for many reasons, for example: to reinforce political claims for repatriation
> and the restitution of property; to create symbolic security and permanency
> in conditions of uncertainty and disorder; to retain the bonds of family,
> household or kinship.[6]

The myth or the concept of return, however, is not equally predominant among all refugees. In a study of Iraqi refugees in London, Al-Rasheed found that those who belonged to the mainstream population of Iraq – Iraqi Arabs – continued to think and dream of return even after many years of exile. In contrast, minorities – such as the Assyrians – had severed their contacts with Iraq and focused on their obligations and responsibilities to the host country.[7] In the future, this probably will be true for most of the minorities who fled Iraq after the 2003 war, given the shrinkage of their remaining communities and the increase in religious extremism.

UNHCR and most other international organizations often perceive return migration to be the best durable solution to the global refugee problem. The 1990s were known as the decade of repatriation with more than nine million refugees returned to their homes. This included the repatriation of 3.4 million refugees to Afghanistan and more than a million refugees and displaced persons to Bosnia and Herzegovina.[8] The cessation of hostilities often prompts these large-scale repatriations, but history also indicates that many countries do not possess the capacity to absorb large returnee populations. In many cases, returnees have faced renewed violence leading to further displacement.

Unsuccessful returns include the Burundians returning from Tanzania and Afghans returning from Iran.

International comparisons demonstrate that truly successful returns cannot take place in the absence of genuine reconciliation between the warring parties, political stability and economic growth with opportunities for employment. In the former Yugoslavia, the return of some people to their homes caused the displacement of others as animosity and ethnic division continued in spite of the cessation of hostilities.[9] For Eritrean refugees, recognition and political inclusion were important factors when considering return migration.[10] Thus, if Iraqis were to return in large numbers, not only does violence have to come to a halt but ethnicity and sectarianism have to contract significantly from daily life.

As UNHCR points out, the return would be safer and more successful if it was based on the 'pull' factors of peace and security in the country of origin rather than the 'push' factors in the country of asylum.[11] In fact, most of the Iraqis who returned from their host countries did so due to 'push' factors such as their lack of legal residency status and dire economic situation.

Who will return and why?

In general, a range of factors induces refugees to return to their own country. Host countries may be weary of the economic and political cost of providing refuge and begin to put pressure on the refugees to repatriate. Refugees may wish to return to assert their rights over their homes or to be reunited with their families who were left behind. Finally, donors may reduce their assistance in expectation of the return of refugees.[12] In the case of Iraqi returnees to date, most of whom have come from Syria, all these factors have been applicable.

As the level of violence decreased in late 2007 compared with the previous 18 months, and given that the host countries started imposing restrictions on Iraqis entering their territories, Iraqi families began to return. The Iraqi government promoted the idea of return by providing financial incentives to the returnees and both the US and Iraqi governments used this issue politically, pointing to the number of returns as an indicator of the success of their strategy.[13] The reality was different. Even IRCO stated that the return of externally displaced Iraqis:

> ...was not only due to the relative improvement in the security situation, but it was the result of high cost of living and limited employment opportunities in the host countries, difficulty in accessing essential services like health and education, and the new regulations regarding obtaining residence permits in Syria.[14]

The UNHCR/Ipsos survey of 110 Iraqis in Damascus asked why they or people they knew were returning to Iraq and the respondents' answers were as follows:

- 46 per cent because they could no longer afford to live in Syria;
- 14 per cent had heard that the security situation in Iraq has improved;
- 26 per cent because their visa had expired;
- 5 per cent answered they had a job in Iraq; and
- the balance, 9 per cent, for unspecified personal reasons.[15]

In a UNHCR analysis of the situation of returns to Iraq made in February 2008, two additional reasons were mentioned: the need to return temporarily in order to collect income/pension/rent; and educational needs.[16] This temporary return is a critical point when one attempts to analyse the statistics of returnees: many Iraqis were going back and forth between Syria and Iraq either to work in Iraq for a couple of months and then return to Syria or, as indicated above, to collect income. Needless to say, statistically this increases the number of returnees but in fact they are not real returnees. Towards the end of 2007, it was reported that about 1,000 people were returning to Iraq and 500 were entering Syria on a daily basis.[17] The number of returnees decreased dramatically by 2008 as those who had returned encountered many problems, and the Iraqi government realized it could not accommodate large numbers of returnees and hence stopped its promotion campaigns: 'In reality, the ministry [MoDM] cannot absorb a return on that scale. If the influx is huge, then neither the ministry nor the government can handle it.'[18] In fact, when the Iraqi government started calling for refugees to return home, both UNHCR and the US military in Iraq reacted with horror as they felt that the government was not coping with the existing unemployment and homelessness levels and that the returnees would threaten the fragile security improvements.[19]

According to another Ipsos survey of 994 Iraqis in Syria during March 2008, only 4 per cent were planning to return to Iraq, while 89.5 per cent said that they had no plans to return and the rest (6.5 per cent) did not know.[20] Thus, the vast majority of those who returned did so either due to their economic despondency or their inability to obtain residency visas in Syria, rather than 'pull' factors in Iraq. The Fafo survey in Jordan indicated a much higher percentage of Iraqis planning to go back to Iraq: 40 per cent.[21] However, not more than a couple of thousand of the estimated 475,000 Iraqis living in Jordan returned permanently.

By the end of 2007, a survey conducted by the MoDM together with IOM estimated the total number of returnees at about 35,000, while the IRCO put the number at 46,000.[22] By the end of March 2008, the MoDM and IOM located about 13,000 families of returnees but only 17 per cent had returned from abroad and the other 83 per cent were families who were internally displaced.[23] There are no accurate statistics of the total number of returnees but it is assumed the vast majority came from Syria. According to Dr Said Hakki, the head of the Iraqi Red Crescent, the estimated number stood at about 55,000 to 60,000 returnees, by the first quarter of 2008.[24] UNHCR reported that over 1,000 Iraqis in Egypt closed their files with UNHCR given their intention to return, and that 86 refugees living on the Iraqi-Syrian border returned to Iraq in March 2008.[25]

A couple of interesting remarks can be gleaned from these two surveys: return movements are mostly happening to areas which have become ethnically/religiously homogenous and only a small percentage of families returned to areas under control of another sect; and almost no member of minority groups (Christians, Sabean-Mandeans and Yazidis) has been among the returnees.

Given that the Iraqi government promised to pay ID 1 million ($850) to every returnee family and in light of their dire economic conditions in Syria, the question is not why so many but why so few Iraqis took that step. There are two parts to the answer: first, it is necessary to understand the considerations of refugees before they decide to return to their country; second, it is important to underline the obstacles that these returnees faced or expected to face after they got back to Iraq.

The myth of return, as powerful as it is, is not a 'static state of affairs'. Studies of refugees, for example in Cyprus, indicated that protracted exile 'profoundly reshaped the social and economic world of refugees'.[26] Refugees undergo dramatic changes given their experiences of many years in exile, and policies by humanitarian organizations and governments to encourage returns rarely acknowledge the complexities of these changes. Hence, the longer refugees are in exile, the less chance there is of their return, and were they to return, the more difficult their reintegration would be. As one Lebanese exile who returned to Lebanon after a long period wrote:

> The transformative powers of war and exile had split the people along additional 'demarcation lines', there now was the culture of war and the culture of exile, and they did not recognize each other.[27]

One complexity is that as time goes by, children who are more adaptable and quick to embrace the new society and language abhor the thought of return, while the older generation continues to cling to the notion of return. One senior Iraqi diplomat in Sweden told me that the issue of language is going to be a severe hurdle for return because most Iraqi children there learn to speak, but not to read and write, Arabic. Many of the Kurds (including those highly educated) who returned to Kurdistan from Europe, or moved from central Iraq, did not master reading or writing Kurdish. Another group that might be reluctant to return is women as Iraq is now dominated by religious dogmas that would affect their lives and careers were they to return. (This happened in Algeria where women encouraged their families to leave and others were reluctant to go back due to the stringent religious environment.)

An assessment of the Iraqi community in Greece confirmed both findings; it pointed out the reluctance of children to return to Iraq, and many women, Christians in particular, stated that under no circumstances would they consider returning to Iraq due to the lawlessness that has made sexual violence and violation of women's rights common features of life in Iraq.[28] Apart from a reduction or cessation of violence in their home countries, refugees regard health conditions and access to health care as a critical determinant for return, especially for families with children or elderly parents. Other important considerations are employment opportunities, access to essential services (water, electricity, etc.) and quality of education. Given the conditions in Iraq, those factors are not conducive to encouraging return.

Iraqis whom I interviewed in the Middle East and Europe felt that the chances for return were very slim for those living in the West, while more of those living in the Arab world would return given the lack of economic and career opportunities in countries such as Syria, Egypt and Jordan. As discussed in the previous chapter, those with the highest professional and academic qualifications are less inclined to return and are usually better integrated in their asylum countries. Studies on an Arab brain drain showed that intraregional migration is different from migration to Organization for Economic Cooperation and Development (OECD) countries; the former is usually temporary while the latter is more permanent.[29]

For those who returned or plan to return, many obstacles stand in their way. The first and most critical obstacle is that despite a reduction in the level of violence from its high of late 2006, the country is still torn by frequent incidents and suicide bomb attacks in many cities. Apart from the generalized violence, major battles such as those in Basra and Sadr City in Baghdad in 2008 illustrated the vulnerability of the situation. The best litmus test for the safety or lack of it is the state of the IDPs discussed in the first chapter. By the end of March 2008, the number of total IDPs, according to the IRCO, stood at 2.25 million emanating from all 18 governorates of Iraq, with Baghdad constituting more than 60 per cent of the total. In fact, given the events in Basra and Mosul during the first three months of 2008, there was an increase in the number of IDPs after the slowdown in late 2007.[30] However, as was noted in Chapter 1, UN agencies estimated IDPs to be 2.78 million by March 2008. Many refugees and IDPs, who returned after the toppling of Saddam's regime, suffered repeated internal displacement due to limited local absorption capacities and renewed sectarian conflict.

After visiting Iraq in February 2008, the UN High Commissioner for Refugees, Antonio Guterres, announced that:

We have clear criteria for the promotion of returns – those criteria are not met by the situation in Iraq now. So we are not promoting returns to Iraq in the present circumstances because we do not believe the conditions are there for that to be possible on a meaningful scale.[31]

In an extensive report on the refugees' crisis, Amnesty International reached a similar conclusion:

At present [June 2008], Amnesty International believes that the time is not right for returns of any kind to Iraq, whether they are explicitly forcible or effectively forcible but disguised as 'voluntary'.[32]

Given the vulnerable security situation, 11 of Iraq's 18 governorates have closed their borders to IDPs, and one reliable source estimated that 20 per cent of the 55,000 refugees who returned became internally displaced as they had no home to return to. Thus, it is clear that Iraqis returned either due to their deteriorating economic conditions or because they could not stay, for visa reasons, in their host countries.

As we saw in the previous chapters, internal and external displacement is taking place not only in a context of violence and insecurity but also in one of unemployment and lack of essential services. Many returnees could not find jobs upon their return and the country is still suffering from shortages of electricity.[33] One Iraqi living in Egypt told me:

Every time I talk to my two children about returning to Iraq, they seem horrified and reply that in Cairo, there is electricity and running water and no bombs. They are very scared even of the thought of going back to Baghdad.[34]

Almost 40 per cent of the Iraqi population are living in 'absolute poverty' and standards of living are lower than before the war.[35] Bureaucracy and sectarianism embedded in different Iraqi ministries constitute another obstacle to return. Many returnees complained of long hours waiting to complete the process of registering and receiving the government's payment of $850 per family. Refugees International said that sectarian differences have further complicated the process of return and that 'the Shia received more support from the Shi'i-run government than did the Sunnis'.[36] A similar report in *USA Today* quoted the MoDM's spokesman criticizing his fellow Shia for discriminating against Sunni refugees after he witnessed a clerk at the MoDM tearing the file of a woman who was applying for compensation because she was a Sunni.[37]

In addition to those obstacles, there was a fundamental problem: the Iraqi government has not yet developed a plan to absorb the influx and prevent it from adding to the woes of the population and leading to a new wave of internal displacement and sectarian violence. Prime Minister Al-Maliki announced that his government hopes that 'our children, especially the experts, who are obliged to emigrate, would return' and promised to give them certain 'privileges'.[38] Again, no details of any plans or the nature of those 'privileges' were announced.

At a meeting between the Iraqi Parliamentarian Committee of Displacement and Migration and the IRCO, the head of the Committee, Abd Al-Khaliq Zankana, informed the IRCO that his committee would have liked to add to the budget for expanding the health facilities but that the government had the final decision.[39] At the same time, it was reported that the government would earmark $195 million to 'repatriate Iraqi refugees from abroad', but again no details were given.[40] The MoDM is overloaded with property dispute cases from Saddam's era and as one official at the Ministry put it:

> We urgently need a plan; the government needs to be involved. We are still working on the old problems [pre-2003] . . . we don't have the mechanism to solve the new ones.[41]

Finally, the housing crisis emanating from millions being displaced, internally and externally, and forced to abandon their homes, is a stumbling block to any serious effort for 'the return', and is the core in every major displacement. In Egypt, for example, Iraqi refugees told an Iraqi newspaper that although their savings are dwindling and there are no employment opportunities, they are not willing to accept Al-Maliki's offer to fly them back to Baghdad at the expense of the Iraqi government as their homes are still occupied by militia groups.[42] This leads us to the next section about property disputes and their resolution.

Restitution of land and property rights

What distinguishes all refugees is 'the loss of continuity with the past – the home as the physical and symbolic representation of what has been irreplaceably lost in exile'.[43] The magnetism of the concept of return is mainly based on returning to one's home.

In Iraq, destruction and occupation of property has become an instrument of warfare in the ethnic cleansing that took place after the 2003 war: 'There are few things more devastating to the human spirit than being forced to flee from home.'[44] Saddam used this weapon effectively in displacing or forcibly relocating his enemies whether they were Kurds, Shia or political enemies, and hundreds of thousands lost their homes. By March 2003, it was estimated that there were about 800,000 Kurds in northern Iraq and roughly 100,000 Shia in central and southern Iraq who were displaced without homes.[45]

Fearing an uncontrolled large scale return of IDPs, the CPA established, in January 2004, the Iraq Property Compensation Commission (IPCC) to review and resolve property disputes related to the Ba'th period. There were many shortcomings in the set up of the IPCC.[46] One omission was that the Commission did not refer to compensation terms, except to assert the original purchase price, rather than current value, as a basic criterion for assessing a lost property.[47] Needless to say, with the inflation Iraq experienced in the 1990s, many people lost a high percentage of the real value of their homes.

When the CPA was disbanded, the IPCC was replaced in early 2006 with the Commission for the Resolution of Real Property Disputes (CRRPD), which essentially had the same mandate as the IPCC. However, a number of important changes were introduced such as the valuation of compensation and the composition of the Judicial Committee reviewing the claims.[48] Apart from technical assistance from the IOM, both commissions were and are staffed exclusively by Iraqis. As van der Auweraert points out, neither the IPCC nor the CRRPD was 'the outcome of an inclusive political debate or reflection on how Iraqi society could best come to terms with a legacy of brutal and violent oppression'.[49] As noted before, whether in economic, social or legal matters, imposing new systems on a local population without addressing issues relating to the history and culture of the country does not produce the right solutions or results. Van der Auweraert underlines a number of problems with regard to the CRRPD: the first issue is that an isolated approach is likely to lead to an unequal treatment of victims; the second issue is that property restitution will not succeed if the state pursues incompatible policies. He stresses that politicized or corrupt state institutions (as they are in Iraq) pose a serious obstacle in tackling the core problem.[50] For instance, with weak governance, it is hard to see how the current practice, whereby the Ministry of Finance appeals all CRRPD decisions in which the state stands to lose, would lead to a fair settlement for all sides. It also seems highly unlikely that the bureaucratic system within which the CRRPD functions would be successful in dealing with a large number of claims. By the end of May 2007, the CRRPD had received 132,038 claims, of which only 34,649 had been decided. The CRRPD had offices in every governorate in Iraq with a staff of more than 1,400 to process the claims.[51]

The challenge for any government to tackle the property problem is immense when it is dealing with almost five million displaced people – internally and externally. About 25 per cent of IDPs cited losing their property as a main reason for their displacement.[52] The report on returnee monitoring (of both IDPs and refugees) indicated that about 46 per cent had their homes completely or partially destroyed or occupied by others. Only 36 per cent still had their movable property while the rest had lost it for different reasons.[53] These percentages reflect huge numbers when one is talking about a large displaced population still waiting or hoping to return.

Property restitution is the basis of restoration of law and order, reconciliation among the different ethnic communities and the return of a measure of normality. Studies outside Iraq have shown, however, that 'repossession or reconstruction of property does not equal return' as returnees often sold or exchanged their homes and moved to settle somewhere else.[54] In Iraq, this is not yet an issue as only a very small percentage succeeded in regaining their property. In essence, repatriation is just the first step in a long process of reintegration and restoration of a normal and economically productive life.

What can Iraq learn from the lessons of other countries who underwent similar episodes of displacement and resettlement? One lesson from Bosnia and Herzegovina is that 'any property rights restitution should be a nationally created, owned and directed process'.[55] In Kosovo, when 800,000 Albanian refugees returned to their homes en masse, the result was an ad hoc occupation of properties and conflict over land and housing along ethnic lines.[56] The question that needs to be addressed in Iraq, similar to these international cases, is whether the Iraqi police and armed forces would have the will or ability to carry out contentious evictions. The American military had been 'very vocal' with the Iraqi authorities on the need to 'establish a system to adjudicate claims about property rights' so as to avoid using Iraqi troops to carry out 'forced evictions'.[57] The policy of the Coalition forces in Iraq is to avoid taking part in resettlement activity, and American forces tend to focus on abandoned houses but leave the Iraqi Army to decide on who should move in. With the prolongation of the crisis, secondary displacement has been growing, and this will further exacerbate the complexities of the problem in the future. One clear lesson comes through many of these international return experiences: certain conditions would have to prevail in the country before return in a significant number can take place. These conditions include a minimal degree of security, ethnic reconciliation and significant commitments by all parties concerned to solve the problem.[58] In mid-2008, Iraq is still very far from meeting any of those conditions.

The Americans and the Iraqis believe that the issue of returnees (if they were to return in large numbers) could be resolved through new housing construction as opposed to eviction and resettlement. The Iraqi newspapers are full of new projects and designs of housing complexes for returnees. The government believes that the construction of new neighbourhoods in Baghdad would dramatically lower the ethnic tension and reduce the potential conflict between returnees and the new occupants of their properties.[59] Iraq is a large country with significant oil wealth, and so in theory it has the means to go ahead with these building projects. But again, this would require tremendous political will, state bureaucracy that functions effectively and most importantly real understanding between the Sunnis and Shia on resolving the crisis. Hence it is doubtful that the government, which does not have a plan to deal with this thorny issue, would undertake such a grand mission.

No one can predict whether many Iraqis will, one day, return home and whether the right conditions for their return will prevail. If and when they return in large numbers, the issue of property rights will be critical to finding a solution to internal and external displacement. As the Economic and Social Council Commission on Human Rights put it:

> The right to housing, land and property restitution is essential to the resolution of the conflict and to post-conflict peace-building, safe and sustainable return and the establishment of the rule of law, and . . . careful monitoring of restitution programmes, on the part of international organizations and affected States, is indispensable to ensuring their effective implementation.[60]

Conclusion

Nearly one in five of all Iraqis has been displaced – internally or externally – since 2003. More than two million had to flee their country. While the Iraqi refugee crisis was unfolding, the world watched with apathy and indolence as it has done throughout most of the world's human-made tragedies. Since the 2003 invasion, the outflow of refugees from Iraq 'is far greater than that resulting from the Indochina War, but it has evoked a dramatically less vigorous response'.[1] Consequently, these refugees have become the responsibility of a few countries, mainly Syria and Jordan, who have had to shoulder the burden of hosting them.

Neither the USA nor the UK wanted to admit there was a refugee crisis because doing so would have meant admitting the failure of their venture in Iraq, and neither has accepted many refugees into their countries. In the UK, to the extent that there has been wide public discussion, it has centred on how many interpreters the government should allow to settle in Britain. Meanwhile in the USA, it seems 'there is a deafening silence from the White House' on the issue of the Iraqi refugees.[2] US policy makers and public opinion are mostly focused on the timing of the withdrawal of US troops from Iraq and rarely about this human tragedy. Morton Abramowitz, a former US ambassador, criticized the USA for its lack of action, saying that 'American actions have unintentionally created three huge refugee crises: the Indochinese in Southeast Asia, the Kurds of northern Iraq and now a third: the Iraqis displaced by today's war'.[3] In the first instance, the USA took action to resettle the refugees (1.2 million Indochinese), and in the second instance the USA sought to help the Kurds by creating the no-fly zone. However, in the third case, 'The US has failed to make Iraq's refugee exodus a focus of national or international attention'.[4]

The USA has donated money to UNHCR but has not placed this issue as a top priority on its agenda. Congress and media are emphasizing the subject more and more (mainly since the beginning of 2007), but the US government is still reluctant to put serious pressure on Al-Maliki and his government to tackle the issue. In addition, the USA is unwilling to help Syria directly in undertaking this responsibility due to the strained political relations between the two countries.[5]

Iraq has not fully acknowledged that there is a crisis, and thus it is doubtful that serious efforts will be made to resolve the issues related to the displaced. Iraq can start by donating more to those in exile directly or indirectly by helping the host countries, particularly Syria and Jordan. Iraq is today a rich country and it is shocking that a country with such reserves has given only $25 million to help its own citizens. This comes at a time when Iraq cannot spend its capital budget and its coffers are flush with reserves estimated at $60 billion. Commenting on the policies of the USA and Iraq, the Chairman of the US House Subcommittee on the Middle East and South Asia stated:

> ...the two governments who should be most concerned . . . are the ones who seem the least interested in helping.
>
> I cannot understand why the Government of Iraq can't, or won't do more to assist its own citizens. The cynical view is that Prime Minister Al-Maliki doesn't want the refugees back because they're mostly ethnic groups he doesn't care about. Some would cite sheer incompetence: that the Government of Iraq simply doesn't know how to take care of its own people.[6]

It is not only American Congressmen who feel that the Iraqi government is not paying sufficient attention; the head of the Displacement and Migration Committee in the Iraqi parliament threatened to resign 'because there are no appropriate measures to solve this problem'.[7] He warned that 'it would take as long as a decade for Iraq to deal with its refugee and displacement problem'.[8] In his address to the Committee he said:

> The government's obvious inability to solve the problem of IDPs and refugees could lead to serious regional and international problems, as there is no clear and comprehensive policy to get them back into their homes. These problems will hit Iraqi security and society.[9]

Iraqi legislators have also urged the government to set aside 5 per cent of the country's oil revenues to provide humanitarian assistance to the refugees, but again to no avail.[10] It should be noted that although violent incidents have dropped, only 1 per cent of displaced people – internal and external – have returned to their homes.

The US occupation of Iraq sought to topple Saddam and create democracy. While it succeeded in the former, its invasion led to the fleeing of the secular, educated middle class who tend to form the backbone of democratic regimes. The USA wanted to set up a free-market economy but ended up having hundreds of business people and entrepreneurs leaving the country with their capital and knowledge. The Americans wanted a pluralistic and multi-ethnic society but the result was that the minorities, who had lived and prospered in Iraq for centuries, found themselves a prime target of the religious groups and their militias, and hence a high percentage of them were forced to leave the country. The Americans aspired to make Iraq an example of modernization for the rest of the Arab world, but what took place set Iraq back a long way. Some have argued that the 'American occupation has been more disastrous than the Mongols' sack of Baghdad in the thirteenth century'.[11] On many levels, Iraq has regressed dramatically: education, health, the state of women and children. The government is dysfunctional, crippled by the lack of bureau-cratic competence, and corrosive corruption has become an integral part of the government mechanism.

The American failure was due not only to lack of planning and mismanage-ment after the occupation, but also to other fundamental factors: the USA wanted to impose values and systems on a country without understanding the complexities and peculiarities of Iraq. There was never a real grasp of Iraqi culture.[12] Iraqis talk about the humiliation they feel at checkpoints and at air-ports as the Americans and their allies lack understanding of Iraqi values such as pride and honour. Iraqis not only feel humiliated in their own country, but even more that they need the help of other Arab countries to give them a safe haven.[13] One wonders whether America's venture in Iraq will have the same long-term implications for the USA as Britain's failed venture in the 1956 Suez Crisis had for the UK.

The cost of the war and the occupation has been colossal both in human and capital terms. There are, as noted before, no official statistics of the number of Iraqis killed during the five-year period since the invasion, but estimates put it at between 500,000 and 750,000. The USA has lost more than 4,000 soldiers and tens of thousands were injured. Iraq's 'lost generation' has suffered displacement, humiliation and a deterioration of almost every aspect of its daily life in the five years following the invasion. This generation is severely traumatized by the violence it witnessed and no one knows what the repercussions of the trauma will augur for the future. Then there is the human cost for the dispossessed who lost their homes, and for the two million in exile who became rootless.

The cost to America and its people was also huge: apart from the human cost, two American economists estimated the 'true' cost of the conflict to be three trillion dollars. This estimate sounds somewhat exaggerated, given that it is very difficult to define the 'true' cost.[14] However, even one trillion dollars is a massive sum for the USA.

The tragedy of the dispossession of more than 4.7 million people spans across Iraqi society and no one was spared:

> The dispossessed are sometimes disoriented, often dependent, and ever conscience of their foreignness. For those who are refugees, that persistent

awareness of difference is something that colors thoughts, feelings, and
interactions with others throughout the life course.[15]

Having lost their homes and livelihoods, they became hapless pawns in the
conflicts between the USA and the insurgents on the one hand, and the many
militias representing religious or gang groups on the other hand. Aid workers
in Iraq expressed a sense of awe that life is so wretched, yet people are willing
to live. Women and children were amongst the biggest losers but many young
men paid with their lives, being the most vulnerable group in the sectarian
conflict and the military operations of the USA and its allies. Health and
education, which began deteriorating after the first Gulf War of 1991, were
severely degraded following the invasion in 2003. Minorities who lived for
centuries in Iraq suffered a major blow and many had to flee the country. The
economy was negatively affected not only by the violence but due to mismanagement, corruption, unemployment and inflation. The brain drain exacerbated the situation as Iraq's best minds left the country to find a safe haven
elsewhere.

Iraq's economy was already in a dire state in 2003. Five years after the war,
the level of oil production is unchanged (revenues are five times the pre-war
level but that is only due to the dramatic increase in oil prices), and the electricity supply is not back to the pre-2003 levels, although it improved towards
the end of 2007 after severe shortages in the period between 2004 and mid-
2007. Unemployment is still extremely high, particularly among the young.
Inflation rose to high levels in 2005–06 but has since come down to more man-
ageable rates. No major industries sprung up and an analysis of Iraq's economy
would indicate that oil price hikes, from $25 to $30 per barrel in 2003 to $130
per barrel in 2008, actually masked the government's incompetent management and the corrosive corruption. One could argue that the country would
have probably imploded if oil prices had not gone to $100 and above, and had
the US presence not supported the Iraqi government in spite of all its shortcomings. The rentierism nature of the economy has not changed in the last five
years, while the USA plunged tens of billions into reconstruction with little to
show for such huge investments.

Long-term, the brain drain issue must be addressed since Iraq's oil wealth
and the USA's investments will not be able to compensate for the human capital loss. Apart from paying lip service, the government has to launch the right
projects to attract back Iraqi talent from abroad. This will happen only if
violence ebbs and professionals living in exile feel they could return to work
in a safe environment and without undue pressure from militia groups and
religious fanaticism. Overseas governments and international organizations
must be involved as 'Iraqis need training of civil servants, scholarships and
agreements with foreign universities'.[16]

UNHCR and other NGOs have done a good job in helping the refugees, considering the numerous constraints they faced, but they need more funding from the West, Iraq and the Gulf States to expand their aid programmes. At a time when the war is costing billions and the Iraqi government is sitting on huge cash reserves, it is nothing short of outrageous that UNHCR is facing a shortage in funding for its assistance programmes, such as distribution of food packages to impoverished Iraqi refugees in Syria and Jordan. In fact, there is a fear that UNHCR will have to downsize its operation, which will lead to widespread malnutrition: 'There is a donor fatigue in the international community for anything connected with Iraq.'[17] A number of donor countries were withholding money because the Iraqi government had 'failed to adequately compensate Syria, Lebanon, and Jordan for sheltering refugees'.[18] UN organizations should also receive better access to the refugees in the Arab world with less intervention by the governments of the host countries.

The impact of the displacement of Iraqis on the region will be felt for years to come. By mid-2008, the fact that relatively few Iraqis have returned home raises many questions over their future status in the host countries. As we have seen, the Iraqis who have left following the 2003 war have not been integrated, unlike previous waves of migration to Jordan and Syria. It may be that the politicization of this crisis has prevented their integration or that the governments of those countries are more fearful of a Palestinization of this crisis than they were in the 1980s or 1990s because of the sheer numbers arriving after 2003. It is also possible that the increase in Sunni–Shi'i polarization in the Arab world during the first decade of 2000 has played a significant role in the lack of integration of the Iraqi refugees into their new countries of refuge. As discussed, security is paramount for all the governments in the Arab world, and the issue of sectarianism has become higher on the agenda given that the displacement of Iraqis was both the consequence and the cause of the sectarian schism. Many observers have pointed out that if the refugees continue not to receive support from host governments and the international community, 'there is a very real danger that political actors will seek to fill the gap'.[19] It should be remembered that the militias in Iraq began providing humanitarian assistance to many of the internally displaced when the Iraqi government failed to do so.

Two important factors that are interrelated to security and the geo-political situation of the region are poverty and deterioration of education. Lacking employment opportunities and denied legal residency status, the standard of living of Iraqis, particularly in Syria and Jordan, has been dropping dramatically. Poverty and malnutrition have pushed many families to engage in dubious activities and prostitution among Iraqi women increased significantly. At the same time, as discussed previously, many children are dropping out of school and the new generation of Iraqi refugees is probably less educated than any Iraqi generation since the 1950s. Needless to say, the ramifications of having a generation of poor and uneducated youth will indeed be severe for the whole region.

The political consequences for the two main host countries are also serious. If the economic conditions were to deteriorate further as a result of a world economic recession or continuation of spiralling commodity prices, the governments of Syria and Jordan would face heavy internal pressure from a population with already low GDP per capita (see Appendix) to remedy the situation by taking the necessary measures against the Iraqi refugees. That would not necessarily mean deporting them en masse, but it could signify imposing drastic restrictive measures on the refugees which in turn would force them to return home even if the right conditions for return do not exist.

What will happen to Iraq and its refugees? Some say that what happened in Lebanon in 1975–76 could offer insights into what is likely to happen in Iraq.[20] Others predict that Iraq will be like Mogadishu, with warlords controlling different areas rich with resources.[21] There is a chance that Iraq could put its house in order if its government and politicians act to reduce sectarianism and promote a culture of tolerance (and the emphasis here is on action not just statements[22]), tackle corruption and begin to plan to help the IDPs and refugees. Without solving this crisis, the future of Iraq is bleak.

At the time of writing this book (mid-2008), there has been tentative progress in certain areas. Iraq, still lacerated by the invasion and its aftermath, is beginning to show a glimmer of light after the darkness of the first five years of occupation. Attacks have plummeted and there is a degree of hope that did not exist in early to mid-2007. There is also the possibility of the USA withdrawing most of its troops by late 2010 or early 2011.[23] Time will tell if Iraq will be able to overcome its major problems and reopen its doors to the millions of its displaced people.

Appendix

Iraq and the host countries – a comparative table

Country	Exchange rate ($1 equivalent)	Population	Number of Iraqi refugees	Iraqi refugees (as a percentage of the total population)	GDP per capita ($)	Rate of inflation
Iraq	1196 Iraqi Dinar	27,100,000	5,030,000*	18.560%	1,723	15.00%
Jordan	0.714 Jordanian Dinar	5,500,000	475,000	8.636%	2,533	6.50%
Syria	51 Syrian Pounds	18,900,000	1,300,000	6.878%	1,464	10.00%
Egypt	5.34 Egyptian Pounds	75,000,000	90,000	0.120%	1,500	11.00%
Lebanon	1508 Lebanese Pounds	4,250,000	50,000	1.176%	4,800	2.00%
Iran	9240 Iranian Rial	69,400,000	57,000	0.082%	3,659	17.10%
Sweden	5.98 Swedish Krona	9,000,000	40,000	0.444%	49,643	2.20%
United States	$1	301,000,000	6,000	0.002%	45,963	2.90%

* Internally and Externally Displaced Iraqis.

Sources: Based on averages of the data in table 1; information provided throughout the different chapters; UNHCR reports; IMF reports; UNDP reports; World Bank Development Indicators; the Economist; and Bloomberg.

Notes

Introduction

1 Human Rights Watch (HRW), *Iraqi Refugees, Asylum Seekers and Displaced Persons: Current Conditions and Concerns in the Event of War*, February 2003.
2 United Nations, *Likely Humanitarian Scenarios*, 10 December 2003, in archives of Campaign Against Sanctions on Iraq (CASI). www.casi.org.info.
3 Chandrasekaran, Rajiv, 'This Time Around War Would Hit Iraq Harder', *The Washington Post*, 29 October 2002.
4 World Health Organization (WHO), *Social Determinants of Health in Countries in Conflict: The Eastern Mediterranean Perspective*, Cairo, June 2007, p. 16. www.emro.who.int; International Rescue Committee (IRC), *Five Years Later, A Hidden Crisis: Report of the IRC Commission on Iraqi Refugees*, March 2008, Appendix 1, p. 18.
5 Owen, Roger, 'Reconstructing the performance of the Iraqi economy 1950–2006: an essay with some hypotheses and many questions', *International Journal of Contemporary Iraqi Studies* 1/1 (2007), pp. 93–101.
6 Davis, Eric, *Memories of State: Politics, History, and Collective Identity in Modern Iraq* (Berkeley, University of California Press, 2005).
7 Batatu, Hanna, *The Old Social Classes and the Revolutionary Movement of Iraq*, New Jersey, Princeton University Press, 1978, p. 45.
8 See, for example, Abbud, Salam, *Thaqaft Al-'Unf fi Al-Iraq* (The Culture of Violence in Iraq), Köln, Germany, Al-Kamel Verlay, 2002; Sharara, Hayat, *Itha Al-Ayyam Agsagat* (When Darkness Fell), Beirut, Arabic Institute for Studies and Publications, 2000.
9 Mazloom, Mohamed, 'Nightmare of the Returning Gilgamesh', in Wollenberg A. and Glenewinkel K. (eds) *Shahadat: Witnessing Iraq's Transformation After 2003*, Berlin, Friedrich Ebert Foundation, 2007, p. 84.
10 Zolberg, Aristide R., Suhrke, Astri and Aguayo, Sergio, *Escape From Violence: Conflict and the Refugee Crisis in the Developing World*, New York, Oxford University Press, 1992, p. 33.
11 Moore, Will H. and Shellman, Stephen M., 'Fear of Persecution: Forced Migration, 1952–1995', *Journal of Conflict Resolutions*, 48/5 (2004), p. 723.
12 WHO, *Social Determinants of Health in Countries in Conflict*, p. 13.
13 Zolberg, et al., *Escape From Violence*, p. 33.
14 Said, Edward, *Reflections on Exile and Other Essays*, Cambridge, Mass., Harvard University Press, 2000, p. 181.

15 Article 1A(2) of the 1951 Convention Relating to the Status of Refugees.
16 Ibid.
17 Marfleet, Philip, 'Iraq's refugees: "exit" from the state', *International Journal of Contemporary Iraqi Studies*, 1/3 (2007), p. 408.
18 Stansfield, Gareth, *Accepting Realities in Iraq*, Chatham House, MEP BP 07/02, 2007.
19 Permanent Mission of Sweden, 'Statement by H.E. Mr. Tobias Billström, Minister for Migration and Asylum Policy at the International Conference hosted by UNHCR', Geneva, 17–18 April 2007.
20 Kushner, Tony and Knox, Katherine, *Refugees in an age of genocide: Global, National and Local Perspectives during the Twentieth Century*, London, Frank Cass, 1999, p. 406.
21 Ferris, Elizabeth, *Iraqi Refugees: Our Problem or Sweden's?*, The Brookings Institution, 18 June 2007.
22 Ferris, Elizabeth, *Security, Displacement and Iraq: A Deadly Combination*, The Brookings-Bern Project on Internal Displacement, 2007, p. 10.

Chapter 1: Internal displacement

1 Sophocles, *Oedipus the King* (translated by Ian Johnston), Virginia, Richer Resources Publication, 2007 lines 98–102.
2 Internal Displacement Monitoring Centre (IDMC), *Iraq: Population Figures and Profiles*, September 2007, see www.internal-displacement.org; IOM mentions 105,619 families or 630,000 individuals while Fawcett, John and Tanner, Victor estimate 805,000 individuals, in their study: *The Internally Displaced People of Iraq*, The Brookings Institution, 2002, p. 16.
3 IDMC, *Iraq: Population Figures*; Fawcett and Tanner, *Internally Displaced*, p. 16. *Anfal* (The spoils) is the name of a *sura* in the Koran, a name given to the military operations against the Kurds towards the end of the war with Iran in 1988.
4 IDMC, *Iraq: Population Figures*; Fawcett and Tanner, *Internally Displaced*, p. 33.
5 UNHCR, *Report on the Situation of Human Rights in Iraq*, submitted by the Special Rapporteur, Mr Max van der Stoel, 10 March 1998, p. 7. E/CN.4/1998/67.
6 Fawcett and Tanner, *Internally Displaced*, p. 42.
7 Tavernise, Sabrina, 'Sectarian Hatred Pulls Apart Iraq's Mixed Towns', *The New York Times*, 20 November 2005.
8 Ibid.
9 The Brookings Institution which launched an Iraq Index to track events and progress in Iraq began to include statistics about displaced persons only after the Samarra bombing. In its report of 30 May 2006, it indicated 3,000 families were displaced (21,000–30,000 individuals) before the Mosque bombing. See The Brookings Institution, *Iraq index*, 30 May 2006, p. 26. www.brookings/edu/iraqindex.
10 UNHCR, *Iraq Operation 2006 Supplementary Appeal*, April 2006, p. 4. www.unhcr.org.

11 SIGIR, *Quarterly Report to the United States Congress*, 30 April 2007, p. 51. www.sigir.mil.

12 UNAMI, *Iraq Situation Report*, 15–28 November 2004, p. 8. www.uniraq.org/ documents.

13 UNHCR, *Iraq Operation 2006*, p. 10.

14 Ibid.

15 UNAMI, *Iraq Situation Report*, p. 1.

16 IDMC, *Iraq: Sectarian violence, military operations spark new displacement, as humanitarian access deteriorates*, 23 May 2006, pp. 48–49.

17 *IRIN*, 'Iraq: Attacks on churches spur Christians to move to Kurdish north', 22 November 2004. www.irinnews.org.

18 International Crisis Group, *The Next Iraq War? Sectarianism and Civil Conflict*, Middle East Report no. 52, 27 February 2006, p. 5. www.crisisgroup.org.

19 IRCO, *The Internally Displaced People in Iraq*, Update 27, 4 November 2007, p. 6. www.iraqiredcrescent.org.

20 IDMC, *Iraq: a displacement crisis*, 30 March 2007, p. 9.

21 Ferris, Elizabeth and Hall, Matthew, *Update on Humanitarian Issues and Politics in Iraq*, The Brookings-Bern Project on Internal Displacement, 6 July 2007. www.brookings.edu/projects/idp.aspx.

22 Ferris, *Security, Displacement and Iraq*, p. 6.

23 Cordesman, Anthony H., *Iraq's Sectarian and Ethnic Violence and Its Evolving Insurgency: Development through Spring 2007*, Center for Strategic and International Studies (CSIS), 2 April 2007. www.cisi.org.

24 al-Khalidi, Ashraf and Tanner, Victor, *Sectarian Violence: Radical Groups Drive Internal Displacement in Iraq*, The Brookings–Bern Project on Internal Displacement, October 2006.

25 Maples, Lt. Gen. Michael, Defense Intelligence Agency, 'Testimony for the Senate Armed Service Committee', 27 February 2007. www.house.gov.

26 See, for example, IDMC, *Iraq: Population Figures*; IOM, 1 September 2007 Report. www.iom-iraq.net.

27 IDP Working Group, *Internally Displaced Persons in Iraq*, 24 March 2008.

28 Interview on file with an Iraqi lawyer, Arbil, 22 September 2008. See also: Refugees International, *The World's Fastest Growing Displacement Crisis*, March 2007. www.refugees.international.org. See also: Wong, Edward, 'Thousands of Iraqis Flee to Kurdish Region to Escape War Face Harsh Living Conditions', *The New York Times*, 21 March 2007.

29 Glanz, James and Rubin, Alissa J., 'Future Look of Iraq Complicated by Internal Migration', *The New York Times*, 19 September 2007.

30 IOM, *Iraq Displacement 2007 Mid-Year Review*, 2007, pp. 2–3.

31 *Azzaman*, 8 January 2008. The paper was quoting Said Hakki, head of the Iraqi Red Crescent.

32 Yousef, Nancy A. and Fadel, Leila, 'What Crocker and Petraeus didn't say', *McClatchy Newspapers*, 11 September 2007.

33 Harper, Andrew, 'Iraq: growing needs amid continuing displacement', *Forced Migration Review*, Issue 29 (December 2007), pp. 51–53.

34 *IRIN*, 'Iraq: Government to give financial aid to displaced in north', 31 December 2007.

35 Farrell, Stephen and Moore, Solomon, 'Iraq Attacks Fall 60 per cent, Petraeus Says', *The New York Times*, 30 December 2007.
36 Rubin, Alissa J., 'A Calmer Iraq: Fragile, and Possibly Fleeting', *The New York Times*, 5 December 2007.
37 IOM, *Iraq Displacement 2007 Mid-Year*, p. 2.
38 See, for example, Dodge, Toby, 'State Collapse and the Rise of Identity Politics', in Bouillon, Markus E., Malone, David M. and Rowswell, Ben (eds), *Iraq: Preventing A New Generation of Conflict*, Colorado, Reinner, 2007, pp. 23–39.
39 For a historical background during the Ba'th era, see Baram, Amatzia, 'Neo-Tribalism in Iraq: Saddam Hussein's Tribal Policies 1991–96', *International Journal of Middle East Studies*, 29/1 (February 1997), pp. 1–31.
40 Herring, Eric and Rangwala, Glen, *Iraq in Fragments: The Occupation and Its Legacy*, London, Hurst & Company, 2006, p. 148.
41 Marfleet, 'Iraq's refugees', p. 410.
42 One of the exceptions has been the Grand Ayatollah Ali Al-Sistani who has urged all sides to stop the bloodshed and called on Shia to protect their Sunni brothers. See *Azzaman*, 27 November 2007; *Al-Hayat*, 7 January 2008.
43 al-Khalidi and Tanner, *Sectarian Violence*, October 2006, p. 12.
44 Iraqi Family Health Study Group (IFHS), 'Violence-Related Mortality in Iraq from 2002 to 2006', *The New England Journal of Medicine*, 31 January 2008, p. 487. www.nejm.org.
45 Anderson, John Lee, 'Inside the Surge', Letter from Iraq, *The New Yorker*, 19 November 2007, p. 68.
46 Ibid., p. 65.
47 See Tavernise, Sabrina, 'Sectarian Hatred Pulls Apart Iraq's Mixed Towns', *The New York Times*, 20 November 2005; Raghavan, Sudarsan, 'Distrust Breaks the Bonds of a Baghdad Neighbourhood', *The Washington Post*, 27 September 2006.
48 Rubin, Alissa J., 'Sunni Baghdad Becomes Land of Silent Ruins', *The New York Times*, 26 March 2007.
49 See report of the Geneva Centre for the Democratic Control of Armed Forces (DCAF), *Sexual Violence in Armed Conflict: Global Overview and Implications for the Security Sector*, Geneva, 2007; *The Economist*, 8 December 2007.
50 Al-Ali, Nadje Sadig, *Iraqi Women: Untold Stories from 1948 to the Present*, London, Zed Books, 2007, p. 267. For a detailed analysis of the impact of sanctions on women, see Al-Jawaheri, Yasmin Husein, *Women in Iraq: The Gender Impact of International Sanctions*, London, I.B.Tauris, 2008.
51 Marfleet, Philip, *Refugees in a Global Era*, New York, Palgrave Macmillan, 2006, p. 198.
52 MADRE, *Promising Democracy, Imposing Theocracy: Gender-Based Violence and the US War on Iraq*, New York, 2007. www.madre.org.
53 *The Guardian*, 13 December 2007.
54 UNAMI, *Human Rights Report*, 1 April–30 June 2007, pp. 14–17. www.uniraq.org.
55 Dakkak, Henia, 'Tackling sexual violence, abuse and exploitation', *Forced Migration Review*, Special issue (June 2007), pp. 39–40.

56 Republic of Iraq and WHO, *Iraq Family Health Survey Report*, IFHS 2006/2007, January 2008, p. 25 and Table 20. www.who.int.

57 Al-Ali, *Iraqi Women*, p. 244.

58 Ibid., pp. 240–244.

59 MADRE, *Promising Democracy*, p. 7.

60 Mahmoud, Mona and Lauchin, Mike, 'Basra Militias targeting women', *BBC World Service*, 15 November 2007.

61 *IRIN*, 'Iraq: Extremists fuel anti-women violence in Basra', 20 November 2007. See also *Azzaman*, 6 December 2007.

62 *IRIN*, 'Iraq: Number of girls attending school dropping, say analysts', 29 October 2007.

63 Sarhan, Rfif, 'Sex for Survival', Al-Jazeera, 13 August 2007. www.aljazeera.net.

64 Dakkak, 'Tackling sexual violence', p. 40.

65 *IRIN*, 'Iraq: Conflict jeopardising children's physical, mental health', 15 August 2007.

66 UNICEF, News note: *Little respite for Iraq's children in 2007*, 21 December 2007. www.unicef.org.

67 UNICEF, *Iraq: Children suffer as food insecurity persists*, 12 May 2006. www.unicef.org. See also: Billing, Leila, 'Iraq's children pay the price of war', *Forced Migration Review*, Special Issue (June 2007), pp. 42–43.

68 IFHS, 'Violence-Related Mortality in Iraq', pp. 488–489.

69 OCHA, *Humanitarian Crisis in Iraq, Facts and Figures*, 13 November 2007. www.ochaonline.org.

70 Figures released by the Ministry of Planning and Development Corporation put it at three to four million, see Voices of Iraq (VOI), 14 December 2007; the figure of five million was reported by Iraq anti-corruption board, see VOI, 15 December 2007.

71 ICRC, *Civilians Without Protection: The ever-worsening humanitarian crisis in Iraq*, 24 October 2007. www.icrc.org.

72 WHO, *Social Determinants of Health*, p. 23.

73 Palmer, James, 'Trauma severe for Iraqi Children', *USA Today*, 16 April 2007.

74 Ibid. *USA Today*, quotes Dr Said Al-Hashimi.

75 WHO, *Healing Minds: Mental Health progress report 2004–2006*, 2006. p. 8, www.emro.who.int/iraq. The report gives a good overview of the mental health of the population.

76 Burham, Gilbert, Doocy, Shannon, Dzeng, Elizabeth, Lafta, Riyadh and Roberts, Les, *The Human Cost of the War in Iraq: A Mortality Study, 2002–2006*, John Hopkins University, October 2006; Burham, Gilbert, Doocy, Shannon, Lafta, Riyadh and Roberts, Les, 'Mortality after the 2003 invasion of Iraq: a cross-sectional cluster sample survey', *The Lancet*, 11 October 2006, pp. 1–9. www.thelancet.com.

77 IFHS, 'Violence-Related Mortality in Iraq', pp. 484–493.

78 Fidler, Stephen and Negus, Steve, 'Iraq death toll exceeds 150,000', *Financial Times*, 10 January 2008. For accessing Iraq Body Count project, see www.iraqbodycount.org.

79 See: Brownstein, Catherine A. and Brownstein, John S., 'Estimating Excess Mortality in Post-Invasion Iraq', *The New England Journal of Medicine*, 31 January 2008, pp. 445–447.

80 Alwan, Ala'din, *Health in Iraq: The Current Situation, Our vision for the Future, and Areas of Work*, Ministry of Health, Second Edition, December 2004.

81 WFP, *The extent and geographic distribution of chronic poverty in Iraq's Center/South Region*, May 2003. www.wfp.org.

82 WFP, *Food Survey Shows High Prevalence of Food Insecurity in Iraq*, 28 September 2004.

83 Ibid.

84 UNHCR, *Country of Origin Information Iraq*, October 2005, p. 93.

85 SIGIR, *Quarterly Report and Semiannual Report to the United States Congress*, 30 January 2006, p. 32.

86 UNICEF, *Iraq Situation Report March 2007*.

87 Oxfam, *Rising to the Humanitarian Challenge in Iraq*, 30 July 2007, p. 3. www.oxfam.org.uk.

88 Alwan, *Health in Iraq*, p. 43.

89 Oxfam, *Rising to the Humanitarian Challenge*, p. 11.

90 *IRIN*, 'Iraq: Country's health care system rapidly deteriorating', 7 November 2006.

91 Médecins Sans Frontières, *Responding to Iraq's Emergency*, 4 February 2007. www.msf.org.

92 Oxfam, *Rising to the Humanitarian Challenge*, p. 12.

93 *IRIN*, 'Blood sellers find market niche in Baghdad', 3 September 2007.

94 *IRIN*, 'Iraq: Insecurity and lack of funds prevent cleaning of polluted sites', 20 October 2007.

95 For the public health approach in countries that suffered violence like Colombia and a typology of violence, see, WHO, *World report on violence and health*, Geneva, 2002, pp. 4–7.

96 UNESCO, *Iraq: Education in Transition, Needs and Challenges*, 2004, p. 4. This is a comprehensive survey with data on secondary and higher education. www.portal.unesco.org.

97 Oxfam, *Rising to the Humanitarian Challenge*, p. 12.

98 UNICEF, *Little respite for Iraq's children*.

99 UNHCR, *Country of Origin Information Iraq*, p. 108.

100 UNICEF, *Little respite for Iraq's children*.

101 BBC News, 'Iraqi scholars fighting for an education', 24 March 2007. www.bbcnews.co.uk.

102 Oxfam, *Rising to the Humanitarian Challenge*, p. 12.

103 Taneja, Preti, *Assimilation, Exodus, Eradication: Iraq's minority communities since 2003*, Minority Rights Group International, February 2007. www.minorityrights.org.

104 HRW, *Iraq: Forcible Expulsion of Ethnic Minorities*, 15/3(E) (March 2003). www.hrw.org.

105 Howard, Michael, 'As violence grows, oil rich Kirkuk could hold key to Iraq's future', *The Guardian*, 27 October 2006.

106 Ibid.
107 Unrepresented Nations and Peoples Organization (UNPO), *Iraqi Turkmen: Indigenous Peoples and Current Human Rights Situation in Iraq*, 7 August 2006.
108 Ibid.
109 Verney, Marie-Helen, 'The Road Home: The Faili Kurds', *Refugee Magazine*, Issue 134 (20 March 2007).
110 Taneja, *Assimilation, Exodus*, p. 8.
111 Rubin, Alissa J., 'Around Baghdad, Signs of Normal Life Creep Back', *The New York Times*, 20 December 2007.
112 Taneja, *Assimilation, Exodus*, p. 9. See also Sengupta, Somini and Fisher, Ian, 'The Reach of War: Violence; Bombs Explode Near Churches in 2 Iraqi Cities', *The New York Times*, 2 August 2004.
113 Goode, Erica, 'Kidnapped Iraqi Archbishop is Dead', *The New York Times*, 14 March 2008.
114 *Azzaman*, 24 May 2007.
115 *IRIN*, 'Iraq: Baghdad Christians flee as violence against them mounts', 3 May 2007.
116 Ibid.
117 *IRIN*, 'Iraq: Christians seek new life in Europe', 5 November 2007.
118 Lattimer, Mark, 'In 20 years, there will be no more Christians in Iraq', *The Guardian*, 6 October 2006.
119 Ibid.
120 Taneja, *Assimilation, Exodus*, pp. 11–12.
121 Haynes, Deborah, 'Al-Qaeda bombing kills and maims 600', *The Times*, 16 August 2007.
122 Rubin, Alissa J., 'Persecuted Sect in Iraq Avoids Its Shrine', *The New York Times*, 14 October 2007.
123 Ibid. See also *Azzaman*, 26 August 2007.
124 Farrell, Stephen, 'Iraq Bomber Aimed at Alcohol Sellers', *The New York Times*, 21 December 2007.
125 Taneja, *Assimilation, Exodus*, p. 20.
126 Lamassu, Nineb, 'The plight of the Iraqi Christians', *Forced Migration Review*, Special Issue (June 2007), pp. 44–45.
127 Kino, Nuri, *By God: Six days in Amman*, 16 June 2007. www.humanrightsblog. org.
128 HRW, *Nowhere to Flee, the Perilous Situation of Palestinians in Iraq*, August 2006.
129 Rosen, Nir, 'The Flight from Iraq', *The New York Times*, 13 May 2007.
130 *Alarabiya*, 'Palestinians in Iraq tortured, ill-treated: report', 1 October 2007. www.alarabiya.net.
131 HRW, *Nowhere to Flee*.
132 Pollack, Kenneth M., *A Switch in Time: A New Strategy for America in Iraq*, Saban Centre for Middle East Policy at the Brookings Institution, February 2006, p. 2.
133 Allawi, Ali, *The Occupation of Iraq: Winning the War, Losing Peace*, New Haven, Yale University Press 2007, p. 348.

134 National Intelligence Council (NIC), 'Prospect for Iraq's Stability: Some Security Progress but Political Reconciliation Elusive', *National Intelligence Estimate*, August 2007. www.dni.gov.

135 The Independent Commission on the Security Forces of Iraq, *The Report of the Independent Commission on the Security Forces of Iraq*, 6 September 2007, p. 17. media.csis.org/isf.pdf.

136 Ibid., p. 18.

137 UNAMI, *Human Rights Report*, 1 April–30 June 2007, p. 4.

138 Allawi, *The Occupation of Iraq*, p. 423.

139 See www.modm-iraq.org.

140 Sultan, Abed Al-Samad Rahman, 'An unenviable task', *Forced Migration Review*, Special Issue (June 2007), p. 16.

141 Cohen, Roberta, 'Iraq: The Human Cost of War', Panel Discussion on the Humanitarian Situation in Iraq, Georgetown University, 21 March 2007. Dr Alwan was Minister of Health from June 2004 to March 2005. Prior to that he was Minister of Education for nine months.

142 Gordon, Michael R. and Rubin, Alissa J., 'Trial Nearer for Shiite Ex-Officials in Sunni Killings', *The New York Times*, 5 November 2007.

143 WHO, *Annual Report 2006: Working Together for a Healthier Iraq*, February 2007, p. 44.

144 IOM, *Capacity Building in Migration Management Programme* (CBMMP), 2005. See also report to Congress by the Department of Defense, *Measuring Stability and Security in Iraq*, 14 September 2007, p. 4. www.defenselink.mil.

145 Allawi, *The Occupation of Iraq*, p. 349.

146 *Azzaman*, 6 September 2007.

147 VOI, the agency quoting *Al-Muwatin* newspaper, 14 December 2007.

148 *Azzaman*, 19 September 2007.

149 Ricks, Thomas E., quotes Brig. Gen. John F. Campbell, deputy commanding general of the 1st Cavalry Division in, 'Iraqis Wasting An Opportunity, US Officers Say', *The Washington Post*, 15 November 2005.

150 Oxfam, *Rising to the Humanitarian Challenge*, p. 17.

151 *Azzaman*, 6 September 2007.

152 Gallager, Tom, *The Balkans in the New Millenium: In the Shadow of War and Peace*, New York, Routledge, 2005, p. 15. The book quotes the UNHCR chief Dennis McNamara's statement to the press in June 2000 after completing a one-year assignment in Kosovo.

153 al-Khalidi and Tanner, *Sectarian Violence*, p. 13.

Chapter 2: Iraqi refugees in Jordan

1 Brecht, Bertolt, 'Concerning the Label Emigrant', in Willett, John and Manheim, Ralph (eds), *Bertolt Brecht Poems*, London, Eyre Methuen Ltd, 1976, p. 301.

2 HRW estimated 250,000 to 300,000. See HRW, *Iraqi Refugees, Asylum Seekers and Displaced Persons*, p. 15. Chatelard estimated 350,000. See Chatelard, Géraldine, *From One War to Another: Iraqi Emigration to Jordan*, Institute for the Study of International Migration (ISIM), Newsletter 13, December 2003, p. 26.

3 US Committee for Refugees and Immigrants, *World Refugee Survey 2007*. www.refugees.org.

4 Chatelard, Géraldine, *Incentives to Transit: Policy Responses to Influxes of Iraqi Forced Migrants in Jordan*, Robert Schuman Centre for Advanced Studies, European University Institute, Working Papers, RSC no. 2002/50, pp. 3–4.

5 Chatelard, Géraldine, *Iraqi Forced Migrants in Jordan: Conditions, Religious Networks, and the Smuggling Process*, Robert Schuman Centre for Advanced Studies, European University Institute, Working Papers, RSC no. 2002/49, pp. 8–9.

6 Ibid., p. 11.

7 McDonald, Mark, 'Iraqis May Not Welcome Invading U.S. Troops as Liberators', *Miami Herald*, Knight Ridder News Service, 17 December 2002. The article quotes Mohammad Adwan, Jordan's Minister of State for Political Affairs and Information.

8 HRW, *Iraqi Refugees*, p. 12.

9 US Committee for Refugees and Immigrants, 'Country Report: Jordan', *World Refugee Survey 2007*. www.refugees.org/countryreports.

10 Chatelard, *Incentives to Transit*, p. 8.

11 Amnesty International, *Refugee crisis unfolds amid global apathy*, 24 September 2007, p. 1. www.amnesty.org.

12 Tabori, Paul, *The Anatomy of Exile*, London, Harrap, 1972, p. 27.

13 Chatelard, *Iraqi Forced Migrants*, p. 21.

14 Ibid., p. 13.

15 Pre-2003, only one-third of the respondents in Chatelard's survey indicated that they had come to Jordan with the idea of transit in mind. See Chatelard, *Iraqi Forced Migrants*, p. 13.

16 Ibid., p. 14.

17 *Al-Sabil*, 22 January 2007, quoted in BBC Monitoring Online. www.bbcmonitoringonline.com.

18 Al-Jazeera, 'Jordan booms as Iraqis flee hardships', 12 October 2005. www.aljazeera.net.

19 Congressional Research Service (CRS), *Iraqi Refugees and Internally Displaced Persons: A Deepening Humanitarian Crisis*, CRS Report for Congress, 3 October 2007, p. 7. www.fas.org.

20 Al-Jazeera, 'Jordan booms'.

21 Husaka, Anna, *With Iraqi Refugees in Jordan*, International Rescue Committee (IRC), 8 February 2007. www.theirc.org.

22 Fafo, *Iraqis in Jordan: Their Number and Characteristics*, November 2007. www.fafo.no.

23 Ibid., p. 18.

24 Ibid., p. 18 and Table 2.10. The vast majority of those who have residency permits tend to have a one-year renewable permit and very few have a five-year permit.

25 Chatelard, Géraldine, *Jordan as a transit country: semi protectionist immigration policies and their effects on Iraqi forced migrants*, Robert Schuman Centre for Advanced Studies, European University Institute, Working Paper no. 61, August 2002, p. 21.
26 Fagen, Patricia Weiss, *Iraqi Refugees: Seeking Stability in Syria and Jordan*, Institution for the Study of International Migration (ISIM), 2007, p. 7. www.georgetown.edu.
27 Interview on file with a diplomat, Amman, 29 January 2008.
28 Interview on file with a Jordanian official, Amman, 29 January 2008.
29 Fafo, *Iraqis in Jordan*, p. 7.
30 Ibid., p. 8.
31 Interview on file with a Jordanian official, Amman, 29 January 2008.
32 Fafo, *Iraqis in Jordan*, p. 16 and Table 1.3.
33 Ibid., p. 15 and Table 2.2.
34 Ibid., p. 25.
35 Ibid.
36 Women's Commission for Refugee Women and Children, *Iraqi Refugees in Jordan: Desperate and Alone*, 11 July 2007. www.womenscommission.org.
37 Women's Commission, *Iraqi Refugee Women and Youth in Jordan: Reproductive Health Findings*, A snapshot from the field, September 2007, p. 6.
38 Ibid., p. 7.
39 Interview on file with a psychologist, Amman, 27 January 2008.
40 Women's Commission, *Iraqi Refugee Women*, p. 7.
41 Interview on file with a Jordanian consultant, Amman, 29 January 2008.
42 HRW, *The Silent Treatment: Fleeing Iraq, Surviving in Jordan*, 18/10(E), November 2006, p. 69. www.hrw.org.
43 See Women's Commission: *From the Field, 'Can You Help Us?' Iraqi Refugees in Jordan*, 15 June 2007.
44 Interview on file with an Iraqi woman who completed her medical studies at Baghdad University, but cannot work in Jordan partly for lacking the necessary documents, Amman, 27 January 2008.
45 Women's Commission, *Iraqi Refugee Women*, pp. 5–6.
46 Ibid., p. 7.
47 Ibid.
48 E-mail from Harper, Andrew, Head of Iraq Support Unit, UNHCR, 14 November 2007.
49 Saif, Ibrahim and DeBartolo, David M., *The Iraq War's Impact on Growth and Inflation in Jordan*, Center for Strategic Studies, University of Jordan, 2007, p. 35. www.css-jordan.org.
50 HRW, *The Silent Treatment*, p. 58.
51 Ibid., p. 60.
52 Women's Commission, *Iraqi Refugee Women*, p. 9.
53 HRW, *The Silent Treatment*, p. 61.
54 Women's Commission, *Iraqi Refugee Women*, p. 9.
55 *The Jordan Times*, 'UNHCR estimates at least 250,000 school age Iraqis in Jordan', 22 August 2007.

56 Interview with UNHCR, Amman, 28 January 2008.
57 Chatelard, Géraldine, Washington, Kate and El-Abed, Oroub, *An Assessment of Services Provided for Vulnerable Iraqis in Jordan*, Austcare, January 2008.
58 *The Jordan Times*, 'UNHCR estimates'.
59 UNICEF/UNHCR, *Providing Education Opportunities to Iraqi Children in Host Countries: A Regional perspective*, July 2007.
60 Amnesty International, *Refugee crisis unfolds*, p. 22.
61 Fafo, *Iraqis in Jordan*, p. 21 and Table 2.2.
62 Ibid., p. 22.
63 Video by Women's Commission, 'Overview of Iraqi Refugees in Jordan', November 2007. www.youtube.com/watch?v=ICI06BbD53I&eurl.
64 Women's Commission, *Iraqi Refugees in Jordan*.
65 The World Bank, *The World Not Traveled: Education Reform in the Middle East and Africa*, MENA Development Report, Washington DC, 2008. See Tables 1.9 and 1.5 respectively. www.worldbank.org.
66 Interview on file with WHO, Amman, 28 January 2008.
67 HRW, *The Silent Treatment*, p. 63.
68 Fafo, *Iraqis in Jordan*, p. 20 and Table 2.17.
69 *The Jordan Times*, 29 January 2008.
70 Amnesty International, *Refugee crisis unfolds*, p. 23.
71 UNFPA, UNHCR, UNICEF, WFP and WHO, *Meeting the Health Needs of Iraqis Displaced in Neighbouring Countries*, Health Sector Appeal, 18 September 2007. www.who.int.
72 Fafo, *Iraqis in Jordan*, Table 2.23.
73 Women's Commission, *Iraqi Refugee Women*, p. 5.
74 Saif and DeBartolo, *The Iraq War's Impact*, p. 35.
75 UNFPA, et al., *Meeting the Health Needs*, p. 9.
76 Ibid., p. 7.
77 Ibid., p. 8.
78 Interview on file with WHO, Amman, 28 January 2008.
79 Ministry of Health, Ministry of Planning and WHO, *Chronic Non-Communicable Diseases: Risk Factors Survey in Iraq*, 2006. www.emro.who.int/iraq.
80 Shami, Seteney and McCann, Lisa, 'The Social Implications of Population Displacement and Resettlement in the Middle East', *International Migration Review*, 27 (Summer 1993), p. 429. The article quotes Dr El-Fatih El-Samani [sic] who presented at a conference at Yarmouk University.
81 Interview on file with a psychologist, Amman, 27 January 2008.
82 During 2007, UNHCR referred 216 individuals for psycho-social counselling services. See UNHCR, *Iraq Situation Update*, 4 January 2008.
83 Interview on file with a psychologist, Amman, 27 January 2008.
84 *Al-Himaya*, Foundation for Trauma Recovery, Growth and Resilience.
85 Fafo, *Iraqis in Jordan*, Table 2.6.
86 Snyder, David, *Another Easter Away, Iraqi Family Marks Another Year as Refugees*, Caritas Internationalis, 11 April 2007. www.caritas.org.
87 Kino, *By God*, p. 28.

88 Additionally, there is the possibility that since 9/11 it has become more difficult for Muslims to get asylum in the West.

89 Fafo, *Iraqis in Jordan*, p. 24.

90 Struck, Doug, 'Professionals Fleeing Iraq As Violence, Threats Persist', *The Washington Post*, 23 January 2006.

91 *Al-Perleman Al-Iraqi*, 'The State of Iraqi Doctors in Amman', 8 September 2007. www.drweb4u.net.

92 HRW, *The Silent Treatment*, p. 55. See other stories, pp. 55–57.

93 Al-Jazeera TV, '"Suffering" of Iraqi doctors in Iraq, abroad', 7 September 2007. BBC Monitoring Online.

94 Fafo, *Iraqis in Jordan*, Table 2.36.

95 Ibid., p. 13 and Table 1.20.

96 Tavernise, Sabrina, 'Jordan Yields Poverty and Pain for the Well-Off Fleeing Iraq', *The New York Times*, 10 August 2007.

97 *IRIN*, 'Jordan: Some Iraqi refugees resort to begging', 1 October 2007.

98 Fafo, *Iraqis in Jordan*, p. 11.

99 Ibid.

100 Seely, Nicholas, 'For Some Iraqi War Refugees, Business is Booming', *Christian Science Monitor*, 10 June 2008. The story tells about Ali Hussein Al-Hassona who fled Iraq in 2005 and set up in Amman a successful sports collectibles shop.

101 World Vision Middle East/Eastern European Office (MEERO), *Blankets for Iraqi Refugees in Jordan*, 14 April 2008. www.meero.worldvision.org.

102 Fafo, *Iraqis in Jordan*, p. 12.

103 Ibid., p. 14.

104 *Al-Hayat*, 'Iraqis top the foreign investors in Jordan', 11 December 2006. www.daralhayat.net.

105 Ibid.

106 Fafo, *Iraqis in Jordan*, Table 1.24.

107 Saif and DeBartolo, *The Iraq War's Impact*, p. 20. See also Royal Scientific Society, Friedrich Ebert Stiftung, *The Iraqi Status and its effect on the Jordanian Economy*, Amman, June 2005.

108 Saif and DeBartolo, *The Iraq War's Impact*, p. 20.

109 *IRIN*, 'Iraq-Jordan: Iraqis cause black market for jobs', 28 March 2007.

110 The report was summarized in *The Jordan Times*, 19–20 May 2006.

111 Ibid.

112 Saif and DeBartolo, *The Iraq War's Impact*, pp. 36–37.

113 Fagen, *Iraqi Refugees*, p. 13.

114 Al-Jazeera, 'Rise in price of staples in Jordan causing hardship', 6 December 2007, quoted in BBC Monitoring Online.

115 Saif and DeBartolo, p. 36.

116 Ibid., p. 37.

117 Mansur, Yusuf, 'Improving the Economy', *The Jordan Times*, 9 October 2007.

118 Saif and DeBartolo, *The Iraq War's Impact*, pp. 23–24.

119 Ibid., p. 26.

120 *The Jordan Times*, 14 March 2005.

121 Saif and DeBartolo, *The Iraq War's Impact*, p. 30.

122 Ibid., p. 31.

123 Royal Scientific Society, *The Iraqi Status*.

124 Van Hear, Nicholas, 'The Impact of the Involuntary Mass "Return" to Jordan in the Wake of the Gulf Crisis', *International Migration Review*, 29/2 (Summer 1995), pp. 352–374.

125 Brand, Laurie A., *Jordan's Inter-Arab Relations: The Political Economy of Alliance Making*, New York, Columbia University Press, pp. 196–241.

126 HRW, *The Silent Treatment*, p. 3.

127 Chatelard, *Incentives to Transit*, p. 23.

128 Chatelard, *From One War to Another*, p. 26.

129 Chatelard, *Incentives to Transit*, p. 8.

130 Fagen, *Iraqi Refugees*, p. 5.

131 Zaiotti, Ruben, 'Dealing with non-Palestinian refugees in the Middle-East: Policies and Practices in an Uncertain Environment', *International Journal of Refugee Law*,18(2) (2006), p. 338.

132 Interview on file with a Jordanian official, Amman, 29 January 2008.

133 Ibid.

134 *The Jordan Times*, 23 January 2007.

135 Hodson, Nathan, *Iraqi Refugees in Jordan: Cause for Concern in a Pivotal State*, The Washington Institute for Near East Policy, no. 13, April 2007.

136 *Al-Arab Al-Yawm*, 14 July 2007, quoted in BBC Monitoring Service.

137 Interview on file with an Iraqi academic, Amman, 29 January 2008.

138 Murad, Nermeen, 'Jordan's legacy', *The Jordan Times*, 30 July 2007.

139 Al-Jazeera quoting Ahmad Uwaidi Abbadi who heads a small right-wing group called the National Jordanian Movement, 12 October 2005.

140 Wright, Robin and Baker, Peter, 'Iraq, Jordan see Threat to Election from Iran – Leaders Warn Against Forming Religious State', *The Washington Post*, 8 December 2004.

141 See, for example, interview with Prince Hassan in the Turkish Daily, *Todays Zaman*, 25 March 2007. www.todayszaman.com.

142 HRW, *The Silent Treatment*, p. 21. See also: Hodson, *Iraqi Refugees in Jordan*, pp. 4–5.

143 HRW, *Iraq: From a Flood to a Trickle*, Neighboring States Stop Iraqis Fleeing War and Persecution, 1, April 2007, pp. 12–13.

144 US Committee for Refugees and Immigrants, *World Refugee Survey 2007*.

145 Chatelard, *Incentives to Transit*, pp. 14–15.

146 Ibid., p. 15.

147 See *IRIN*, 'Iraq-Jordan: Government introduces entry visas for Iraqis', 13 December 2007; *The Jordan Times*, 12 December 2007.

148 Rosen, 'The Flight from Iraq'.

149 *Al-Ahram Weekly*, 'The need to move fast', interview with King Abdullah II of Jordan, Issue 844, 10–16 May 2007.

150 Buck, Tobias, 'Oil price poses threat to Jordan's stability', *Financial Times*, 5–6 April 2008.

151 *Al-Ra'y*, 'They are not Refugees', 10 July 2007, quoted in BBC Monitoring Online.

152 Royal Scientific Society, *The Iraqi Status*.

153 *The Jordan Times*, 'Who should compensate Jordan for the massive Iraqi influx?', 12 February 2007.

154 Interview on file with a Jordanian official, Amman, 29 January 2008.

155 *The Jordan Times*, 12 February 2007.

156 *Al-Dustour*, 'The Iraqis in Jordan: The need to control influx while simultaneously respecting human rights', 17 March 2007, quoted in BBC Monitoring Online.

157 Ibid.

158 Van Hear, 'The Impact of the Involuntary Mass Return', p. 359.

159 *Al-Ra'y*, 'The Iraqis in Jordan: What kind of Addition', 24 February 2007, quoted in BBC Monitoring Online.

160 Lasensky, Scott, *Jordan and Iraq – Between Cooperation and Crisis*, United States Institute of Peace, Special Report 178, December 2006. www.usip.org.

161 Saif and DeBartolo, *The Iraq War's Impact*, p. 10.

162 Ibid., pp. 5–11.

163 Hodson, *Iraqi Refugees in Jordan*, p. 5.

164 *IRIN*, 'Jordan: Water contamination incidents highlight water shortage problem', 19 November 2007.

165 *Al-Arab Al-Yawm*, 'The Iraqis in Jordan', 10 February 2007, quoted in BBC Monitoring Online.

166 *IRIN*, 'Iraq-Jordan: Iraq to give $8 million to Jordan for hosting refugees', 28 November 2007.

167 Aswat Al-Iraq, 'Officials: Iraqis' situation in Jordan will improve after granting Jordan favourable oil prices', 22 September 2007. www.aswataliraq.info.

168 Interview on file with an Iraqi family, Amman, 25 January 2008.

169 UNHCR, *Objectives of UNHCR in Jordan*, August 2007.

170 For an overview of these organizations and their activities and locations, see a map produced by UNHCR, *Ongoing and Planned Activities in Amman/Jordan*. www.unhcr.org. For an interesting analysis of the Christian organizations operating in Jordan, and their attitude to Muslims, particularly Shia, see Chatelard, *Jordan as a Transit Country*, pp. 21–22. See also Chatelard, Washington, El-Abed, *An Assessment of Services Provided*, for an extensive overview of local and international humanitarian organizations.

171 Fagen, *Iraqi Refugees*, p. 11.

172 HRW, *The Silent Treatment*, p. 7.

173 The procedure of UNHCR is as follows (based on UNHCR brochures):
a) registration whereby a UNHCR official takes the details of the story of the individual/family;
b) a decision is made whether an individual is vulnerable and qualifies for resettlement, and this is done on a case by case basis;
c) further check ups are done before a decision is made to refer the individual/family for resettlement;
d) once an individual is referred to a country, then that country will begin its own procedure to decide whether to grant a visa or not. This could take anywhere from three months to two years (particularly in the case of the USA).

174 Fafo, *Iraqis in Jordan*, Table 2.12.
175 Ibid., Table 2.14.
176 HRW, *The Silent Treatment*, p. 99.
177 Ibid., p. 159.

Chapter 3: Iraqi refugees in Syria

1 Poem by an anonymous Afghan worker being deported from Iran, translated by Olszewska, Zuzanna, 'Selected Poems by Afghan Refugees in Iran', from lecture given at The British Academy Conference on Dispossession and Displacement, London, 28–29 February 2008.
2 Tiltnes, Åge A., *Keeping Up: A Brief on the Living Conditions of Palestinian Refugees in Syria*, Fafo, 2007. UNRWA has estimated 383,000, but Fafo believes that some of those moved to the Gulf or Europe but stayed registered with UNRWA in Syria.
3 Ibid., p. 8.
4 Perthes, Volker, 'Syrian Regional Policy under Bashar Al-Asad: Realignment or Economic Rationalization?', *Middle East Report*, 220 (Fall 2001), p. 38.
5 Dorai, Mohamed Kamel, 'The Social Networks of Iraqis in Damascus', Presentation at the Second Conference of the International Association of Contemporary Iraqi Studies (IACIS) held at Philadelphia University, Jordan, 11–13 June 2007. Dorai based his estimates on data of the Central Bureau of Statistics in Syria.
6 US Committee for Refugees and Immigrants, 'Country Report: Syria', *World Refugee Survey 2007*.
7 Ibid.
8 al-Khalidi, Ashraf, Hoffman, Sophia and Tanner, Victor, *Iraqi Refugees in The Syrian Arab Republic: A Field-Based Snapshot*, The Brookings Institution–University of Bern Project on Internal Displacement, June 2007, p. 46. www.brookings.edu/projects/idp.aspx.
9 Amnesty International, *The Situation of Iraqi Refugees in Syria*, 26 July 2007.
10 al-Khalidi, et al., *Iraqi Refugees*, p. 17.
11 Ibid.
12 Ibid.
13 Rosen, 'The Flight from Iraq'.
14 Ibid.
15 al-Khalidi, et al., *Iraqi Refugees*, pp. 20–21.
16 Chatelard, Géraldine, 'Emigrating from Iraq in the period 1991–2007: social networks as alternatives for international protection', Presentation at IACIS Conference, Amman, 11–13 June 2007.
17 'Alawi suggests an adherent of Ali (The Prophet's Cousin) and 'Alawi doctrine derives from Shi'i Islam. See Pipes, Daniel, 'The Alawi Capture of Power in Syria', *Middle Eastern Studies*, 25/4 (October 1989), pp. 429–450.
18 al-Khalidi, et al., *Iraqi Refugees*, p. 21.

19 Ezzat, Dina, 'Problems by the dozen', *Al-Ahram Weekly*, Issue 842, 26 April–2 May 2007.
20 al-Khalidi, et al., *Iraqi Refugees*, pp. 22–23.
21 UNHCR, *Iraq Situation Update*, 23 January 2008.
22 Syrian News Agency (SANA), 'Syria hosts the majority of Iraqi refugees, Interior Minister says', 11 July 2008. The agency quotes Minister Bassam Abdul-Majeed.
23 Jacobsen, Karen, 'Refugees and Asylum Seekers in Urban Areas: A Livelihoods Perspective', Editorial Introduction, *Journal of Refugee Studies*, 19/3 (September 2006), p. 275.
24 SANA, 'Syrian Population over 19 million by End of 2007', 14 January 2008, quoted in BBC Monitoring Online. In Damascus and its suburbs live about 4.15 million, followed by Aleppo and its countryside areas with about 3.4 million people.
25 Jacobsen, 'Refugees and Asylum Seekers', p. 275.
26 UNHCR, UNICEF, WFP, *Assessment on the Situation of Iraqi Refugees in Syria*, March 2006. www.ncciraq.org.
27 Ipsos Public Affairs & Opinion Research, UNHCR Syria, *Survey of Iraqi Refugees*, Final Results, 31 October–25 November 2007.
28 Mervin, Sabrina, 'Sayyida Zaynab [sic], Banlieue de Damas ou nouvelle ville sainte chiite?' *Cemoti*, vol. 22, July–December 1996.
29 BBC Background Briefing, 'Iraqi Refugees in Syria – an overview'. The briefing is partly based on a paper presented by the Syrian Ministry of Foreign Affairs to the Geneva conference in April 2007.
30 *Ipsos Survey*.
31 UNHCR, et al., *Assessment*, p. 14.
32 UNHCR, *Syria Update*, June 2008.
33 UNHCR, et al., *Assessment*, p. 15; *Ipsos Survey*.
34 al-Khalidi, et al., *Iraqi Refugees*, p. 29.
35 *Ipsos Survey*.
36 Ibid.
37 Al-Jazeera TV, 'Special programme on Iraqi refugees in Syria', 7 September 2007. Quoted in BBC Monitoring Online.
38 *Ipsos Survey*. A Microfund project was launched to help Iraqi female heads of households in Jordan and Syria, which is designed to provide soft loans to these women who are able to propose a micro or small business project. See Chatelard, Géraldine, Washington, Kate and el-Abed, Oroub, *Iraqi Refugees and Exiles in Jordan and Syria: A Proposal for Initiatives on the Part of the Open Society Institute*, November 2007, pp. 26–27.
39 Phillips, Joshua E.S., 'Unveiling Iraq's teenage prostitutes', 24 June 2005. www.salon.com.
40 UNHCR, *SGBV Update*, Damascus, 15 November 2007.
41 Firmo-Fontan, Victoria, 'Abducted, Beaten and Sold into Prostitution: A Tale from Iraq', *The Independent*, 26 July 2004.
42 UNHCR, *SGBV Update*.
43 UNHCR, et al., *Assessment*, p. 37.

44 Zoepf, Katherine, 'Iraqi Refugees Turn to the Sex Trade in Syria', *The New York Times*, 29 May 2007.
45 Hassan, Nihal, '50,000 Iraqi refugees forced into prostitution', *The Independent*, 24 June 2007. See also DVD on Iraqi Prostitutes. www.journeyman.tv.
46 Zoepf, 'Iraqi Refugees'.
47 Sinan, Omar, 'Iraqi Refugees Turn to Prostitution', *The Washington Post*, 24 October 2007.
48 SANA, 'Syrian minister discusses Iraqi female refugees with Iraqi delegation', 15 December 2007, quoted in BBC Monitoring Online.
49 McLeod, Hugh, 'Despair of Baghdad turns into a life of shame in Damascus', *The Guardian*, 24 October 2006.
50 *Al-Mashriq*, 5 December 2007.
51 UNHCR, UNICEF, *Providing Education*.
52 Amnesty International, *Refugee Crisis*.
53 UNHCR, UNICEF, *Providing Education*.
54 al-Khalidi, et al., *Iraqi Refugees*, p. 33.
55 *Ipsos Survey*.
56 Amnesty International, *Refugee Crisis*.
57 Alam, Hannah, 'Illiteracy increasing among Iraq's refugee children', *McClatchy Newspapers*, 11 December 2007. www.mcclatchydc.com.
58 UNHCR, UNICEF, *Providing Education*.
59 The World Bank, *The Road Not Traveled*, p. 23; p. 15.
60 Amnesty International, *Refugee Crisis*.
61 al-Khalidi, et al., *Iraqi Refugees*, p. 34.
62 Sinjab, Lina, 'Iraqi refugees struggle in Syria', BBC News, 23 August 2007.
63 UNHCR, et al., *Assessment*, p. 38.
64 Amnesty International, *Refugee Crisis*.
65 al-Khalidi, et al., *Iraqi Refugees*, p. 31.
66 Interview with an Iraqi family living in Damascus, 12 February 2008.
67 al-Khalidi, et al., *Iraqi Refugees*, p. 32.
68 UNHCR, et al., *Assessment*, p. 30.
69 *Ipsos Survey*.
70 UNHCR, et al., *Assessment*, p. 30.
71 Ibid.
72 UNFPA, et al., *Meeting the Health Needs*, p. 8. Recent research indicated that malnutrition in the first two years of a child's life is irreversible and that hunger causes disease as well as death. See *The Economist*, 26 January 2008.
73 UNFPA, et al., *Meeting the Health Needs*, p. 8.
74 UNHCR, *Trauma Survey in Syria highlights suffering of Iraqi refugees*, quoting UNHCR Representative in Syria, Laurens Jolles, 22 January 2008.
75 Ibid.
76 al-Khalidi, et al., *Iraqi Refugees*, p. 32.
77 *The Economist*, 17 November 2007.
78 *Ipsos Survey*.
79 Interview with NGO on file, Amman, 27 January 2008.

80 See, for example, *Syria Times*, 30 July 2008.

81 Interview with a Mandean family living in Syria, via telephone, 12 February 2008.

82 Zoepf, Katherine, 'The Reach of War: Exodus; Many Christians Flee Iraq, with Syria the Haven of Choice', *The New York Times*, 5 August 2004.

83 International Catholic Migration Commission (ICMC) and United States Conference of Catholic Bishops (USCCB), *Iraqi Refugees in Syria*, A Report of the ICMC-USCCB Mission to Assess the Protection Needs of Iraqi Refugees in Syria, April 2008, p. 23. www.icmc.net.

84 Van Hear, Nicholas, 'Refugees in Diaspora; From Durable Solutions to Transnational Relations', *Refuge*, 23/1 (Winter 2006), p. 12.

85 See interesting case studies of the social networks of the Iraqi minorities in Dorai, 'Social Network'.

86 *The New York Times*, 'Iraqi Refugees Shed Sectarian Bitterness', from Associated Press in Damascus, 13 October 2007.

87 Interview with a Mandean family living in Syria.

88 *The New York Times*, 'Iraq: Refugees Shed Sectarianism'.

89 HRW, *Syria: Give Refuge to Palestinians Fleeing Threats in Iraq*, 2 February 2007.

90 *IRIN*, 'Iraq-Syria: Plight of Palestinian refugees in border camps worsens', 27 June 2007. See also the description of life in the camps in Rosen, 'The Flight from Iraq'.

91 UNHCR, *Conditions deteriorate for 2,000 Palestinians stuck at Iraq-Syria border*, 9 November 2007.

92 UNHCR, *Palestinians at the Iraq-Syria border*, 9 November 2007.

93 The World Bank, *World Development Indicators database*, April 2007. devdata.worldbank.org.

94 Raphaeli, Nimrod, 'Syria's Fragile Economy', *Middle East Review of International Affairs (MERIA)*, vol. 11 (June 2007), p. 45.

95 ILO: *2003–2004 Key Indicators of the Labour Market*, Geneva, 2003. www.ilo.org/kilm.

96 Fafo, *The Syrian Labour Market: Findings from the 2003 Unemployment Survey*, Fafo-report 2007:02. Among Palestinians, Fafo estimated 9 per cent unemployed and actively looking for work. See Tiltnes, *Keeping Up*, p. 48.

97 al-Khalidi, et al., *Iraqi Refugees*, p. 41.

98 Interview with a Damascus-based social researcher, by telephone, 14 February 2008.

99 UNDP, *Poverty in Syria: 1996–2004: Diagnosis and Pro-Poor Policy Considerations*, June 2005. www.undp.org.

100 UNHCR, et al., *Assessment*, p. 21. Many young Iraqis spend their days in internet cafes to contact their families and friends and 'to kill time'. See VOI, 'Iraqi Refugees in Damascus find consolation in Internet Cafes', 29 January 2008. www.iraqupdates.com.

101 UNHCR, et al., *Assessment*, p. 21.

102 Ibid.

103 al-Khalidi, et al., *Iraqi Refugees*, p. 25.

104 BBC Background Briefing, 17 November 2007.

105 al-Khalidi, et al., *Iraqi Refugees*, p. 19.

106 UNHCR, *UNHCR issues ATM cards to 7,000 needy Iraqi families in Syria*, 17 December 2007.

107 Ibid.

108 *IRIN*, 'Iraq-Syria: Starving to survive: Iraqi refugees resort to desperate measures', 2 January 2008.

109 UNHCR, *Iraq Situation*, 25 April 2008.

110 *IRIN*, 'Iraq-Syria: Starving to survive'. *IRIN* was quoting Sybella Wilkes, spokesperson for UNHCR in Syria.

111 International Monetary Fund, *IMF Executive Board Concludes 2007 Article IV Consultation with the Syrian Arab Republic*, Public Information Notice (PIN) no. 07/104, 15 August 2007. www.imf.org.

112 al-Khalidi, et al., *Iraqi Refugees*, p. 41.

113 *Syria Today*, 'The Price of Refuge', April 2007. The Syrian magazine quotes Deputy Prime Minister for Economic Affairs, Abdullah Al-Dardari in an interview with the German magazine Spiegel. www.syria-today.com.

114 International Monetary Fund, *Syrian Arab Republic: 2007 Article IV Consultation – Staff Report; and Public Information Notice on the Executive Board Discussion*, IMF Country Report no. 07/280, August 2007.

115 IMF, *IMF Executive Board*.

116 *IRIN*, 'Iraq-Syria: Iraqi doctors welcome refugee agency contributions to hospitals', 1 May 2007.

117 IMF, *IMF Executive Board*.

118 *IRIN*, 'Syria: Wealth gap widening as inflation hits poor', 7 February 2008.

119 UNDP, *Poverty in Syria*.

120 Fagen, *Iraqi Refugees*, p. 21.

121 IMF, *Syrian Arab Republic: Selected Issues*, IMF Country Report no. 06/295, August 2006.

122 *Syria Today*, April 2007. The IMF says the cost is $1.3 billion, representing 3.7 per cent of Syria's GDP. See also *Asharq Alawsat*, 31 August 2007, quoted in BBC Monitoring Online.

123 Roug, Louise, 'Iraq accuses Syria of helping rebels', *Los Angeles Times*, 5 February 2007.

124 Department of Defense, *Measuring Stability and Security in Iraq*, Report to Congress, March 2007, p. 17.

125 *Tishreen*, 19 April 2007.

126 Ferris, *Security, Displacement and Iraq*, p. 15.

127 BBC Briefing, 'Iraqi refugees in Syria'.

128 HRW, *No Room to Breathe*, State Repression of Human Rights Activism in Syria, 19/6(E) (October 2007), p. 1.

129 Al-Miqdad, Faisal, 'Iraq Refugees in Syria', *Forced Migration Review*, Special Issue (June 2007), p. 20.

130 Ibid., p. 19.

131 *Al-Baath*, 'Iraq's refugees in Syria', 22 February 2007.

132 International Crisis Group, *Failed Responsibility: Iraqi Refugees in Syria, Jordan and Lebanon*, Middle East Report no. 77, 10 July 2008, p. 16.

133 Al-Khalidi, et al., *Iraqi Refugees*, p. 42.
134 *Al-Thawrah*, 'Iraqis and the open doors', 17 April 2007.
135 *Al-Thawrah*, 'Interview with Dr Bashar Al-Sha'ar, Minister of State for Syrian Red Crescent Affairs', 31 October 2007.
136 *Al-Thawrah*, 10 September 2007.
137 *IRIN*, 'Syria: Warning looming crisis as Iraqi refugee influx continues', 28 June 2007. See also Reuters, 'New rules make Syrian border a dead-end for Iraqis', 7 November 2007. www.reliefweb.int.
138 UNHCR, *Iraq Situation Update*, 23 January 2008. See also Associated Press, 'Syria displays new security measures along Iraqi border', 11 November 2007.
139 Cambanis, Thanassis, 'Syria Shuts main Exit from War for Iraqis', *The New York Times*, 20 October 2007.
140 Al-Sharqiyah TV, Dubai, 'Iraqi MPs unaware of Syria's decision to impose entry visas on Iraqis', 1 September 2007, quoted in BBC Monitoring Online.
141 Interview by telephone with an Iraqi family, Damascus, 12 February 2008.
142 *IRIN*, 'Iraq-Syria: Iraqi pledge to Syria fails to assuage refugees', 23 August 2007.
143 Al-Sharqiyah TV, Dubai, 'Iraqi Speaker asks Syria to revise residency rules for refugees', 17 February 2007, quoted in BBC Monitoring Online.
144 VOI, 'Iraq pays Syria $15M to host refugees', 20 November 2007. www.iraqupdates.com.
145 *Asharq Alawsat*, 'Syrian-Iraqi Committee to assess cost of Iraqi refugees to compensate Syria', 31 August 2007.
146 *Al-Thawrah*, 'Interview with Deputy Foreign Minister, Dr Faysal Al-Miqdad', 31 October 2007.
147 Cordesman, *Iraq's Sectarian and Ethnic Violence*, p. 111. Based on ABC News/USA Today/BBC/ARD Poll, 19 March 2007. The survey interviewed 2,212 randomly selected Iraqis from 25 February to 5 March 2007. See also www.abcnews.go.com.
148 Frelick, Bill, 'Talk to Syria for the Sake of Iraqi Refugees', *HRW*, 16 October 2007.
149 Al-Muhammad, Muhyi Al-Din, 'The Iraqis are not looking for repatriation because that is not a solution', *Tishreen*, 22 April 2007.
150 *Syrian Times*, 'Syrian, Iraqi, WHO officials comment on health needs of Iraqi refugees', 30 July 2007.
151 *Al-Thawrah*, 'Syrian officials discuss "modest" international aid for Iraqi refugees', 31 October 2007.
152 Refugees International, *A lot of Talk, Little Action*, 14 November 2007. www.refugeesinternational.org.
153 Ibid.
154 O'Donnell, Kelly and Newland, Kathleen, *The Iraqi Refugee Crisis: The Need For Action*, Migration Policy Institute, 2008, p. 12. www.migrationpolicy.org.
155 Reuters, 'Syria, U.S. agree on processing Iraqi refugees', 8 November 2007. www.reliefweb.int. For an interesting analysis of the 'political game' between the US and Syria, see Moubayed, Sami, 'Back in Damascus', *Al-Ahram Weekly*, Issue 839, 5–11 April 2007.
156 *Azzaman*, 3 October 2007.
157 Fagen, *Iraqi Refugees*, p. 27.

158 International Crisis Group, *Failed Responsibility*, p. 24.
159 UNHCR, *Iraq Situation Update*, March 2008.
160 UNHCR, *Syria Update*, June 2008.
161 Ibid.
162 Refugees International, *Iraqi refugees: Time for the UN system to fully engage*, 27 July 2007.
163 Ibid.
164 ICMC-USCCB, *Iraqi Refugees in Syria*, p. 21.
165 Al-Jazeera TV, 7 September 2007, quoted in BBC Monitoring Online.
166 *IRIN*, 'Iraq: Refugees forced home as funds dry up', 13 November 2007.

Chapter 4: Iraqi refugees in the rest of the world

1 Lazarus, Emma, 'The New Colosssus', poem on the Statue of Liberty National Monument.
2 Grabska, Katarzyna, 'Marginalization in Urban Spaces of the Global South: Urban Refugees in Cairo', *Journal of Refugee Studies*, 19/3 (2006), p. 288.
3 Ibid., p. 292.
4 UNHCR mentioned two different estimates: 20,000 to 40,000 in *Iraq Situation Update*, 23 January 2008; and 80,000 to 100,000 in *Global Appeal 2008–2009*, 1 December 2007, p. 208. US Committee for Refugees and Immigration *World Refugee Survey 2007* in its country report, Egypt, has an estimate of 80,000; Refugees International in *Egypt: Respond to the needs of Iraqi refugees*, 12 April 2007, talks about a number of up to 150,000.
5 VOI, 'Politics and Security', 27 October 2006.
6 Sperl, Stefan, *Evaluation of UNHCR's policy on refugees in urban areas: A case study review of Cairo*, UNHCR Evaluation and Policy Analysis Unit, June 2001, p. 29.
7 Al-Shalchi, Hadeel, 'Down the line', *Al-Ahram Weekly*, Issue 844, 10–16 May 2007.
8 Rosen, 'The Flight from Iraq'.
9 UNFPA, et al., *Meeting the Health Needs*, p. 4.
10 IMF, *Arab Republic of Egypt: 2007 Article IV Consultation Staff Report; Staff Statement; Public Information Notice on the Executive Board Discussion; and Statement by the Executive Director for the Arab Republic of Egypt*, IMF Country Report no. 07/380, December 2007.
11 Megiffin, Janet, 'No Work for Doctors', The American University in Cairo website, 12 March 2008. www.aucegypt.edu.
12 Al-Shalchi, 'Down the line'.
13 IMF, *Arab Republic of Egypt: 2007 Article IV*, p. 11; p. 22.
14 England, Andrew, 'Riyadh and Cairo to cut import duties', *Financial Times*, 2 April 2008.
15 Slackman, Michael, 'Day of angry protest stuns Egypt', *International Herald Tribune*, 7 April 2008.
16 Immigration Here & There, *Iraqi refugees in Egypt seek secure education*, 24 July 2007. www.immigrationhereandthere.org.

17 Ibid.
18 US Committee for Refugees, *World Refugee Survey*.
19 Immigration Here & There, *Iraqi refugees in Egypt*.
20 UNHCR, *Iraq Situation Update*, 23 January 2008.
21 *IRIN*, 'Egypt: High rates of trauma, sickness among Iraqi refugees', 27 February 2008. The report quotes Dr Ahlam Tobia who works with refugees in Cairo.
22 Yoshikawa, Lynn, 'Iraqi refugees in Egypt', *Forced Migration Review*, Issue 29 (December 2007), p. 54.
23 UNFPA, et al., *Meeting the Health Needs*, pp. 5–6.
24 Ibid., p. 8.
25 HRW, *Iraq: From a Flood to a Trickle*, p. 14.
26 Refugees International, *Egypt: Respond*.
27 Ezzat, 'Problems by the dozen'.
28 Grabska, 'Marginalization in Urban Spaces', p. 294.
29 Telephone interview with an Iraqi living in Cairo, 2 March 2008.
30 Voutira, Effie, a talk given at a conference on 'Dispossession and Displacement: Forced migration in the Middle East and Africa', The British Academy, London, 28–29 February 2008.
31 Bancroft-March, Carolyn, 'Becoming a Refugee', The American University in Cairo website, 12 March 2008. www.aucegypt.edu.
32 Ezzat, 'Problems by the dozen'.
33 Yosikawa, 'Iraqi refugees in Egypt'.
34 Refugees International, *Egypt: Respond*. See also Egypt's emergency rule and freedom of association in HRW, *Egypt*, Country Summary, January 2007.
35 UNHCR, *Iraq Situation Update*, 25 April 2008.
36 HRW, *Rot Here or Die There: Bleak Choices for Iraqi Refugees in Lebanon*, 19/8(E) (November 2007), p. 12.
37 Danish Refugee Council, *Iraqi population in Lebanon*, Survey report, Beirut, July 2005, p. 14.
38 Ibid.
39 Danish Refugee Council, *Iraqi Population Survey in Lebanon*, November 2007, p. 23.
40 Ibid., p. 19.
41 Ibid., p. 24. The survey encompassed 1,015 households which was 2,895 individuals.
42 *IRIN*, 'Lebanon: Iraqi refugees face prison and deportation', 6 November 2007.
43 Danish Refugee Council, *Iraqi Population Survey*, pp. 28–29.
44 HRW, *Rot Here*, p. 14.
45 Ibid., p. 15.
46 *IRIN*, 'Lebanon: Iraqi refugees'.
47 Danish Refugee Council, *Iraqi Population Survey*, p. 40.
48 Ibid., pp. 34–36.
49 HRW, *Rot Here*, p. 58.
50 Danish Refugee Council, *Iraqi Population Survey*, p. 57.
51 Ibid., pp. 43–45.

52 IMF, *Lebanon: 2007 Article IV Consultation – Staff Report; Staff Statement; Public Information Notice on the Executive Board Discussion; and Statement by the Executive Director of Lebanon*, IMF Country Report no. 07/382, December 2007, p. 24.

53 Ibid., pp. 5–6.

54 HRW, *Rot Here*, p. 52. See the testimonies of Iraqi workers, pp. 52–54.

55 Trad, Samira and Frangieh, Ghida, 'Iraqi refugees in Lebanon: continuous lack of protection', *Forced Migration Review*, Special Issue (June 2007), p. 35.

56 Frontiers Association, *Legality vs. Legitimacy: Detention of Refugees and Asylum Seekers in Lebanon*, Legal Study, Beirut, May 2006. www.frontierassociation.org.

57 O'Donnell and Newland, *The Iraqi Refugee Crisis*, p. 16.

58 UNHCR, *Iraq Situation Update*.

59 Danish Refugee Council, *Iraq Population Survey*, p. 67. For conditions in prison, see HRW, *Rot Here*, pp. 28–30.

60 HRW, *Rot Here*, pp. 31–33.

61 Ibid., p. 26.

62 UNHCR, *UNHCR welcomes Lebanon's recognition of Iraqi refugees*, 20 February 2008.

63 HRW, *Rot Here*, p. 58.

64 Ibid., p. 49.

65 Danish Refugee Council, *Iraqi population in Lebanon*, p. 34; *Iraqi Population Survey*, p. 72.

66 *The Daily Star* (Beirut), 20 November 2007, quoted in BBC Monitoring Online.

67 HRW, *Rot Here*, p. 34.

68 Ibid., p. 31.

69 UNHCR, *Iraq Situation Update*, April 2008.

70 HRW, *Kuwait, Promised Betrayed: Denial of Rights of Bidun, Women and Freedom of Expression*, 12/2(E) (October 2000).

71 HRW, *The Silent Treatment*, p. 93 puts the estimate at 10,000–13,000, while a March 2008 update of UNHCR estimated 50,000. See UNHCR, *Iraq Situation Update*, March 2008.

72 HRW, *The Silent Treatment*, p. 93.

73 UNHCR, *Iraqis prepare to leave remote desert camp*, 28 July 2003. www.reliefweb.int.

74 Country Report: Saudi Arabia, *World Refugee Survey 2007*.

75 VOI, 'Saudi Arabia to build security fence on borders with Iraq', 14 September 2007.

76 Ibid.

77 UNHCR, *Iraq Situation Update*, March 2008.

78 IRIN, 'Yemeni Iraqi migrants, refugees await brighter future', 1 July 2007.

79 HRW, *The Silent Treatment*, p. 97.

80 Ibid., p. 98.

81 IRIN, 'Yemeni Iraqi migrants'.

82 UNHCR, *Iraq Situation Update*, March 2008.

83 UNHCR, *Arab League to launch fund-raising campaign for Iraqi refugees*, 10 January 2008.

84 Ibid. UNHCR quotes the Arab Iraqi musician Naseer Shamma.
85 Rajee, Bahram, 'The Politics of Refugee Policy in Post-revolutionary Iran', *Middle East Journal*, 54/1 (Winter 2000), pp. 44–63.
86 Chatelard, Géraldine, 'L'émigration des Irakiens de la guerre du Golfe à la guerre d'Irak (1990–2003)', in Jaber, H. and Métral, F. (eds), *Mondes en mouvements, Migrants et migration au Moyen-Orient au tournant du XXIe siècle*, Institut Français du Proche Orient, Beirut, 2005, pp. 115–116; pp. 143–146.
87 HRW, *The Silent Treatment*, p. 94. HRW was quoting Ahmad Hosseini, advisor to the Minister and director general of the Bureau for Aliens and Foreign Immigrants' Affairs.
88 Sassoon, Joseph, 'Management of Iraq's Economy Pre and Post the 2003 War: An Assessment', in Baram, Amatzia, Rohd, Achim and Zeidel, Ronen (eds), *Iraq, Past and Present* (to be published by Routledge, 2009).
89 UNHCR, *Over half of Iraqi refugees in Iran have gone home*, 16 December 2004.
90 MaximsNews Network, 'Iraqi Refugees in Iran Held Up by Red Tape and Border Closures, UN says', 13 June 2008. www.maximsnews.com.
91 UNHCR, *Iraq Situation Update*, April 2008.
92 Al-Jazeera, 'Rare sanctuary for Iraqi pilgrims', 12 September 2007. www.aljazeera.net.
93 Gordon, Michael R., 'Iraq Needs Strides in Economy and Government to Cut Attacks, a Top General Says', *The New York Times*, 3 March 2008. The paper quotes Lt. Gen. Raymond T. Odierno.
94 VOI, 'Iran builds security barrier along borders with Iraq', 14 September 2007.
95 Sherwood-Randall, Elizabeth, 'Tend to Turkey', *Journal of Democracy*, Issue no. 6, Fall 2007.
96 HRW, *The Silent Treatment*, pp. 96–97.
97 Kuwait News Agency (KUNA), 'Turkey plans to build fence on its borders with Iraq', 14 September 2007, quoted in Iraq Updates.
98 UNHCR, *Iraq Situation Update*, April 2008.
99 *Hurriyet*, 'Turkey warns of impending refugee wave from Iraq', 5 October 2007. The Turkish daily was quoted in BBC Monitoring Online.
100 Rose, Peter I. (ed.) *The Dispossessed: An Anatomy of Exile*, Boston, University of Massachusetts Press, 2005, p. 231.
101 Based on interviews in Stockholm with Swedish officials in Ministry of Justice, Iraqi embassy officials and Federation of Iraqi Associates, April 2008.
102 Estimates given by Iraqi officials at the Iraqi Embassy in Stockholm, 4 April 2008.
103 Swedish Migration Board, *Facts & Figures 2006*, March 2007. www.migrationsverket.se.
104 Interview with an Iraqi woman, Stockholm, 12 November 2007.
105 BBC News, 'Iraqis who left: Mohammed', 17 March 2008.
106 Interview in Södertälje, 5 April 2008.
107 Swedish Radio, Gothenberg. www.sr.se/p1/kaliber.
108 Backer, Stina, 'Iraqis choose Sweden as new home', BBC News, 6 July 2007.
109 Ekman, Ivar, 'Far From War, a Town with a Well-Used Welcome Mat', *The New York Times*, 13 June 2007.

110 'FIAS: History and Activity'. www.iraqifias.org.

111 Interview with an official from the municipality of Södertälje, 4 April 2008.

112 Engel, Matthew, 'The new face of Sweden', *Financial Times*, 19–20 January 2008.

113 Interview with an official at Södertälje Municipality, 7 April 2008.

114 Mongalvy, Sophie, 'Transition classes ease Iraqi kids into Swedish way of life', Middle East Online, quoted in Iraq Updates, 18 February 2008.

115 Apps, Peter, 'Alone, Iraq's teenage migrants head for Sweden', Reuters, 17 October 2007. www.alertnet.org.

116 Al-Arabiya, 'The dangerous journey from Iraq to Europe', 17 October 2007. www.alarabiya.net.

117 Lee, Laurence, 'Little solace for Iraqis in Sweden', Al-Jazeera, 20 August 2007. www.aljazeera.net.

118 *Swedish Press Review*, 19 October 2007.

119 *Dagens Nyheter*, 21 December 2007, quoted in BBC Monitoring Online.

120 Meeting with Secretary of State, Gustaf Lind, Ministry of Justice, Stockholm, 4 April 2008.

121 *Financial Times*, 19 February 2008.

122 *Dagens Nyheter*, 'Swedish foreign minister visits Baghdad, discusses refugees, reconciliation', 2 September 2007, quoted in BBC Monitoring Online.

123 Betts, Alexander, 'International Cooperation Between North and South to Enhance Refugee Protection in Regions of Origin', Working Paper Series, Refugee Studies Centre, University of Oxford, July 2005, p. 4.

124 Wanche, Sophia I., *An Assessment of the Iraqi Community in Greece*, Commissioned by UNHCR, January 2004, p. 12.

125 World Organization Against Torture, 'Greece: Alleged ill-treatment and fear of forcible deportation of Iraqi refugees', Press Release, 5 April 2007. cm.greekhelsinki.gr.

126 Press Release by 16 NGOs, 1 August 2007. Among the NGOs are Amnesty International, Greek Council for Refugees, Hellenic Red Cross. cm.greekhelsinki.gr.

127 Sperl, Markus, *Fortress Europe and the Iraqi 'intruders': Iraqi asylum-seekers and the EU, 2003–2007*, New Issues in Refugee Research, UNHCR, Research Paper no. 144, October 2007. www.unhcr.org/research.

128 UNCHR, *Global Overview*, April 2007.

129 ECRE, *Guidelines on The Treatment of Iraqi Asylum Seekers and Refugees in Europe*, April 2007. www.ecre.org/resources.

130 Sperl, *Fortress Europe*, p. 9.

131 Dempsey, Judy, 'Germany to press EU over Iraqi refugees', *International Herald Tribune*, 17 April 2008.

132 Reuters, 'No priority for Christian Iraqi refugees – EU presidency', 18 April 2008.

133 ECRE, *Guidelines on the Treatment*, p. 4.

134 Gardiner, Beth, 'Iraqi refugees receive cold greeting in Britain', *International Herald Tribune*, 18 May 2007.

135 Travis, Alan, 'Iraqi asylum seekers given deadline to go home or face destitution in UK', *The Guardian*, 13 March 2008.

136 Quote of Bjarte Vandvik, secretary general of ECRE, is from Godfrey, Hannah, 'From Baghdad to Britain', *The Guardian*, 20 March 2008.
137 Sperl, *Fortress Europe*, pp. 7–8.
138 Doward, Jamie, 'Refugees fight forced return to Iraq war zones', *The Observer*, 13 April 2008.
139 BBC News, 'Asylum system "shameful for UK"', 27 March 2008; Dugan, Emily, '"Inhumane and oppressive": the final verdict on Britain's asylum policy', *The Independent*, 27 March 2008.
140 *The Times*, 'Iraqi interpreters seeking asylum in Britain will be refused entry until 2009', 13 December 2007.
141 *The Times*, 'Breach of honour', the paper quoted the Liberal Democrat MP Lynne Featherstone, 12 December 2007.
142 *The Times*, 'Iraqi interpreters and families prepare for new lives in Britain', 14 March 2008.
143 Al-Rasheed, Madawi, 'Political migration and downward socio-economic mobility: The Iraqi community in London', *New Community*, 18/4 (July 1992), pp. 537–550.
144 French News Agency (AFP), 'France moves closer to asylum offer for Iraqi Christians', 11 December 2007, quoted in BBC Monitoring Online.
145 *Le Figaro*, 'Le maire PS de Cherbourg demande l'expulsion d'un Squat d'Irakiens', 20 September 2007.
146 Spinder, William, 'Are Iraqis getting a Fair Deal', *Refugees*, no. 146, Issue 2, 2007, pp. 20–23.
147 *The Economist*, 23 February 2008.
148 UNHCR, *Iraqis top latest asylum figures for industrialized countries*, 21 September 2007; BBC News, 'Iraqi asylum seeker numbers jump', 18 March 2008.
149 For a historical review of Iraqi asylum applications for the years 1980–2002, see Sirkeci, Ibrahim, 'War in Iraq: Environment of Insecurity and International Migration', *International Migration*, 43/4 (2005).
150 Spindler, 'Are Iraqis getting a Fair Deal'.
151 UNHCR, *Asylum Levels and Trends in Industrialized Countries, 2007*, 18 March 2008, p. 9.
152 Ibid., p. 4.
153 Sperl, *Fortress Europe*, p. 14.
154 Kushner and Knox, *Refugees in An Age of Genocide*, p. 335.
155 Hearing before the Committee on the Judiciary United States Senate, 'The Plight of Iraqi Refugees', One Hundred Tenth Congress, First Session, 16 January 2007, p. 2.
156 Ibid., p. 4.
157 Ibid., p. 15. Statement of Ellen Sauerbrey, Assistant Secretary of State for Population, Refugees and Migration, Department of State.
158 US Department of State, *United States Humanitarian Assistance for Displaced Iraqis*, 9 November 2007. www.state.gov.
159 US Department of State, *US Contributes More Than $125 Million to International Organizations to Aid Displaced Iraqis*, 14 February 2008.

160 Hearing, 'The Plight of Iraqi Refugees', p. 10.
161 State House News Service, 'Representative Waters Calls For Leadership On Iraqi Refugee Crisis', 11 April 2008. California Representative Maxine Waters is Chairwoman and co-founder of the Out of Iraq Congressional Caucus.
162 Rosen, 'The Flight from Iraq'.
163 Lee, Matthew, 'US Falls Short of Iraqi Refugees Goal', *The Washington Post*, 31 October 2007.
164 Associated Press, 20 August 2008. For previous months of 2008, see: Human rights first, *US Resettles 974 Iraqi Refugees in April; Improvement Welcome but Comprehensive Response Still Needed*, 1 May 2008. www.humanrightsfirst. org.
165 Pew Research Center Publications, *Iraq Portrait: How the Press Has Covered Events on the Ground*, 19 December 2007. www.pewresearch.org. Full report at www.journalism.org.
166 Pérez-Peña, Richard, 'The War Endures, but Where's the Media?', *The New York Times*, 24 March 2008.
167 Raghavan, Sudarsan, 'Iraqis with Ties to U.S. Cross Border Into Despair', *The Washington Post*, 17 November 2007.
168 Tavernise, Sabrina, 'In Life of Lies, Iraqis Conceal Work for U.S.', *The New York Times*, 6 October 2007.
169 Raghavan, 'Iraqis with Ties to U.S.'.
170 Hearing, 'The Plight of Iraqi Refugees', p. 28. The statement was of Captain Zachary J. Iscol, Foreign Military Training Unit.
171 Packer, George, 'Planning for Defeat', *The New Yorker*, 17 September 2007. 'Betrayed' was presented in February 2008 at the Culture Project Theater in Soho, New York.
172 US Department of State, *Special Immigrant Visas for Iraqis – Employed by/on behalf of U.S. Government*, March 2008. travel.state.gov/visa/immigrants.
173 Raghavan, 'Iraqis with Ties to U.S.'.
174 Cohen, Roger, 'Closing the door to an Iraqi Mandela', *International Herald Tribune*, 27 September 2007.
175 BBC News, 'Australian homes for Iraqi workers', 9 April 2008.
176 Harper, Andrew, 'Iraq's Refugees: Ignored and Unwanted', Unpublished Paper by UNHCR's head of Iraq unit, January 2008.
177 *IRIN*, 'Iraq-Brazil: First group of Palestinians arrive in Brazil from desert camp', 23 September 2007.

Chapter 5: The role of humanitarian organizations

1 Tabori, 'Song of Exile', in *The Anatomy of Exile*, p. 9.
2 Fawcett, John and Tanner, Victor, *The Internally Displaced People of Iraq*, The Brookings Institution, 2002, pp. 35–40.
3 de Torrente, Nicholas, 'Humanitarian Action Under Attack: Reflections on the Iraq War', *Harvard Human Rights Journal*, vol. 17 (Spring 2004), p. 3.

4 Carle, Alexandre and Chkam, Hakim, *Humanitarian action in the new security environment: policy and operational implications in Iraq*, Humanitarian Policy Group, September 2006, p. iii.

5 For the details of the attack and UN's work in Iraq, see Power, Samantha, 'The Envoy', The United Nations' doomed mission to Iraq, *The New Yorker*, 7 January 2008.

6 BBC News, 'Baghdad Terror Blast Kills Dozens', 27 October 2003.

7 de Torrente, 'Humanitarian Action Under Attack', p. 2.

8 Hansen, Greg, *Coming to Terms with the Humanitarian Imperative in Iraq*, Feinstein International Center, January 2007, pp. 8–9.

9 HRW, *Iraqi Refugees, Asylum Seekers, and Displaced Persons*, p. 12.

10 Ibid., pp. 12–13.

11 Ibid., p. 18.

12 Ibid.

13 Refugees International, *Iraqi Refugees: Time for the UN*.

14 Loesher, Gil, *The UNHCR and World Politics*, Oxford, Oxford University Press, 2001, p. 329.

15 Ibid.

16 Refugees International, *Iraqi Refugees: Time for the UN*.

17 UNHCR, *Humanitarian Needs of Persons Displaced Within Iraq and Across the Country's Borders: An International Response*, HCR/ICI/2007/2, 30 March 2007.

18 Ibid.

19 UNHCR, *Country Operations Plan*, Country: Lebanon, Planning Year 2006, 1 September 2006.

20 HRW, *The Silent Treatment*, p. 42.

21 Ibid., p. 46. Interview with a Shi'i barber from Sadr City, Baghdad who fled Iraq in early 2004.

22 HRW, *Rot Here*, p. 19.

23 UNHCR, *Humanitarian Needs*.

24 UNHCR, *Iraq Situation Response*, Update on revised activities under the January 2007 Supplementary Appeal, July 2007.

25 UNHCR, *2008 Iraq Situation Supplementary Appeal*, 2 January 2008.

26 UNHCR, *Syria Update*.

27 Ladek, Dana Graber, 'IOM – building Iraqi capacity and assisting IDPs', *Forced Migration Review*, Special Issue (June 2007), p. 51. See also website of the programme 'Iraqis Rebuilding Iraq' at www.iraq_iri.org.

28 Hansen, Greg, *Taking Sides or Saving Lives: Existential Choices for the Humanitarian Enterprise in Iraq*, Humanitarian Agenda 2015, Iraq Country Study, Feinstein International Center, June 2007, p. 38.

29 UNHCR, *Iraq Situation Update*, November 2006.

30 Hansen, *Coming to Terms*, p. 15.

31 UNHCR, *UN agency Appeals for Urgent Aid to Support Countries Hosting Iraqi Refugees*, 6 July 2007. The quote is of UNHCR spokesperson Ron Redmond.

32 Ibid.

33 Amnesty International, *Iraq: Rhetoric and Reality: The Iraqi Refugee Crisis*, 15 June 2008, p. 48.

34 UNHCR, *Iraq Situation Response*, July 2007.

35 AlertNet, 'UNHCR seeks donor help amid funding shortfall for Iraq Operation', 9 May 2008.

36 Amnesty, *Iraq: Rhetoric and Reality*, p. 49.

37 FMR authors, 'Delivering is never remote: NGOs' vital role', *Forced Migration Review*, Special Issue (June 2007), p. 28.

38 UNHCR, *Iraq Situation*, 2008.

39 Ibid.

40 Ezzat, Dina, 'From one hell to another', *Al-Ahram Weekly*, Issue 845 (17–23 May 2007).

41 Peteet, Julie, 'Unsettling the Categories of Displacement', *Middle East Report*, no. 244 (Fall 2007).

42 Hansen, *Taking Sides*, p. 44.

43 Gidley, Ruth, 'Aid world rethinks role in Iraq', AlertNet, 8 April 2004. The agency quotes Larry Minear of Tufts University. www.alertnet.org.

44 Oxfam, *Rising to the Humanitarian Challenge*, p. 5.

45 Al-Adhami, Mundher, 'Refugees or angry citizens', *Al-Ahram Weekly*, Issue 838, 29 March–4 April 2007.

46 Loescher, *The UNHCR and World Politics*, p. 330.

47 Ezzat, 'From one hell to another'.

48 Betts, 'International Cooperation', p. 4.

49 Ibid., p. 5.

50 Carle and Chkam, *Humanitarian action*, p. 7.

51 UNHCR has a more detailed split of services (centralized and decentralized) according to geographical clusters. See UNHCR, *Ongoing and planned activities*.

52 *Mizan*, 'Know your rights and protect yourself Campaign'. www.mizangroup.jo.

53 *IRIN*, 'Jordan: Limited access to justice for women', 23 February 2006.

54 Chatelard, et al., *An Assessment of Services Provided*.

55 See www.terredeshommes.org.

56 Mokbel, Madona, 'Refugees in Limbo: The Plight of Iraqis in Bordering States', *Middle East Report*, no. 244 (Fall 2007), p. 13.

57 Ibid. See also www.caritas.org.

58 UNHCR, *Ongoing and planned activities*. This is a map showing UNHCR's main partners in Jordan.

59 Mokbel, 'Refugees in Limbo', pp. 13–14.

60 Chatelard, et al., *An Assessment of Services Provided*.

61 Ibid.

62 This is not a complete list. For a more comprehensive list, see ICMC – USCCB, *Iraqi Refugees in Syria* and Chatelard, et al., *Iraqi Refugees and Exiles in Jordan and Syria*.

63 Correspondence with UNHCR, Damascus, 16 March 2008 (e-mail on file).

64 UNHCR, *Syria Update*.

65 Patience, Martin, 'UN staff relive Iraqi refugee horror', BBC News, Damascus, 19 September 2007.

66 Carle and Chkam carried out an interesting risk/threat analysis involving human-
    itarian actors in Iraq. See Carle and Chkam, *Humanitarian action*, pp. 8–10.

Chapter 6: Iraq's economy and its brain drain

1 Bendix, Reinhard, 'The Lost Status', *From Berlin to Berkeley*, New Jersey, New
   Brunswick, 1986, p. 276.
2 Sassoon, 'Management of Iraq's Economy'.
3 For a detailed analysis of rentierism, see the different articles by Isam Al-Khafaji.
   See, for example, his article: 'A Few Days After: State and society in a post-Saddam
   Iraq', in Toby Dodge and Steven Simon (eds), *Iraq at the Crossroads: State and
   Security in the Shadow of Regime Change*, London, Adelphi Papers, 2003, pp.
   77–92.
4 Owen, 'Reconstructing the performance of the Iraqi economy', p. 97.
5 For a review of the impact of wars and sanctions, see Alnasrawi, Abbas, 'Long-
   term Consequences of War and Sanctions', in Mahdi, Kamil A. (ed.), *Iraq's
   Economic Predicament*, Reading, Ithaca Press, 2002, pp. 343–348.
6 Packer, George, *The Assassin's Gate*, New York, Farrar, Straus and Giroux, 2005,
   p. 139.
7 Phillips, David L., *Losing Iraq*, New York, Westview Press, 2005, pp. 143–153. For
   Bremer's point of view, see Bremer III, L. Paul, *My Year in Iraq: The Struggle to
   Build a Future of Hope*, New York, Simon & Schuster, 2006, pp. 39–42.
8 Bremer, *My Year in Iraq*, p. 200.
9 Foote, Christopher, Block, William, Crane, Keith and Gray, Simon, 'Economic
   Policy and Prospects in Iraq', *Journal of Economic Perspectives*, 18/3 (Summer
   2004), p. 59.
10 Hoff, Karla and Stiglitz, Joseph E., 'After the Big Bang? Obstacles to the Emergence
   of the Rule of Law in Post-Communist Societies', *The American Economic Review*,
   94/3 (June 2004), p. 762.
11 Owen, 'Reconstructing the performance', pp. 98–99.
12 International Advisory and Monitoring Board (IAMB) of the Development Fund
   for Iraq (DFI), *Report for the period 22 May 2003 to 28 June 2004*. The IAMB was
   set up by the United Nations as an independent oversight body for the DFI to
   ensure that Iraq's oil export sales were made consistent with international best
   practices.
13 Parker, Christopher and Moore, Pete W., 'The War Economy of Iraq', *Middle East
   Report*, no. 243 (Summer 2007), p. 13.
14 Alnasrawi, Ali, *Iraq's Burdens: Oil, Sanctions and Underdevelopment*, Connecticut,
   Greenwood Press, 2002, p. 104.
15 Al-Shabibi, Sinan, 'An Economic Agenda For a Future Iraq', *Studies on the Iraqi
   Economy*, Iraqi Economic Forum, London, 2002, pp. 24–25.
16 *Azzaman*, 20 November 2006.
17 International Monetary Fund, *Iraq: 2007 Article IV Consultation, Fifth Review
   Under the Stand-By Agreement, Staff Report; Public Information and Press Release*

on the Executive Board Discussion; and Statement by the Executive Director for Iraq, IMF Country Report no. 07/301, August 2007.

18 Iraq Directory, 2 January 2008.

19 The Brookings Institution, *Iraq Index*, 31 March 2008. www.brookings.edu/saban/iraq-index.aspx.

20 UNDP/Ministry of Planning and Development Cooperation, *Iraq Living Conditions Survey 2004*, vol. II, Analytical Report, p. 120, Baghdad, 2005.

21 Herring and Rangwalla, *Iraq in Fragments*, p. 131.

22 Women's International League for Peace and Freedom, *Iraq: Unemployment Forces Female Professionals Into Domestic Work*, 25 July 2006. www.peacewomen.org.

23 Milligan, Rebecca, 'The Other Casualties of War in Iraq', *Middle East Report*, no. 239 (Summer 2006), pp. 26–27.

24 UNDP/Ministry of Planning, *Iraq Living Conditions*, II, p. 133.

25 *Financial Times*, Interview with Zalmay Khalilzad, 29–30 April 2006.

26 Weiss, Stanley A., 'Iraq needs a job surge', *International Herald Tribune*, 27 December 2007.

27 Glantz, James, 'Iraqi Factories, Aging and Shut, Now Give Hope', *The New York Times*, 18 January 2007; Jelinek, Pauline, 'Pentagon Helping Restart Iraqi Factories', *The Washington Post*, 4 January 2007.

28 Glanz, James, 'Iraqi shoe manufacturers survive through persistence and ingenuity', *International Herald Tribune*, 15 April 2008.

29 *Al-Hayat*, 23 July 2004.

30 IMF, *Iraq: Country Report No. 07/301*, August 2007.

31 SIGIR, *Quarterly Report to the United States Congress*, 30 October 2007, p. 63.

32 SIGIR, *Quarterly Report and Semiannual Report to the United States Congress*, 30 January 2008, figure 2.27.

33 The Brookings Institution, *Iraq Index*, March 2008. See also *Financial Times*, 'Black-outs sap public faith in Baghdad', 17 June 2007.

34 Al-Khalisi, Isam, 'Ministry doctors figures on power output', *Azzaman*, 7 April 2008.

35 GAO, *Iraq Reconstruction: Better Data Needed to Assess Iraq's Budget Execution*, Report to Congressional Committees, January 2008.

36 Ibid.

37 O'Hanlon, Michael, *Iraq's Unknown Economy*, The Brookings Institution, 6 January 2008.

38 Billion, Philippe Le, 'Corruption, Reconstruction and Oil Governance in Iraq', *Third World Quarterly*, 26/4–5 (2005), p. 698.

39 Stewart, Rory, *Occupational Hazards: My Time Governing in Iraq*, London, Picador, 2006, p. 82.

40 Barakat, Sultan, 'Post-Saddam Iraq: deconstructing a regime, reconstructing a nation', *Third World Quarterly*, 26/4–5 (2005), p. 577.

41 Merza, Ali, 'Iraq: reconstruction under uncertainty', *International Journal of Contemporary Iraqi Studies*, 1/2 (2007), p. 173. The article analyses extensively the different scenarios of reconstruction.

42 A list of 270 names is published in a website called: Friends of Saddam – Al-Mada list of 270. See www.acepilots.com/unscam/. See also Foote, et al., 'Economic Policy and Prospects', pp. 53–55. For the many culprits involved in this scandal, see *The Economist*, 15 March 2008.

43 Billon, 'Corruption, Reconstruction', p. 689.

44 Allawi, *The Occupation of Iraq*, pp. 353–369. For a general review of corruption in Iraq, see: Harriman, Ed, 'The Least Accountable Regime in the Middle East', *London Review of Books*, 2 November 2006.

45 Ibid., p. 349.

46 House of Representatives, Resolution 734, 110th Congress, First Session, 11 October 2007. www.oversight.house.gov.

47 CNN, 'Draft report: Iraq government "not capable" of fighting corruption', 27 September 2007. www.cnn.com.

48 Pollack, *A Switch in Time*, p. XIII.

49 Oppel, Richard A., 'Iraq Insurgency Runs on Stolen Oil Profits', *The New York Times*, 16 March 2008.

50 Ibid.

51 Glantz, James and Worth, Robert F., 'Attacks on Iraq Oil Industry Aid Vast Smuggling Scheme', *The New York Times*, 4 June 2006. See also *Financial Times*, 6 May 2006.

52 Lando, Ben, 'Analysis: Iraq's Oil Smuggling', Parts I and II, United Press International, quoted in Iraq Updates, 15 December 2006. See also Glantz, James, 'Billions in Oil Missing in Iraq, US Study Says', *The New York Times*, 12 May 2007.

53 The CPA was criticized for not putting in place the right metering systems despite its awareness of the problem at a very early stage in 2003. See KPMG, *Reports submitted to DFI for the period 1 January 2004 to 28 June 2004*. www.iamb.info/dfiaudit.htm.

54 According to Allawi, the spread ranged from 10 times to 80 times making it extremely lucrative for smugglers. Allawi, *The Occupation of Iraq*, pp. 358–359.

55 Glantz, James, 'Senate Committee Seeks Audit of Iraq Oil Money', *The New York Times*, 9 March 2008. The article quotes a letter from Senator Carl Levin and Senator John W. Warner, both members of the Senate Armed Service Committee.

56 Moore, Solomon, 'Secret Iraqi Deal Shows Problems in Arms Orders', *The New York Times*, 13 April 2008.

57 Kessler, Glenn, 'Ex-Investigator Details Iraqi Corruption', *The Washington Post*, 5 October 2007.

58 VOI, 'Forum in Baghdad on administrative corruption', 2 January 2008.

59 Hansen, *Taking Sides*, pp. 39–40.

60 Clark, Kate, 'Corruption in Iraqi Kurdistan', BBC News, 11 January 2008.

61 Interview with a senior Kurdish official in Europe, 4 April 2008.

62 Clark, 'Corruption in Iraqi Kurdistan'.

63 Although there was a unification of ministries between the two parties, each still has its independent ministries: finance, *peshmerga* (the military Kurdish units) and the interior. See: Aswat Al-Iraq, 13 April 2008.

64 Based on information provided by an Iraqi entrepreneur with extensive business interests in Kurdistan. Material on file.

65 For an interesting discussion of the issues relating to granting oil and gas concessions, see Foroohar, Kambiz, 'The Fight For Kurdistan's Oil', *Bloomberg Markets*, August 2007, pp. 96–105. www.bloomberg.com.

66 Zulal, Shwan, 'Economic successes or incompetence in Kurdistan regional government', Kurdish Media, 10 April 2008. www.kurdmedia.com.

67 IMF, *Iraq: Country Report*, August 2007.

68 Al-Ali, Zaid, 'The IMF and the Future of Iraq', *Middle East Report Online*, 7 December 2004. www.merip.org.

69 Zawya, 21 April 2008. Zawya is an economic and finance portal based in Dubai. It quotes spokesman Ali Al-Dabbagh.

70 *Asharq Alawsat*, 'The Iraqi Debt: One Down, Still Many to Go', 8 July 2008.

71 NIC, 'Prospect for Iraq's Stability', August 2007.

72 Interview with a senior Iraqi diplomat in Europe, 4 April 2008. Interview on file.

73 Chen, Siyan, Loayza, Norman V. and Reynal-Querol, Marta, 'The Aftermath of Civil War', *The World Bank Economic Review*, 22/1 (2008), pp. 63–85.

74 Tripp, Charles, *A History of Iraq*, Cambridge, Cambridge University Press, 2000, p. 281.

75 Merza, 'Iraq: reconstruction under scrutiny', p. 173.

76 Al Saraf, Hala and Garfield, Richard, 'The Brain Drain of Health Capital: Iraq as a Case Study', in Cholewka, Patricia A. and Motlagh, Mitra M. (eds), *Health Capital and Sustainable Socioeconomic Development*, Boca Raton, CRC Press, 2008, p. 158.

77 Marr, Phebe, *The Modern History of Iraq*, Boulder, Westview Press, 1985, p. 289.

78 Allawi, *The Occupation of Iraq*, p. 127.

79 Ibid., p. 128.

80 See, for example Middle East Online, 'Best Iraqi Minds Join Exodus', 12 November 2006. Quoted in Iraq Updates.

81 Cave, Damien, 'Cheated of Future, Iraqi Graduates want to Flee', *The New York Times*, 4 June 2007.

82 Middle East Online, 'Iraqi professionals forced to take small jobs', 21 February 2008. Quoted in Iraq Updates.

83 Wong, Edward, 'Sunnis find sanctuary among Iraqi Kurds', *International Herald Tribune*, 2–3 September 2006.

84 *Azzaman*, 26 July 2006.

85 al-Khalidi, et al., *Iraqi Refugees in the Syrian Arab Republic*, p. 7.

86 www.brusselstribunal.org/academicsList.htm

87 Ibid.

88 *IRIN*, 'Iraqis Justice delayed as lawyers live under threat', 30 April 2007.

89 Ibid. See also UNAMI, *Human Rights Report*, 1 April–30 June, p. 11.

90 Pachachi, Adnan, 'Iraq at Crossroads', Lecture given by Dr Pachachi at St. Antony's College, Oxford, 15 November 2006.

91 *IRIN*, 'Iraq: Neglected nurses fight their own war', 19 November 2006.

92 Jalili, Ismail, 'Plight of Iraqi Academics', presentation to the Madrid International Conference on the Assassinations of Iraqi Academics, 23–24 April 2006. Data was updated by Dr Jalili as of 1 May 2006. www.iraqis.org.uk/contents.

93 Brulliard, Karin, 'Saddam-era rule restored to retain doctors', *The Los Angeles Times*, 7 May 2007.

94 Tavernise, Sabrina, 'Facing Chaos, Iraqi Doctors are Quitting', *The New York Times*, 31 May 2005.

95 Al-Iraqiya Television, 'Special Interview: Sultan Abd Al-Samad Rahman, Minister of Immigrants and Displaced [sic] persons', 4 February 2008. Quoted in BBC Monitoring Online.

96 Interview by telephone with Dr Said Hakki, 20 May 2008. It should be noted that many Iraqis who have the means go to see their specialist doctors in Amman.

97 Alwan, *Health in Iraq*, pp. 60–61.

98 WHO, *Country Profiles: Iraq*. www.emro.who.int.

99 Medact, *Communiqué*, no. 43 (Spring 2006).

100 Palmer, James, 'Frequent targets of violence, Iraqi physicians flee in droves', *The Seattle Times*, 4 April 2006. www.seatlletimes.nwsource.com.

101 *IRIN*, 'Iraq: Diyala desperately needs doctors', 18 November 2007.

102 *IRIN*, 'Iraq: Hospitals in Baghdad, Basra lack supplies – ICRC', 1 April 2008.

103 Leyne, John, 'Iraqi medical crisis as doctors flee', BBC News, 22 March 2007.

104 Interview with WHO officials, Geneva, 13 November 2007.

105 BBC News, 'My Iraq: Child Psychiatrist', 23 March 2007.

106 Interview with an Iraqi psychiatrist, London, 28 March 2008. Interview on file.

107 Al-Sheibani, Bassim Irheim Mohammed, Hadi, Najah R. and Hasoon, Tariq, 'Iraq lacks facilities and expertise in emergency medicine', *British Medical Journal*, 333:847, 21 October 2006. www.BMJ.com.

108 Zarocastas, John, 'Exodus of medical staff strains Iraq's health facilities', *BMJ*, 334:865, 28 April 2007.

109 US Agency for International Development, *A Year in Iraq: Restoring Services*, May 2004. www.usaid.gov.

110 Compiled from Tables in Annex 2, Table 2: Teacher/Student Ratio for Universities and Colleges in UNESCO, *Iraq: Education in Transition*, pp. 77–80 of Annex 2.

111 Interview with a senior Iraqi working at WHO, Geneva, 13 November 2007.

112 VOI, 'Seven new universities to be established countrywide', 19 December 2007.

113 Munthe, Turi, 'Will harsh weed-out allow Iraqi academia to flower', *The Times Higher Education Supplement*, 25 July 2003. www.thes.co.uk.

114 United Nations University, *UNU calls for World Help to Repair System*, 27 April 2005. www.unu.edu.

115 Cave, 'Cheated of Future'.

116 Morgan, Tabitha, 'Murder of lecturers threatens Iraqi academia', *The Times Higher Education Supplement*, 10 September 2004; lecture given by Prof. Saad Jawad of Baghdad University at SOAS, London, 22 January 2008.

117 Cave, 'Cheated of Future'.

118 The Iraq War & Archaeology Blog, 'Academics in Iraq: a vanishing breed', 16 November 2006. iwa.univi.ac.at.

119 CARA, *Regional Programme for Iraqi Academics in Exile: a network of learning hubs*, 2008.

120 Stannard, Mathew B., 'Education Ministry kidnappings reflect plight of Iraqi academics', *The San Francisco Chronicle*, 15 November 2006. The professor is Abdul Sattar Jawad.

121 VOI, 'Sex, Religion, Politics – a prohibited Trinity for Iraqi writers', 24 March 2008. Quoted in Iraq Updates.

122 Interview with an Iraqi professor, Amman, 16 March 2008.

123 *IRIN*, 'Iraq: Higher education ministry tempts professionals with security, higher salaries', 31 January 2006.

124 Salusbury, Matt, 'Kurds plan to host American University', *The Times Higher Education Supplement*, 18 March 2007.

125 *Kurdish Globe*, 'Conference on higher education begins', 12 December 2007. Quoted in Iraq Updates.

126 In 2006, migrants from poor countries sent home $300 billion, about three times the world's foreign aid budgets combined. See Deparle, Jason, 'Western Union as a player in immigration debates', *International Herald Tribune*, 22 November 2007.

127 Gulf Centre for Strategic Studies, *Brain drain threatens future of Arab Science*, Cairo, May 2004.

128 BBC News, 'Huge cost of Iranian brain drain', 8 January 2007.

129 Özden, Çağlar and Schiff, Maurice (eds), *International Migration, Remittances & The Brain Drain*, Washington DC, World Bank and Palgrave McMillan, 2006.

130 Nolad, Marcus and Pack, Howard, *The Arab Economies in a Changing World*, Washington DC, Peterson Institute, 2007, pp. 180–181.

131 Ibid.

132 Acemoglu, Daron and Robinson, James A., *Economic Origins of Dictatorship and Democracy*, New York, Cambridge University Press, 2006, pp. 38–43.

133 Vedentam, Shankar, 'One Thing We Can't Build Alone in Iraq', *The Washington Post*, 29 October 2007. The article quotes Joseph Kopser an army major who was serving in Iraq.

134 *Financial Times*, 16 August 2007.

135 Shinn, David, 'Reversing the Brain Drain in Ethiopia', a lecture delivered to the Ethiopian North American Health Professionals Association, 23 November 2002.

136 Özden and Schiff, *International Migration*, pp. 227–244.

137 Testimony by Robert Malley, Middle East and North Africa Program Director, International Crisis Group to the Senate Armed Services Committee, 9 April 2008.

Chapter 7: Return and returnees

1 Kahar, Basim, 'Arabia' in *Shahadat*, p. 33. The play about Iraqis in Syria was shown in Damascus in 2004. For an interview with the playwright, see Ibid., pp. 21–26.

2 Dahya, Badr, 'Pakistanis in Britain: Transients or Settlers?', *Race*, 14/3 (1973), pp. 268–269.

3 Al-Rasheed, Madawi, 'The Myth of Return: Iraqi Arab and Assyrian Refugees in London', *Journal of Refugee Studies*, 7/2–3 (1994), p. 200.

4 Shoeb, Marwa, Weinstein, Harvey M. and Halpern, Jodi, 'Living in Religious Time and Space: Iraqi Refugees in Dearborn, Michigan', *Journal of Refugee Studies*, 20/3 (2007), pp. 441–460.

5 Zetter, Roger, 'Reconceptualizing the Myth of Return: Continuity and Transition Amongst the Greek-Cypriot Refugees of 1974', *Journal of Refugee Studies*, 12/1 (1999), p. 6.

6 Ibid.

7 Al-Rasheed, 'The Myth of Return', pp. 217–218.

8 UNHCR, *The State of the World's Refugees 2006*, Oxford, Oxford University Press, 2006, p. 18. See also Loescher, *The UNHCR and World Politics*, pp. 280–293.

9 UNHCR and International Peace Academy, *Healing the Wounds, Refugees, Reconstruction and Reconciliation*, Report of a conference, 30 June–1 July 1996.

10 Hassanen, Sadia, *Repatriation, Integration or Resettlement: The Dilemmas of Migration among Eritrean Refugees in Eastern Sudan*, Asmara, The Red Sea Press, 2007, pp. 175–176.

11 UNHCR, *The State of the World's Refugees*, p. 19.

12 Martin, Susan, 'Forced Migration and the Humanitarian Regime', in Kacowicz, Arie M. and Lutomski, Pawel (eds), *Population Resettlement in International Conflicts*, Maryland, Lexington Books, 2007, pp. 3–4.

13 Refugees International, *Uprooted and Unstable*, April 2008.

14 IRCO, *Iraqi Returnees From Syria*, Update 3, 19 February 2008.

15 UNHCR, *Iraq Situation Update*, 21 November 2007.

16 UNHCR, *Analysis of the Situation of Returns to Iraq*, February 2008.

17 *IRIN*, 'Iraq-Syria: More Iraqi refugees leaving Syria than entering', 28 November 2007.

18 DeYoung, Karen, 'Balkanized Homecoming', *The Washington Post*, 16 December 2006. The paper quotes MoDM's Minister, Abdul-Samad Rahman.

19 Ibid.

20 UNHCR, *Assessment on Returns to Iraq Amongst the Iraqi Refugee Population in Syria*, April 2008.

21 Fafo, *Iraqis in Jordan*, Table 2.14.

22 MoDM and IOM, *Returnee Monitoring and Needs Assessments*, Baghdad, January 2008; IRCO, *Iraqi Returnees from Syria*, Update 2, 30 December 2007.

23 MoDM and IOM, *Returnee Monitoring and Needs Assessments*, Tabulation Report, Baghdad March 2008.

24 Interview by telephone with Dr Said Hakki, Head of Iraqi Red Crescent, 20 May 2008.

25 UNHCR, *Iraq Situation*, April 2008.

26 Zetter, 'Reconceptualizing the Myth of Return', p. 5.

27 Habib, Naila, 'The Search for Home', *Journal of Refugee Studies*, 9/1 (1996), p. 101.

28 Wanche, *An Assessment of the Iraqi Community*, pp. 51–53.

29 The World Bank, *The Road Not Traveled*, pp. 266–267.

30 IRCO, *The Internally Displaced People in Iraq*, Update 33, 30 April 2008.

31 *IRIN*, 'Syria: Not safe enough for Iraqi refugees to return – UNHCR Chief', 14 February 2008.

32 Amnesty International, *Iraq: Rhetoric and Reality*, p. 30.

33 Aswat Al-Iraq, 'Investigations', 4 December 2007. www.aswataliraq.info.

34 Interview with an Iraqi doctor in Cairo, 26 April 2008.

35 Elizabeth Ferris, *The Looming Crisis: Iraqi Displacement and Security*, The Brookings Institution, April 2008, p. 3.

36 Pincus, Walter, 'Iraq's Slow Refugee Funding Has Ripple Effect', *The Washington Post*, 17 May 2008. The article quotes Kristele Younes from Refugees International.

37 Levinson, Charles, 'Fall in violence lures Iraqis back to homes they fled', *USA Today*, 5 May 2008.

38 VOI, 'Iraq wants refugees to return home – PM', 31 May 2008. The statements were made during a visit to Sweden.

39 Majlis Al-Nuwab (Council of Representatives), 'Head of Displacement and Migration Committee meets Iraqi Red Crescent', 2 June 2008. Details of sessions and activities of parliament can be found on: www.parliament.iq.

40 *Al-Sabaah*, 2 June 2008.

41 Buckley, Cara, 'Iraqi Refugees Return, and Are Stranded', *The New York Times*, 20 December 2007.

42 *Azzaman*, 18 August 2008.

43 Zetter, 'Reconceptualizing the Myth of Return', p. 9.

44 Rose, *The Dispossessed*, p. 1.

45 For a general background of this period, see Romano, David, 'Whose House is this Anyway? IDP and Refugee Return in Post-Saddam Iraq', *Journal of Refugee Studies*, 18/4 (December 2005), pp. 430–453.

46 For a comprehensive review of the IPCC and its shortcomings, see Housing and Land Rights Network, Habitat International Coalition, *Restoring Values*, August 2005.

47 Section Four – General Principles, Article Eight, L. For the full law, see Scott, Leakie (ed.), *Housing, Land and Property Restitution of Rights of Refugees and Displaced Persons: Laws, Cases and Materials*, New York, Cambridge University Press, 2007, pp. 319–334.

48 Ibid., pp. 334–340.

49 Van der Auweraert, Peter, 'Property Restitution in Iraq', Presentation at the Symposium on Post-Conflict Property Restitution, Hosted by the Bureau of Population, Refugees, and Migration, US Department of State, Arlington, Virginia, 6–7 September 2007, p. 4.

50 Ibid., p. 10.

51 IOM, *Iraq Property Claims Programme*, June 2007.

52 Ferris, *The Looming Crisis*, p. 51.

53 MoDM & IOM, *Returnee Monitoring*, Tables 15 and 16.

54 Prettitore, Paul, 'Return and Resettlement as a Result of Ethnic Cleansing in Post-Conflict Former Yugoslavia', in Kacowicz, Arie M. and Lutomski, Pawel (eds), *Population Resettlement in International Conflicts*, Maryland, Lexington Books, 2007, p. 94.

55 Housing and Land Rights, *Restoring Values*, p. 34. See also Williams, Rhodri C., 'The Significance of Property Restitution to Sustainable Return in Bosnia and Herzegovina', *International Migration*, 44/3 (2006), pp. 39–61.

56 Davies, Ann, 'Restitution of land and property rights', *Forced Migration Review*, Issue 21 (September 2004), pp. 12–14.

57 Gordon, Michael R. and Farrell, Stephen, 'Iraq Lacks Plan on the Return of Refugees, Military Says', *The New York Times*, 30 November 2007.

58 Williams, Rhodri C., *Applying the lessons of Bosnia in Iraq: Whatever the Solution, Property Rights Should be Secured*, The Brookings Institution, 18 March 2008.

59 See, for example *Al-Sabaah*, 'Plans to build houses for displaced people', 22 January 2008; *Al-Sabaah*, 'Babel governor: building 10,000 houses in Babel', 19 March 2008.

60 Economic and Social Council Commission on Human Rights, 'Housing and Property Restitution in the Context of the Return of Refugees and Internally Displaced Persons', 28 June 2005, E/CN.4/Sub.2/2005/17, *Refugee Survey Quarterly*, 24/3 (2005), p. 139.

Conclusion

1 Sanders, Ben and Smith, Merrill, 'The Iraqi Refugee Disaster', *World Policy Journal*, Fall 2007, p. 23.

2 Rubin, Trudy, 'Worldview: Bush shamefully flees Iraqi refugees crisis', *The Philadelphia Inquirer*, 2 April 2008.

3 Abramowitz, Morton, 'The shortchanging of Iraqi refugees', *Los Angeles Times*, 23 June 2008.

4 Ibid.

5 For advice to US Presidential candidates, see Ferris, Elizabeth, *Prepare for the Iraqi Humanitarian Crisis: Open Letter to the U.S. Presidential Candidates*, The Brookings Institution, 29 February 2008.

6 Ackerman, Gary L., Chairman, House Subcommittee on the Middle East & South Asia, 'No Direction Home: An NGO Perspective on Iraqi Refugees and IDPs', in Joint Hearing with the Subcommittee on International Organizations, Human Rights and Oversight, 1 May 2008.

7 *IRIN*, 'Iraq: Government negligent in tackling human displacement – MP', 13 May 2008. *IRIN* quotes MP Abdul-Khaliq Zankana.

8 United Press International, 'MP: Region at risk from Iraqi refugees', 21 June 2008.

9 Ibid.

10 *Azzaman*, 8 May 2008.

11 Rosen, Nir, 'No Going Back', *Boston Review*, September/October 2007. www.bostonreview.net.

12 See interesting anecdotes in Massing, Michael, 'As Iraqis See It', *The New York Review of Books*, 17 January 2008. The McClatchy blog, 'Inside Iraq', mentioned above, has many stories about daily life under the occupation. washingtonbureau.typepad.com.

13 Al-Mufti, Nermeen, 'No place to go', *Al-Ahram Weekly*, Issue 842, 26 April–2 May 2007.

14 Stiglitz, Joseph and Bilmes, Linda J., *The Three Trillion Dollar War: The True Cost of the Iraq Conflict*, New York, Norton, 2008. See reviews of the book in *The Economist*, 15 March 2008; *Financial Times*, 3 March 2008.

15 Rose, *The Dispossessed*, p. 329.

16 Malley, 'Testimony to Senate Armed Services'.

17 Rubin, 'Worldview: Bush'.

18 Bruno, Greg, 'A Long Road for Iraq's Refugees', *The Washington Post*, 27 May 2008.

19 Ferris, *Security, Displacement and Iraq*, p. 17.

20 Fearson, James, 'Iraq's Civil Affairs', *Foreign Affairs*, March/April 2007.

21 Rosen, 'No Going Back'.

22 See, for example VOI, 'Iraq must promote culture of tolerance over violence – Al-Maliki', 20 March 2008.

23 *Financial Times*, 'Interview with General David Petraeus, the top US Commander in Iraq', 4 September 2008.

Bibliography

Published works

Abbud, Salam, *Thaqaft Al-'Unf fi Al-Iraq* (The Culture of Violence in Iraq), Köln, Germany, Al-Kamel Verlay, 2002.

Abramowitz, Morton, 'The shortchanging of Iraqi refugees', *Los Angeles Times*, 23 June 2008.

Acemoglu, Daron and Robinson, James A., *Economic Origins of Dictatorship and Democracy*, New York, Cambridge University Press, 2006.

Ackerman, Gary L., 'No Direction Home: An NGO Perspective on Iraqi Refugees and IDPs', in Joint Hearing with the Subcommittee on International Organizations, Human Rights and Oversight, 1 May 2008.

Al-Adhami, Mundher, 'Refugees or angry citizens', *Al-Ahram Weekly*, Issue 838, 29 March–4 April 2007.

Al-Ahram Weekly, 'The need to move fast', interview with King Abdullah II of Jordan, Issue 844, 10–16 May 2007. http://weekly.ahram.org.eg.

Alam, Hannah, 'Illiteracy increasing among Iraq's refugee children', *McClatchy Newspapers*, 11 December 2007. www.mcclatchydc.com.

Al-Ali, Nadje Sadig, *Iraqi Women: Untold Stories from 1948 to the Present* London, Zed Books, 2007.

Al-Ali, Zaid, 'The IMF and the Future of Iraq', *Middle East Report Online*, 7 December 2004. www.merip.org.

Allawi, Ali, *The Occupation of Iraq: Winning the War, Losing the Peace*, New Haven, Yale University Press, 2007.

Alnasrawi, Abbas, 'Long-term Consequences of War and Sanctions', in Mahdi Kamil A. (ed.), *Iraq's Economic Predicament*, Reading, Ithaca Press, 2002, pp. 343–348.

———, *Iraq's Burdens: Oil, Sanctions and Underdevelopment*, Connecticut, Greenwood Press, 2002.

Alwan, Ala'din, *Health in Iraq: The Current Situation, Our vision for the Future, and Areas of Work*, Ministry of Health, Second Edition, December 2004.

Amnesty International, *The Situation of Iraqi Refugees in Syria*, 26 July 2007. www.amnesty.org.

————, *Refugee crisis unfolds amid global apathy*, 24 September 2007.

————, *Iraq: Rhetoric and Reality: The Iraqi Refugee Crisis*, 15 June 2008.

Anderson, John Lee, 'Inside the Surge', Letter from Iraq, *The New Yorker*, 19 November 2007, pp. 58–69.

Apps, Peter, 'Alone, Iraq's teenage migrants head for Sweden', Reuters, 17 October 2007. www.alertnet.org.

Backer, Stina, 'Iraqis choose Sweden as new home', BBC News, 6 July 2007.

Bancroft-March, Carolyn, 'Becoming a Refugee', The American University in Cairo website, 12 March 2008. www.aucegypt.edu.

Barakat, Sultan, 'Post-Saddam Iraq: deconstructing a regime, reconstructing a nation', *Third World Quarterly*, 26/4–5 (2005), pp. 571–591.

Baram, Amatzia, 'Neo-Tribalism in Iraq: Saddam Hussein's Tribal Policies 1991–96', *International Journal of Middle East Studies*, 29/1 (February 1997), pp. 1–31.

Batatu, Hanna, *The Old Social Classes and the Revolutionary Movement of Iraq*, New Jersey, Princeton University Press, 1978.

Bendix, Reinhard, *From Berlin to Berkeley*, New Jersey, New Brunswick, 1986.

Betts, Alexander, 'International Cooperation Between North and South to Enhance Refugee Protection in Regions of Origin', Working Paper Series, Refugee Studies Centre, University of Oxford, July 2005.

Billing, Leila, 'Iraq's children pay the price of war', *Forced Migration Review*, Special Issue (June 2007), pp. 42–43.

Billion, Philippe Le, 'Corruption, Reconstruction and Oil Governance in Iraq', *Third World Quarterly*, 26/4–5 (2005), pp. 685–703.

Billström, Tobias, 'Statement at the International Conference hosted by UNHCR', Geneva, 17–18 April 2007.

Brand, Laurie A., *Jordan's Inter-Arab Relations: The Political Economy of Alliance Making*, New York, Columbia University Press, 1994.

Bremer III, L. Paul, *My Year in Iraq: The Struggle to Build a Future of Hope*, New York, Simon & Schuster, 2006.

The Brookings Institution, *Iraq Index*, Tracking Variables of Reconstruction & Security in Post-Saddam Iraq, 30 May 2006–29 May 2008. www.brookings/edu/iraqindex.

Brownstein, Catherine A. and Brownstein, John S., 'Estimating Excess Mortality in Post-Invasion Iraq', *The New England Journal of Medicine*, 31 January 2008, pp. 445–447.

Brulliard, Karin, 'Saddam-era rule restored to retain doctors', *Los Angeles Times*, 7 May 2007.

Bruno, Greg, 'A Long Road for Iraq's Refugees', *The Washington Post*, 27 May 2008.

BRussells Tribunal, People vs Total War Incorporated. www.brusselstribunal.org/academicsList.htm.

Buck, Tobias, 'Oil price poses threat to Jordan's stability', *Financial Times*, 5–6 April 2008.

Buckley, Cara, 'Iraqi Refugees Return, and Are Stranded', *The New York Times*, 20 December 2007.

Burham, Gilbert, Doocy, Shannon, Dzeng, Elizabeth, Lafta, Riyadh and Roberts, Les, *The Human Cost of the War in Iraq: A Mortality Study, 2002–2006*, Johns Hopkins University, 2006.

———, Doocy, Shannon, Lafta, Riyadh and Roberts, Les, 'Mortality after the 2003 invasion of Iraq: a cross-sectional cluster sample survey', *The Lancet*, 11 October 2006, pp. 1–9. www.thelancet.com.

Cambanis, Thanassis, 'Syria Shuts main Exit from War for Iraqis', *The New York Times*, 20 October 2007.

Council for Assisting Refugee Academics (CARA), *Regional Programme for Iraqi Academics in Exile: a network of learning hubs* (2008).

Carle, Alexandre and Chkam Hakim, *Humanitarian action in the new security environment: policy and operational implications in Iraq*, Humanitarian Policy Group, 2006.

Cave, Damien, 'Cheated of Future, Iraqi Graduates want to Flee', *The New York Times*, 4 June 2007.

Chandrasekaran, Rajiv, 'This Time Around War Would Hit Iraq Harder', *The Washington Post*, 29 October 2002.

Chatelard, Géraldine, *Iraqi Forced Migrants in Jordan: Conditions, Religious Networks, and the Smuggling Process*, Robert Schuman Centre for Advanced Studies, European University Institute, Working Papers, RSC no. 2002/49.

———, *Incentives to Transit: Policy Responses to Influxes of Iraqi Forced Migrants in Jordan*, Robert Schuman Centre for Advanced Studies, European University Institute, Working Papers, RSC no. 2002/50.

———, *Jordan as a transit country: semi protectionist immigration policies and their effects on Iraqi forced migrants*, Robert Schuman Centre for Advanced Studies, European University Institute, Working Paper no. 61, August 2002.

———, *From One War to Another: Iraqi Emigration to Jordan*, Institute for the Study of International Migration (ISIM), Newsletter 13, December 2003.

———, 'L'émigration des Irakiens de la guerre du Golfe à la guerre d'Irak (1990–2003)', in Jaber, H. and Métral, F. (eds), *Mondes en mouvements, Migrants et migration au Moyen-Orient au tournant du XXIe siècle*, Institut Français du Proche Orient, Beirut, 2005, pp. 113–155.

———, 'Emigrating from Iraq in the period 1991–2007: social networks as alternatives for international protection', Presentation at IACIS Conference, Amman, 11–13 June 2007.

————, Washington, Kate and El-Abed, Oroub, *Iraqi Refugees and Exiles in Jordan and Syria: A Proposal for Initiatives on the Part of the Open Society Institute*, November 2007.

————, Washington, Kate and El-Abed, Oroub, *An Assessment of Services Provided for Vulnerable Iraqis in Jordan*, Austcare, January 2008.

Chen, Siyan, Loayza, Norman V. and Reynal-Querol, Marta, 'The Aftermath of Civil War', *The World Bank Economic Review*, 22/1 (2008), pp. 63–85.

Clark, Kate, 'Corruption in Iraqi Kurdistan', BBC News, 11 January 2008.

Cohen, Roberta, 'Iraq: The Human Cost of War', Panel Discussion on the Humanitarian Situation in Iraq, Georgetown University, 21 March 2007.

Cohen, Roger, 'Closing the door to an Iraqi Mandela', *International Herald Tribune*, 27 September 2007.

Committee on the Judiciary United States Senate, 'The Plight of Iraqi Refugees', One Hundred Tenth Congress, First Session, 16 January 2007.

Congressional Research Service (CRS), *Iraqi Refugees and Internally Displaced Persons: A Deepening Humanitarian Crisis?*, CRS Report for Congress, 3 October 2007. www.fas.org.

Cordesman, Anthony H., *Iraq's Sectarian and Ethnic Violence and Its Evolving Insurgency: Development through Spring 2007*, Center for Strategic and International Studies (CSIS), 2 April 2007. www.cisi.org.

Dahya, Badr, 'Pakistanis in Britain: Transients or Settlers?' *Race*, 14/3 (1973), pp. 241–277.

Dakkak, Henia, 'Tackling sexual violence, abuse and exploitation, *Forced Migration Review*, Special Issue (June 2007), pp. 39–40.

Danish Refugee Council, *Iraqi population in Lebanon*, Survey report, Beirut, July 2005. www.drc.dk.

————, *Iraqi population Survey in Lebanon*, November 2007.

Davies, Ann, 'Restitution of land and property rights', *Forced Migration Review*, Issue 21 (September 2004), pp. 12–14.

Davis, Eric, *Memories of State: Politics, History, and Collective Identity in Modern Iraq*, Berkeley, University of California Press, 2005.

de Torrente, Nicholas, 'Humanitarian Action Under Attack: Reflections on the Iraq War', *Harvard Human Rights Journal*, vol. 17 (Spring 2004), pp. 1–29.

Dempsey, Judy, 'Germany to press EU over Iraqi refugees', *International Herald Tribune*, 17 April 2008.

Deparle, Jason, 'Western Union as a player in immigration debates', *International Herald Tribune*, 22 November 2007.

Department of Defense, *Measuring Stability and Security in Iraq*, Report to Congress, March 2007. www.defenselink.mil.

———, *Measuring Stability and Security in Iraq*, Report to Congress, 14 September 2007.

DeYoung, Karen, 'Balkanized Homecoming', *The Washington Post*, 16 December 2006.

Dodge, Toby, 'State Collapse and the Rise of Identity Politics', in Bouillon, Markus, E., Malone, David M. and Rowswell, Ben (eds), *Iraq, Preventing A New Generation of Conflict*, Colorado, Reinner, 2007.

Dorai, Mohamed Kamel, 'The Social Networks of Iraqis in Damascus', Presentation at the Second Conference of the International Association of Contemporary Iraqi Studies (IACIS), Philadelphia University, Jordan, 11–13 June 2007.

Doward, Jamie, 'Refugees fight forced return to Iraq war zones', *The Observer*, 13 April 2008.

Dugan, Emily, '"Inhumane and oppressive": the final verdict on Britain's asylum policy', *The Independent*, 27 March 2008.

Economic and Social Council Commission on Human Rights, 'Housing and Property Restitution in the Context of the Return of Refugees and Internally Displaced Persons', 28 June 2005, E/CN.4/Sub.2/2005/17, *Refugee Survey Quarterly*, 24/3 (2005), pp. 136–149.

Ekman, Ivar, 'Far From War, a Town with a Well-Used Welcome Mat', *The New York Times*, 13 June 2007.

Engel, Matthew, 'The new face of Sweden', *Financial Times*, 19–20 January 2008.

England, Andrew, 'Riyadh and Cairo to cut import duties', *Financial Times*, 2 April 2008.

European Council on Refugees and Exiles (ECRE), *Guidelines on The Treatment of Iraqi Asylum Seekers and Refugees in Europe*, April 2007. www.ecre.org/resources.

Ezzat, Dina, 'Problems by the dozen', *Al-Ahram Weekly*, Issue 842, 26 April–2 May 2007.

———, 'From one hell to another', *Al-Ahram Weekly*, Issue 845, 17–23 May 2007.

Fafo, *Iraqis in Jordan, Their Number and Characteristics*, November 2007. www.fafo.no.

———, *The Syrian Labour Market, Findings from the 2003 Unemployment Survey*, Fafo-report 2007:02.

Fagen, Patricia Weiss, *Iraqi Refugees: Seeking Stability in Syria and Jordan*, Institution for the Study of International Migration (ISIM), 2007. www.georgetown.edu.

Farrell, Stephen, 'Iraq Bomber Aimed at Alcohol Sellers', *The New York Times*, 21 December 2007.

——— and Moore, Solomon, 'Iraq Attacks Fall 60 per cent, Petraeus Says', *The New York Times*, 30 December 2007.

Fawcett, John and Tanner, Victor, *The Internally Displaced People of Iraq*, The Brookings Institution, October 2002.

Fearson, James, 'Iraq's Civil Affairs', *Foreign Affairs*, March/April 2007.

Ferris, Elizabeth, *Iraqi Refugees: Our Problem or Sweden's?*, The Brookings Institution, 18 June 2007.

———, *Security, Displacement and Iraq: A Deadly Combination*, The Brookings-Bern Project on Internal Displacement, 27 August 2007. www.brookings.edu.

———, *Prepare for the Iraqi Humanitarian Crisis: Open Letter to the U.S. Presidential Candidates*, The Brookings Institution, 29 February 2008.

———, *The Looming Crisis: Iraqi Displacement and Security*, The Brookings Institution, April 2008.

——— and Hall, Matthew, *Update on Humanitarian Issues and Politics in Iraq*, The Brookings-Bern Project on Internal Displacement, 6 July 2007.

'The Federation of Iraqi Association Sweden (FIAS): History and Activity'. www.iraqifias.org.

Fidler, Stephen and Negus, Steve, 'Iraq death toll exceeds 150,000', *Financial Times*, 10 January 2008.

Firmo-Fontan, Victoria, 'Abducted, Beaten and Sold into Prostitution: A Tale from Iraq', *The Independent*, 26 July 2004.

FMR authors, 'Delivering is never remote: NGOs' vital role', *Forced Migration Review*, Special Issue (June 2007), pp. 27–29.

Foote, Christopher, Block, William, Crane, Keith and Gray, Simon, 'Economic Policy and Prospects in Iraq', *Journal of Economic Perspectives*, 18/3 (Summer 2004), pp. 47–70.

Foroohar, Kambiz, 'The Fight For Kurdistan's Oil', *Bloomberg Markets*, August 2007, pp. 96–105. www.bloomberg.com.

Frelick, Bill, 'Talk to Syria for the Sake of Iraqi Refugees', *HRW*, 16 October 2007.

Frontiers Association, *Legality vs. Legitimacy: Detention of Refugees and Asylum Seekers in Lebanon*, Legal Study, Beirut, May 2006. www.frontierassociation.org.

Gallager, Tom, *The Balkans in the New Millenium: In the Shadow of War and Peace*, New York, Routledge, 2005.

Gardiner, Beth, 'Iraqi refugees receive cold greeting in Britain', *International Herald Tribune*, 18 May 2007.

The Geneva Centre for the Democratic Control of Armed Forces (DCAF), *Sexual Violence in Armed Conflict*, Global Overview and Implications for the Security Sector, Geneva, 2007.

Gidley, Ruth, 'Aid world rethinks role in Iraq', AlertNet, 8 April 2004. www.alertnet.org.

Glantz, James, 'Iraqi Factories, Aging and Shut, Now Give Hope', *The New York Times*, 18 January 2007.

————, 'Billions in Oil Missing in Iraq, US Study Says', *The New York Times*, 12 May 2007.

————, 'Senate Committee Seeks Audit of Iraq Oil Money', *The New York Times*, 9 March 2008.

————, 'Iraqi shoe manufacturers survive through persistence and ingenuity', *International Herald Tribune*, 15 April 2008.

———— and Rubin, Alissa J., 'Future Look of Iraq Complicated by Internal Migration', *The New York Times*, 19 September 2007.

———— and Worth, Robert F., 'Attacks on Iraq Oil Industry Aid Vast Smuggling Scheme', *The New York Times*, 4 June 2006.

Godfrey, Hannah, 'From Baghdad to Britain', *The Guardian*, 20 March 2008.

Goode, Erica, 'Kidnapped Iraqi Archbishop is Dead', *The New York Times*, 14 March 2008.

Gordon, Michael R., 'Iraq Needs Strides in Economy and Government to Cut Attacks, a Top General Says', *The New York Times*, 3 March 2008.

———— and Farrell, Stephen, 'Iraq Lacks Plan on the Return of Refugees, Military Says', *The New York Times*, 30 November 2007.

———— and Rubin, Alissa J., 'Trial Nearer for Shiite Ex-Officials in Sunni Killings', *The New York Times*, 5 November 2007.

Grabska, Katarzyna, 'Marginalization in Urban Spaces of the Global South: Urban Refugees in Cairo', *Journal of Refugee Studies*, 19/3 (2006), pp. 287–307.

Greek Helsinki Monitor, 'Press Release: Refoulement of Iraqi Citizens to Greece–Common Statement by 16 NGOs', 1 August 2007. www.greekhelsinki.gr.

Gulf Centre for Strategic Studies, *Brain drain threatens future of Arab Science*, Cairo, May 2004.

Habib, Naila, 'The Search for Home', *Journal of Refugee Studies*, 9/1 (1996), pp. 96–102.

Hansen, Greg, *Coming to Terms with the Humanitarian Imperative in Iraq*, Feinstein International Center, January 2007.

————, *Taking Sides or Saving Lives: Existential Choices for the Humanitarian Enterprise in Iraq*, Humanitarian Agenda 2015, Iraq Country Study, Feinstein International Center, June 2007.

Harper, Andrew, 'Iraq: growing needs amid continuing displacement', *Forced Migration Review*, Issue 29 (December 2007), pp. 51–53.

————, 'Iraq's Refugees: Ignored and Unwanted', Unpublished Paper, January 2008.

Harriman, Ed, 'The Least Accountable Regime in the Middle East', *London Review of Books*, 2 November 2006.

Hassan, Nihal, '50,000 Iraqi refugees forced into prostitution', *The Independent*, 24 June 2007.

Hassanen, Sadia, *Repatriation, Integration or Resettlement: The Dilemmas of Migration among Eritrean Refugees in Eastern Sudan*, Asmara, The Red Sea Press, 2007.

Haynes, Deborah, 'Al-Qaeda bombing kills and maims 600', *The Times*, 16 August 2007.

Herring, Eric and Rangwala, Glen, *Iraq in Fragments: The Occupation and its Legacy*, London, Hurst & Company, 2006.

Al-Himaya, Foundation for Trauma Recovery, Growth and Resilience.

Hodson, Nathan, *Iraqi Refugees in Jordan: Cause for Concern in a Pivotal State*, The Washington Institute for Near East Policy, no. 13, April 2007.

Hoff, Karla and Stiglitz, Joseph E., 'After the Big Bang? Obstacles to the Emergence of the Rule of Law in Post-Communist Societies', *The American Economic Review*, 94/3 (June 2004), pp. 753–763.

House of Representatives, Resolution 734, 110th Congress, First Session, 11 October 2007. www.oversight.house.gov.

Housing and Land Rights Network, Habitat International Coalition, *Restoring Values*, August 2005.

Howard, Michael, 'As violence grows, oil rich Kirkuk could hold key to Iraq's future', *The Guardian*, 27 October 2006.

Human rights first, *US Resettles 974 Iraqi Refugees in April; Improvement Welcome but Comprehensive Response Still Needed*, 1 May 2008. www.humanrightsfirst.org.

Human Rights Watch (HRW), *Kuwait, Promised Betrayed: Denial of Rights of Bidun, Women and Freedom of Expression*, 12/(E) (October 2000).

——, *Iraqi Refugees, Asylum Seekers and Displaced Persons: Current Conditions and Concerns in the Event of War*, February 2003. www.hrw.org

——, *Iraq: Forcible Expulsion of Ethnic Minorities*, 15/3(E) (March 2003).

——, *Nowhere to Flee, the Perilous Situation of Palestinians in Iraq*, August 2006.

——, *The Silent Treatment: Fleeing Iraq, Surviving in Jordan*, 18/10(E) (November 2006).

——, *Egypt*, Country Summary, January 2007.

——, *Syria: Give Refuge to Palestinians Fleeing Threats in Iraq*, 2 February 2007.

——, *Iraq: From a Flood to a Trickle*, Neighboring States Stop Iraqis Fleeing War and Persecution, no. 1 (April 2007).

——, *No Room to Breathe: State Repression of Human Rights Activism in Syria*, 19/6 (October 2007).

——, *Rot Here or Die There: Bleak Choices for Iraqi Refugees in Lebanon*, 19/8(E) (November 2007).

Husaka, Anna, *With Iraqi Refugees in Jordan*, International Rescue Committee (IRC), 8 February 2007.

Immigration Here & There, *Iraqi refugees in Egypt seek secure education*, 24 July 2007. www.immigrationhereandthere.org.

The Independent Commission on the Security Forces of Iraq, *The Report of the Independent Commission on the Security Forces of Iraq*, 6 September 2007. media.csis.org/isf.pdf.

Integrated Regional Information Networks (IRIN), 'Iraq: Attacks on churches spur Christians to move to Kurdish north', 22 November 2004. www.irinnews.org.

———, 'Iraq: Higher education ministry tempts professionals with security, higher salaries', 31 January 2006.

———, 'Jordan: Limited access to justice for women', 23 February 2006.

———, 'Iraq: Country's healthcare system rapidly deteriorating', 7 November 2006.

———, 'Iraq: Neglected nurses fight their own war', 19 November 2006.

———, 'Iraq-Jordan: Iraqis cause black market for jobs', 28 March 2007.

———, 'Iraqis Justice delayed as lawyers live under threat', 30 April 2007.

———, 'Iraq-Syria: Iraqi doctors welcome refugee agency contributions to hospitals', 1 May 2007.

———, 'Iraq: Baghdad Christians flee as violence against them mounts', 3 May 2007.

———, Iraq-Syria: Plight of Palestinian refugees in border camps worsens', 27 June 2007.

———, 'Syria: Warning looming crisis as Iraqi refugee influx continues', 28 June 2007.

———, 'Yemeni Iraqi migrants, refugees await brighter future', 1 July 2007.

———, 'Iraq: Conflict jeopardising children's physical, mental health', 15 August 2007.

———, 'Iraq-Syria: Iraqi pledge to Syria fails to assuage refugees', 23 August 2007.

———, 'Blood sellers find market niche in Baghdad', 3 September 2007.

———, 'Iraq-Brazil: First group of Palestinians arrive in Brazil from desert camp', 23 September 2007.

———, 'Jordan: Some Iraqi refugees resort to begging', 1 October 2007.

———, 'Iraq: Insecurity and lack of funds prevent cleaning of polluted sites', 20 October 2007.

———, 'Iraq: Number of girls attending school dropping, say analysts', 29 October 2007.

———, 'Iraq: Christians seek new life in Europe', 5 November 2007.

———, 'Lebanon: Iraq refugees face prison and deportation', 6 November 2007.

———, 'Iraq: Refugees forced home as funds dry up', 13 November 2007.

———, 'Iraq: Diyala desperately needs doctors', 18 November 2007.

————, 'Jordan: Water contamination incidents highlight water shortage problem', 19 November 2007.

————, 'Iraq: Extremists fuel anti-women violence in Basra', 20 November 2007.

————, 'Iraq-Jordan: Iraq to give US$8 million to Jordan for hosting refugees', 28 November 2007.

————, 'Iraq-Syria: More Iraqi refugees leaving Syria than entering', 28 November 2007

————, 'Iraq-Jordan: Government introduces entry visas for Iraqis', 13 December 2007.

————, 'Iraq: Government to give financial aid to displaced in north', 31 December 2007.

————, 'Iraq-Syria: Starving to survive: Iraqi refugees resort to desperate measures', 2 January 2008.

————, 'Syria: Wealth gap widening as inflation hits poor', 7 February 2008.

————, 'Syria: Not safe enough for Iraqi refugees to return – UNHCR Chief', 14 February 2008.

————, 'Egypt: High rates of trauma, sickness among Iraqi refugees', 27 February 2008.

————, 'Iraq: Hospitals in Baghdad, Basra lack supplies – ICRC', 1 April 2008.

————, 'Iraq: Government negligent in tackling human displacement–MP', 13 May 2008.

Internal Displacement Monitoring Centre (IDMC), *Iraq: Sectarian violence, military operations spark new displacement, as humanitarian access deteriorates*, 23 May 2006. www.internal-displacement.org.

————, *Iraq: a displacement crisis*, 30 March 2007.

————, *Iraq: Population Figures and Profiles*, September 2007.

IDP Working Group, *Internally Displaced Persons in Iraq*, 24 March 2008.

International Advisory and Monitoring Board (IAMB) of the Development Fund for Iraq (DFI), *Report for the period 22 May 2003 to 28 June 2004*. www.iamb.info/dfiaudit.htm.

International Catholic Migration Commission (ICMC) and United States Conference of Catholic Bishops (USCCB), *Iraqi Refugees in Syria*, A Report of the ICMC-USCCB Mission to Assess the Protection Needs of Iraqi Refugees in Syria, April 2008. www.icmc.net.

International Committee of the Red Cross (ICRC), *Civilians Without Protection: The ever-worsening humanitarian crisis in Iraq*, 24 October 2007. www.icrc.org.

International Crisis Group, *The Next Iraq War? Sectarianism and Civil Conflict*, Middle East Report no. 52, 27 February 2006. www.crisisgroup.org.

————, *Failed Responsibility: Iraqi Refugees in Syria, Jordan and Lebanon*, Middle East Report no. 77, 10 July 2008.

International Labour Organization, *2003–2004 Key Indicators of the Labour Market*, Geneva 2003. www.ilo.org/kilm.

International Monetary Fund (IMF), *Syrian Arab Republic: Selected Issues*, IMF Country Report no. 06/295, August 2006. www.imf.org.

——, *IMF Executive Board Concludes 2007 Article IV Consultation with the Syrian Arab Republic*, Public Information Notice (PIN) no. 07/104, 15 August 2007.

——, *Syrian Arab Republic: 2007 Article IV Consultation–Staff Report: and Public Information Notice on the Executive Board Discussion*, IMF Country Report no. 07/280, August 2007.

——, *Iraq: 2007 Article IV Consultation, Fifth Review Under the Stand-By Agreement, Staff Report; Public Information and Press Release on the Executive Board Discussion; and Statement by the Executive Director for Iraq*, IMF Country Report no. 07/301, August 2007.

——, *Arab Republic of Egypt: 2007 Article IV Consultation Staff Report; Staff Statement; Public Information Notice on the Executive Board Discussion; and Statement by the Executive Director for the Arab Republic of Egypt*, IMF Country Report no. 07/380, December 2007.

——, *Lebanon: 2007 Article IV Consultation–Staff Report; Staff Statement; Public Information Notice on the Executive Board Discussion; and Statement by the Executive Director of Lebanon*, IMF Country Report no. 07/382, December 2007.

International Organization for Migration (IOM), *Capacity Building in Migration Management Programme* (CBMMP), 2005. www.iom-iraq.net.

——, *Iraq Displacement 2007 Mid-Year Review*.

——, *Iraq Property Claims Programme*, June 2007.

International Rescue Committee (IRC), *Five Years Later, A Hidden Crisis: Report of the IRC Commission on Iraqi Refugees*, March 2008.

Ipsos Public Affairs & Opinion Research, UNHCR Syria, *Survey of Iraqi Refugees*, Final Results, 31 October–25 November 2007.

Iraq Body Count project. www.iraqbodycount.org.

The Iraq War & Archaeology Blog, 'Academics in Iraq: a vanishing breed', 16 November 2006. iwa.univi.ac.at.

Iraqi Family Health Study Group (IFHS), 'Violence-Related Mortality in Iraq from 2002 to 2006', *The New England Journal of Medicine*, 31 January 2008, pp. 484–493. www.nejm.org.

Iraqi Red Crescent Organization (IRCO), *The Internally Displaced People in Iraq*, Update 27, 4 November 2007. www.iraqiredcrescent.org.

——, *Iraqi Returns from Syria*, Update 2, 30 December 2007.

——, *Iraqi Returnees From Syria*, Update 3, 19 February 2008.

——, *The Internally Displaced People in Iraq*, Update 33, 30 April 2008.

Jacobsen, Karen, 'Refugees and Asylum Seekers in Urban Areas: A Livelihoods Perspective', *Journal of Refugee Studies*, 19/3 (September 2006), pp. 273–286.

Jalili, Ismail, 'Plight of Iraqi Academics', presentation to the Madrid International Conference on the Assassinations of Iraqi Academics, 23–24 April 2006. www.iraqis.org.uk/contents.

Al-Jawaheri, Yasmin Husein, *Women in Iraq: The Gender Impact of International Sanctions*, London, I.B.Tauris, 2008.

Jelinek, Pauline, 'Pentagon Helping Restart Iraqi Factories', *The Washington Post*, 4 January 2007.

Kahar, Basim, 'Arabia', *Shahadat: Witnessing Iraq's Transformation after 2003*, Berlin, Friedrich Ebert Foundation, 2007, pp. 29–34.

Kessler, Glenn, 'Ex-Investigator Details Iraqi Corruption', *The Washington Post*, 5 October 2007.

Al-Khafaji, Isam, 'A Few Days After: State and society in a post-Saddam Iraq', in Dodge, Toby and Simon, Steven (eds), *Iraq at the Crossroads: State and Security in the Shadow of Regime Change*, London, Adelphi Papers, 2003, pp. 77–92.

al-Khalidi, Ashraf and Tanner, Victor, *Sectarian Violence: Radical Groups Drive Internal Displacement in Iraq*, The Brookings–Bern Project on Internal Displacement, October 2006. www.brookings.edu.

———, Ashraf, Hoffman, Sophia and Tanner, Victor, *Iraqi Refugees in The Syrian Arab Republic: A Field-Based Snapshot*, The Brookings Institute–University of Bern Project on Internal Displacement, June 2007. www.brookings-bern.edu.

Al-Khalisi, Isam, 'Ministry doctors figures on power output', *Azzaman*, 7 April 2008.

Kino, Nuri, *By God: Six days in Amman*, 16 June 2007. www.humanrightsblog.org.

KPMG, *Reports submitted to DFI for the period 1 January 2004 to 28 June 2004*.

Kushner, Tony and Knox, Katherine, *Refugees in an age of genocide: Global, National and Local Perspectives during the Twentieth Century*, London, Frank Cass, 1999.

Ladek, Dana Graber, 'IOM–building Iraqi capacity and assisting IDPs', *Forced Migration Review*, Special Issue (June 2007), pp. 50–51.

Lamassu, Nineb, 'The plight of the Iraqi Christians', *Forced Migration Review*, Special Issue (June 2007), pp. 44–45.

Lando, Ben, 'Analysis: Iraq's Oil Smuggling', Parts I and II, *United Press International*, quoted in Iraq Updates, 15 December 2006.

Lasensky, Scott, *Jordan and Iraq–Between Cooperation and Crisis*, United States Institute of Peace, Special Report 178, December 2006. www.usip.org.

Lattimer, Mark, 'In 20 years, there will be no more Christians in Iraq', *The Guardian*, 6 October 2006.

Lazarus, Emma, 'The New Colosssus', poem on the Statue of Liberty National Monument.

Lee, Laurence, 'Little solace for Iraqis in Sweden', Al-Jazeera, 20 August 2007. www.english.aljazeera.net.

Lee, Matthew, 'US Falls Short of Iraqi Refugees Goal', *The Washington Post*, 31 October 2007.

Levinson, Charles, 'Fall in violence lures Iraqis back to homes they fled', *USA Today*, 5 May 2008.

Leyne, John, 'Iraqi medical crisis as doctors flee', BBC News, 22 March 2007.

Loesher, Gil, *The UNHCR and World Politics*, Oxford, Oxford University Press, 2001.

MADRE, *Promising Democracy, Imposing Theocracy: Gender-Based Violence and the US War on Iraq*, New York, 2007. www.madre.org.

Mahmoud, Mona and Lauchin, Mike, 'Basra Militias targeting women', *BBC World Service*, 15 November 2007.

Majlis Al-Nuwab (Council of Representatives), 'Head of Displacement and Migration Committee meets Iraqi Red Crescent', 2 June 2008. www.parliament.iq.

Malley, Robert, 'Testimony to the Senate Armed Services Committee', 9 April 2008.

Mansur, Yusuf, 'Improving the Economy', *The Jordan Times*, 9 October 2007.

Maples, Lt. Gen. Michael, Defense Intelligence Agency, 'Testimony for the Senate Armed Service Committee', 27 February 2007. www.house.gov.

Marfleet, Philip, *Refugees in a Global Era*, New York, Palgrave Macmillan, 2006.

——, 'Iraq's refugees: "exit" from the state', *International Journal of Contemporary Iraqi Studies*, 1/3 (October 2007), pp. 397–419.

Marr, Phebe, *The Modern History of Iraq*, Boulder, Westview Press 1985.

Martin, Susan, 'Forced Migration and the Humanitarian Regime', in Kacowicz, Arie M. and Lutomski, Pawel (eds), *Population Resettlement in International Conflicts*, Maryland, Lexington Books, 2007, pp. 1–19.

Massing, Michael, 'As Iraqis See It', *The New York Review of Books*, 17 January 2008.

Mazloom, Mohamed, 'Nightmare of the Returning Gilgamesh', *Shahadat: Witnessing Iraq's Transformation after 2003*, Berlin, Friedrich Ebert Foundation, 2007, pp. 81–85.

McDonald, Mark, 'Iraqis May Not Welcome Invading U.S. Troops as Liberators', *Miami Herald*, 17 December 2002.

McLeod, Hugh, 'Despair of Baghdad turns into a life of shame in Damascus', *The Guardian*, 24 October 2006.

Medact, *Communiqué*, no. 43 (Spring 2006). www.medact.org.

Médecins Sans Frontières, *Responding to Iraq's Emergency*, 4 February 2007. www.msf.org.

Megiffin, Janet, 'No Work for Doctors', The American University in Cairo website, 12 March 2008. www.aucegypt.edu.

Mervin, Sabrina, 'Sayyida Zaynab [sic], Banlieue de Damas ou nouvelle ville sainte chiite?' *Cemoti*, no. 22 (July–December 1996).

Merza, Ali, 'Iraq: reconstruction under uncertainty', *International Journal of Contemporary Iraqi Studies*, 1/2 (2007), pp. 173–212.

Milligan, Rebecca, 'The Other Casualties of War in Iraq', *Middle East Report*, no. 239 (Summer 2006), pp. 26–27.

Ministry of Displacement and Migration (MoDM) & International Organization of Migration (IOM), *Returnee Monitoring and Needs Assessments*, Baghdad, January 2008. www.modm-iraq.net.

———, *Returnee Monitoring and Needs Assessments*, Tabulation Report, Baghdad, March 2008.

Ministry of Health, Ministry of Planning and WHO, *Chronic Non-Communicable Diseases: Risk Factors Survey in Iraq*, 2006. www.emro.who.int/iraq.

Al-Miqdad, Faisal, 'Iraq Refugees in Syria, *Forced Migration Review*, Special Issue (June 2007), pp. 19–20.

Mizan, 'Know your rights and protect yourself Campaign'. www.mizangroup. jo.

Mokbel, Madona, 'Refugees in Limbo: The Plight of Iraqis in Bordering States', *Middle East Report*, no. 244 (Fall 2007), pp. 10–17.

Mongalvy, Sophie, 'Transition classes ease Iraqi kids into Swedish way of life', Middle East Online, quoted in Iraq Updates, 18 February 2008. www.iraqupdates.com.

Moore, Solomon, 'Secret Iraqi Deal Shows Problems in Arms Orders', *The New York Times*, 13 April 2008.

Moore, Will H. and Shellman, Stephen M., 'Fear of Persecution: Forced Migration, 1952–1995', *Journal of Conflict Resolutions*, 48/5 (October 2004), pp. 723–745.

Morgan, Tabitha, 'Murder of lecturers threatens Iraqi academia', *The Times Higher Education Supplement*, 10 September 2004.

Moubayed, Sami, 'Back in Damascus', *Al-Ahram Weekly*, Issue 839, 5–11 April 2007.

Al-Mufti, Nermeen, 'No place to go', *Al-Ahram Weekly*, Issue 842, 26 April–2 May 2007.

Al-Muhammad, Muhyi Al-Din, 'The Iraqis are not looking for repatriation because that is not a solution', *Tishreen*, 22 April 2007.

Munthe, Turi, 'Will harsh weed-out allow Iraqi academia to flower', *The Times Higher Education Supplement*, 25 July 2003. www.thes.co.uk.

Murad, Nermeen, 'Jordan's legacy', *The Jordan Times*, 30 July 2007.

National Intelligence Council (NIC), 'Prospect for Iraq's Stability: Some Security Progress but Political Reconciliation Elusive', *National Intelligence Estimate*, August 2007. www.dni.gov.

Nolad, Marcus and Pack, Howard, *The Arab Economies in a Changing World*, Washington DC, Peterson Institute, 2007.

O'Donnell, Kelly and Newland, Kathleen, *The Iraqi Refugee Crisis: The Need for Action*, Migration Policy Institute, 2008. www.migrationpolicy.org.

Office for Coordination of Humanitarian Affairs (OCHA), *Humanitarian Crisis in Iraq: Facts and Figures*, 13 November 2007. www.ochaonline.org.

O'Hanlon, Michael, *Iraq's Unknown Economy*, The Brookings Institution, 6 January 2008.

Olszewska, Zuzanna, 'Selected Poems by Afghan Refugees in Iran', a lecture given at The British Academy Conference on 'Dispossession and Displacement: Forced Migration in the Middle East and Africa', London, 28–29 February 2008.

Oppel, Richard A., 'Iraq Insurgency Runs on Stolen Oil Profits', *The New York Times*, 16 March 2008.

Owen, Roger, 'Reconstructing the performance of the Iraqi economy 1950–2006: an essay with some hypotheses and many questions', *International Journal of Contemporary Iraqi Studies*, 1/1 (2007), pp. 93–101.

Oxfam, *Rising to the Humanitarian Challenge in Iraq*, 30 July 2007. www.oxfam.org.uk.

Özden, Çağlar and Schiff, Maurice (eds), *International Migration, Remittances & The Brain Drain*, Washington DC, World Bank and Palgrave McMillan, 2006.

Pachachi, Adnan, 'Iraq at Crossroads', Lecture given by Dr Pachachi at St Antony's College, Oxford, 15 November 2006.

Packer, George, *The Assassin's Gate*, New York, Farrar, Straus and Giroux, 2005.

———, 'Planning for Defeat', *The New Yorker*, 17 September 2007.

———, *Betrayed*, play at the Culture Project Theater, New York, February 2008.

Palmer, James, 'Frequent targets of violence, Iraqi physicians flee in droves', *The Seattle Times*, 4 April 2006. www.seatlletimes.nwsource.com.

———, 'Trauma severe for Iraqi Children', *USA Today*, 16 April 2007. www.usatoday.com.

Parker, Christopher and Moore, Pete W., 'The War Economy of Iraq', *Middle East Report*, no. 243 (Summer 2007), pp. 6–15.

Patience, Martin, 'UN staff relive Iraqi refugee horror', BBC News, Damascus, 19 September 2007.

Pérez-Peña, Richard, 'The War Endures, but Where's the Media?', *The New York Times*, 24 March 2008.

Al-Perleman Al-Iraqi, 'The State of Iraqi Doctors in Amman', 8 September 2007. www.drweb4u.net.

Perthes, Volker, 'Syrian Regional Policy under Bashar Al-Asad: Realignment or Economic Rationalization?', *Middle East Report*, no. 220 (Fall 2001), pp. 36–41.

Peteet, Julie, 'Unsettling the Categories of Displacement', *Middle East Report*, no. 244 (Fall 2007), pp. 2–9.

Pew Research Center Publications, *Iraq Portrait: How the Press Has Covered Events on the Ground*, 19 December 2007. www.pewresearch.org. Full report at www.journalism.org.

Phillips, David L., *Losing Iraq*, New York, Westview Press, 2005.

Phillips, Joshua E.S., 'Unveiling Iraq's teenage prostitutes', 24 June 2005. www.salon.com.

Pincus, Walter, 'Iraq's Slow Refugee Funding Has Ripple Effect', *The Washington Post*, 17 May 2008.

Pipes, Daniel, 'The Alawi Capture of Power in Syria', *Middle Eastern Studies*, 25/4 (October 1989), pp. 429–450.

Pollack, Kenneth M., *A Switch in Time: A New Strategy for America in Iraq*, Saban Centre for Middle East Policy at the Brookings Institution, February 2006.

Power, Samantha, 'The Envoy', The United Nations' doomed mission to Iraq, *The New Yorker*, 7 January 2008.

Prettitore, Paul, 'Return and Resettlement as a Result of Ethnic Cleansing in Post-Conflict Former Yugoslavia', in Kacowicz & Lutomski (eds), *Population Resettlement in International Conflicts*, Maryland, Lexington Books, 2007, pp. 79–98.

Raghavan, Sudarsan, 'Distrust Breaks the Bonds of a Baghdad Neighbourhood', *The Washington Post*, 27 September 2006.

———, 'Iraqis with Ties to U.S. Cross Border Into Despair', *The Washington Post*, 17 November 2007.

Rajee, Bahram, 'The Politics of Refugee Policy in Post-revolutionary Iran', *Middle East Journal*, 54/1 (Winter 2000), pp. 44–63.

Raphaeli, Nimrod, 'Syria's Fragile Economy', *Middle East Review of International Affairs (MERIA)*, vol. 11 (June 2007), pp. 34–51.

Al-Rasheed, Madawi, 'Political migration and downward socio-economic mobility: The Iraqi community in London', *New Community*, 18/4 (July 1992), pp. 537–550.

———, 'The Myth of Return: Iraqi Arab and Assyrian Refugees in London', *Journal of Refugee Studies*, 7/2–3 (1994), pp. 199–219.

Refugees International, *The World's Fastest Growing Displacement Crisis*, March 2007. www.refugees.international.org.

————, *Egypt: Respond to the needs of Iraqi refugees*, 12 April 2007.

————, *Iraqi refugees: Time for the UN system to fully engage*, 27 July 2007.

————, *A lot of Talk, Little Action*, 14 November 2007.

————, *Uprooted and Unstable*, April 2008.

Republic of Iraq and WHO, *Iraq Family Health Survey Report*, IFHS 2006/2007, January 2008. www.who.int.

Ricks, Thomas E., 'Iraqis Wasting An Opportunity, US Officers Say', *The Washington Post*, 15 November 2005.

Romano, David, 'Whose House is this Anyway? IDP and Refugee Return in Post-Saddam Iraq', *Journal of Refugee Studies*, 18/4 (December 2005) pp. 430–453.

Rose, Peter I. (ed.), *The Dispossessed: An Anatomy of Exile*, Amherst, University of Massachusetts Press, 2005.

Rosen, Nir, 'The Flight from Iraq', *The New York Times*, 13 May 2007.

————, 'No Going Back', *Boston Review*, September/October 2007. www.bostonreview.net.

Roug, Louise, 'Iraq accuses Syria of helping rebels', *Los Angeles Times*, 5 February 2007.

Royal Scientific Society, Friedrich Ebert Stiftung, *The Iraqi Status and its Effect on the Jordanian Economy*, Amman, June 2005.

Rubin, Alissa J., 'Sunni Baghdad Becomes Land of Silent Ruins', *The New York Times*, 26 March 2007.

————, 'Persecuted Sect in Iraq Avoids Its Shrine', *The New York Times*, 14 October 2007.

————, 'A Calmer Iraq: Fragile, and Possibly Fleeting', *The New York Times*, 5 December 2007.

————, 'Around Baghdad, Signs of Normal Life Creep Back', *The New York Times*, 20 December 2007.

Rubin, Trudy, 'Worldview: Bush shamefully flees Iraqi refugees crisis', *The Philadelphia Inquirer*, 2 April 2008. www.philly.com/inquirer/.

Said, Edward, *Reflections on Exile and Other Essays*, Cambridge, Mass., Harvard University Press, 2000.

Saif, Ibrahim and DeBartolo, David M., *The Iraq War's Impact on Growth and Inflation in Jordan*, Center for Strategic Studies, University of Jordan, 2007. www.css-jordan.org.

Salusbury, Matt, 'Kurds plan to host American University', *The Times Higher Education Supplement*, 18 March 2007.

Sanders, Ben and Smith, Merrill, 'The Iraqi Refugee Disaster', *World Policy Journal* (Fall 2007), pp. 23–28.

Al Saraf, Hala and Garfield, Richard, 'The Brain Drain of Health Capital: Iraq as a Case Study', in Cholewka, Patricia A. and Motlagh, Mitra M. (eds),

Health Capital and Sustainable Socioeconomic Development, Boca
  Raton, CRC Press, 2008, pp. 151–167.
Sarhan, Rfif, 'Sex for Survival', Al-Jazeera, 13 August 2007. www.aljazeera.net.
Sassoon, Joseph, 'Management of Iraq's Economy Pre and Post the 2003
  War: An Assessment', in Baram, Amatzia, Rohd, Achim and Zeidel,
  Ronen (eds), *Iraq, Past and Present,* to be published by Routledge,
  2009.
Scott, Leakie (ed.), *Housing, Land and Property Restitution of Rights of Refugees
  and Displaced Persons: Laws, Cases and Materials,* New York,
  Cambridge University Press, 2007.
Sengupta, Somini and Fisher, Ian, 'The Reach of War: Violence; Bombs
  Explode Near Churches in 2 Iraqi Cities', *The New York Times,* 2 August
  2004.
Al-Shabibi, Sinan, 'An Economic Agenda For a Future Iraq', *Studies on the Iraqi
  Economy,* Iraqi Economic Forum, London, 2002, pp. 24–37.
Al-Shalchi, Hadeel, 'Down the line', *Al-Ahram Weekly,* Issue 844, 10–16 May
  2007.
Shami, Seteney and McCann, Lisa, 'The Social Implications of Population
  Displacement and Resettlement in the Middle East', *International
  Migration Review,* vol. 27 (Summer 1993), pp. 425–430.
Sharara, Hayat, *Itha Al-Ayyam Agsagat* (When Darkness Fell), Beirut, Arabic
  Institute for Studies and Publications, 2000.
Al-Sheibani, Bassim Irheim Mohammed, Hadi, Najah R. and Hasoon, Tariq,
  'Iraq lacks facilities and expertise in emergency medicine', *BMJ,*
  333:847, 21 October 2006. www.BMJ.com.
Sherwood-Randall, Elizabeth, 'Tend to Turkey', *Journal of Democracy,* vol. 6
  (Fall 2007).
Shinn, David, 'Reversing the Brain Drain in Ethiopia', a lecture delivered to the
  Ethiopian North American Health Professionals Association, 23
  November 2002.
Shoeb, Marwa, Weinstein, Harvey M. and Halpern, Jodi, 'Living in Religious
  Time and Space: Iraqi Refugees in Dearborn, Michigan', *Journal of
  Refugee Studies,* 20/3 (2007), pp. 441–460.
Sinan, Omar, 'Iraqi Refugees Turn to Prostitution', *The Washington Post,* 24
  October 2007.
Sinjab, Lina, 'Iraqi refugees struggle in Syria', BBC News, 23 August 2007.
Sirkeci, Ibrahim, 'War in Iraq: Environment of Insecurity and International
  Migration', *International Migration,* 43/4 (2005).
Slackman, Michael, 'Day of angry protest stuns Egypt', *International Herald
  Tribune,* 7 April 2008.
Snyder, David, *Another Easter Away, Iraqi Family Marks Another Year as
  Refugees,* Caritas Internationalis, 11 April 2007. www.caritas.org.

Sophocles, *Oedipus the King*, translated by Ian Johnston, Virginia, Richer Resources Publication, 2007.

Special Inspector General for Iraq Reconstruction (SIGIR), *Quarterly Report and Semiannual Report to the United States Congress*, 30 January 2006.

———, *Quarterly Report to the United States Congress*, 30 April 2007.

———, *Quarterly Report to the United States Congress*, 30 October 2007.

———, *Quarterly Report and Semiannual Report to the United States Congress*, 30 January 2008.

Sperl, Markus, *Fortress Europe and the Iraqi 'intruders': Iraqi asylum-seekers and the EU, 2003–2007*, New Issues in Refugee Research, UNHCR, Research Paper no. 144, October 2007, p. 1. www.unhcr.org/research.

Sperl, Stefan, *Evaluation of UNHCR's policy on refugees in urban areas: A case study review of Cairo*, UNHCR Evaluation and Policy Analysis Unit, June 2001.

Spinder, William, 'Are Iraqis getting a Fair Deal', *Refugees*, 146/2 (2007), pp. 20–23.

Stannard, Mathew B., 'Education Ministry kidnappings reflect plight of Iraqi academics', *The San Francisco Chronicle*, 15 November 2006. www.sfgate.com.

Stansfield, Gareth, *Accepting Realities in Iraq*, Middle East Briefing Paper, Chatham House, MEP BP 07/02, May 2007.

Stewart, Rory, *Occupational Hazards: My Time Governing in Iraq*, London, Picador, 2006.

Stiglitz, Joseph and Bilmes, Linda J., *The Three Trillion Dollar War: The True Cost of the Iraq Conflict*, New York, Norton, 2008.

Struck, Doug, 'Professionals Fleeing Iraq As Violence, Threats Persist', *The Washington Post*, 23 January 2006.

Sultan, Abed Al-Samad Rahman, 'An unenviable task', *Forced Migration Review*, Special Issue (June 2007), pp. 16–17.

Swedish Migration Board, *Facts & Figures 2006*, March 2007. www.migrationsverket.se.

Tabori, Paul, *The Anatomy of Exile*, London, Harrap, 1972.

Taneja, Preti, *Assimilation, Exodus, Eradication: Iraq's minority communities since 2003*, Minority Rights Group International, February 2007. www.minorityrights.org.

Tavernise, Sabrina, 'Facing Chaos, Iraqi Doctors are Quitting', *The New York Times*, 31 May 2005.

———, 'Sectarian Hatred Pulls Apart Iraq's Mixed Towns', *The New York Times*, 20 November 2005.

———, 'Jordan Yields Poverty and Pain for the Well-Off Fleeing Iraq', *The New York Times*, 10 August 2007.

———, 'In Life of Lies, Iraqis Conceal Work for U.S.', *The New York Times*, 6 October 2007.

Tiltnes, Åge A., *Keeping Up: A Brief on the Living Conditions of Palestinian Refugees in Syria*, Fafo, 2007.

Trad, Samira and Frangieh, Ghida, 'Iraqi refugees in Lebanon: continuous lack of protection', *Forced Migration Review*, Special Issue (June 2007), pp. 35–36.

Travis, Alan, 'Iraqi asylum seekers given deadline to go home or face destitution in UK', *The Guardian*, 13 March 2008.

Tripp, Charles, *A History of Iraq*, Cambridge, Cambridge University Press, 2000.

United Nations, *Likely Humanitarian Scenarios*, 10 December 2003, www.casi.org.info.

United Nations Assistance Mission for Iraq (UNAMI), *Iraq Situation Report*, 15–28 November 2004. www.uniraq.org.

———, *Human Rights Report*, 1 April–30 June 2007.

United Nations Children's Fund (UNICEF), *Iraq: Children suffer as food insecurity persists*, 12 May 2006. www.unicef.org.

———, *Iraq Situation Report March 2007*.

———, *Little respite for Iraq's children in 2007*, 21 December 2007.

UNICEF/UNHCR, *Providing Education Opportunities to Iraqi Children in Host Countries: A Regional Perspective*, July 2007.

United Nations Development Programme (UNDP), *Poverty in Syria: 1996–2004: Diagnosis and Pro-Poor Policy Considerations*, June 2005, www.undp.org.

———/Ministry of Planning and Development Cooperation, *Iraq Living Conditions Survey 2004*, vol. II, Analytical Report, Baghdad, 2005.

United Nations Educational Scientific and Cultural Organization (UNESCO), *Iraq: Education in Transition*, Needs and Challenges, 2004. www.portal.unesco.org.

UNFPA, UNHCR, UNICEF, WFP and WHO, *Meeting the Health Needs of Iraqis Displaced in Neighbouring Countries*, Health Sector Appeal, 18 September 2007. www.who.int.

United Nations High Commissioner for Refugees (UNHCR), *Report on the Situation of Human Rights in Iraq*, submitted by the Special Rapporteur, Mr Max van der Stoel, 10 March 1998. E/CN.4/1998/67. www.unhcr.org.

———, *Iraqis prepare to leave remote desert camp*, 28 July 2003.

———, *Over half of Iraqi refugees in Iran have gone home*, 16 December 2004.

———, *Country of Origin Information Iraq*, October 2005.

———, *Iraq Operation 2006 Supplementary Appeal*, April 2006.

———, *Country Operations Plan*, Country: Lebanon, Planning Year 2006, 1 September 2006.

———, *Iraq Situation Update*, November 2006.

————, *The State of the World's Refugees 2006*, Oxford, Oxford University Press, 2006.

————, *Humanitarian Needs of Persons Displaced Within Iraq and Across the Country's Borders: An International Response*, HCR/ICI/2007/2, 30 March 2007.

————, *Global Overview*, April 2007.

————, *Iraq Situation Response*, Update on revised activities under the January 2007 Supplementary Appeal, July 2007.

————, *UN agency Appeals for Urgent Aid to Support Countries Hosting Iraqi Refugees*, 6 July 2007.

————, *Objectives of UNHCR in Jordan*, August 2007.

————, *Ongoing and planned activities in Amman/Jordan*, 3 September 2007.

————, *Iraqis top latest asylum figures for industrialized countries*, 21 September 2007.

————, *Conditions deteriorate for 2,000 Palestinians stuck at Iraq-Syria border*, 9 November 2007.

————, *Palestinians at the Iraq-Syria border*, 9 November 2007.

————, *SGBV Update*, Damascus, 15 November 2007.

————, *Iraq Situation Update*, 21 November 2007.

————, *Addendum to UNHCR's Eligibility Guidelines for Assessing the International Protection Needs of Iraqi Asylum-seekers*, December 2007.

————, *Global Appeal 2008–2009*, 1 December 2007.

————, *UNHCR issues ATM cards to 7,000 needy Iraqi families in Syria*, 17 December 2007.

————, *2008 Iraq Situation Supplementary Appeal*, 2 January 2008.

————, *Iraqi Situation Update*, 4 January 2008.

————, *Arab League to launch fund-raising campaign for Iraqi refugees*, 10 January 2008.

————, *Trauma Survey in Syria highlights suffering of Iraqi refugees*, 22 January 2008.

————, *Iraq Situation Update*, 23 January 2008.

————, *Analysis of the Situation of Returns to Iraq*, February 2008.

————, *UNHCR welcomes Lebanon's recognition of Iraqi refugees*, 20 February 2008.

————, *Iraq Situation Update*, March 2008.

————, *Asylum Levels and Trends in Industrialized Countries, 2007*, 18 March 2008.

————, *Assessment on Returns to Iraq Amongst the Iraqi Refugee Population in Syria*, April 2008.

————, *Iraq Situation Update*, 25 April 2008.

————, *Syria Update*, June 2008.

———— and International Peace Academy, *Healing the Wounds, Refugees, Reconstruction and Reconciliation*, Report of a conference, 30 June–1 July 1996.

UNHCR, UNICEF, WFP, *Assessment on the Situation of Iraqi Refugees in Syria*, March 2006. www.ncciraq.org.

United Nations Treaty Series, *Number 189 UNTS 137*, 28 July 1951.

United Nations University, *UNU calls for World Help to Repair System*, 27 April 2005. www.unu.edu.

Unrepresented Nations and Peoples Organization (UNPO), *Iraqi Turkmen: Indigenous Peoples and Current Human Rights Situation in Iraq*, 7 August 2006.

US Agency for International Development, *A Year in Iraq*, Restoring Services, May 2004. www.usaid.gov.

US Committee for Refugees and Immigrants, *World Refugee Survey 2007*. www.refugees.org.

US Department of State, *United States Humanitarian Assistance for Displaced Iraqis*, 9 November 2007. www.state.gov.

————, *US Contributes More Than $125 Million to International Organizations to Aid Displaced Iraqis*, 14 February 2008.

————, *Special Immigrant Visas for Iraqis–Employed by/on behalf of U.S. Government*, March 2008.

United States Government Accountability Office (GAO), *Iraq Reconstruction: Better Data Needed to Assess Iraq's Budget Execution*, Report to Congressional Committees, January 2008.

United States Senate, Hearing before the Committee on the Judiciary, 'The Plight of Iraqi Refugees', One Hundred Tenth Congress, 16 January 2007.

Van der Auweraert, Peter, 'Property Restitution in Iraq', Presentation at the Symposium on Post-Conflict Property Restitution, Hosted by the Bureau of Population, Refugees, and Migration, US Department of State, Arlington, Virginia, 6–7 September 2007.

Van Hear, Nicholas, 'The Impact of the Involuntary Mass "Return" to Jordan in the Wake of the Gulf Crisis', *International Migration Review*, vol. 29 (Summer 1995), pp. 352–374.

————, 'Refugees in Diaspora; From Durable Solutions to Trans-national Relations', *Refuge*, 23/1 (Winter 2006), pp. 9–15.

Vedentam, Shankar, 'One Thing We Can't Build Alone in Iraq', *The Washington Post*, 29 October 2007.

Verney, Marie-Helen, 'The Road Home: The Faili Kurds', *Refugee Magazine*, Issue 134 (20 March 2007).

Voutira, Effie, a lecture given at the British Academy conference on 'Dispossession and Displacement: Forced Migration in the Middle East and Africa', London, 28–29 February 2008.

Wanche, Sophia I., *An Assessment of the Iraqi Community in Greece*, Commissioned by UNHCR, January 2004.

Weiss, Stanley A., 'Iraq needs a job surge', *The International Herald Tribune*, 27 December 2007.

Willett, John and Manheim, Ralph (eds), *Bertolt Brecht Poems*, London, Eyre Methuen Ltd, 1976.

Williams, Rhodri C., 'The Significance of Property Restitution to Sustainable Return in Bosnia and Herzegovina', *International Migration*, 44/3 (2006), pp. 39–61.

———, *Applying the lessons of Bosnia in Iraq: Whatever the Solution, Property Rights Should be Secured*, The Brookings Institution, 18 March 2008.

Women's Commission for Refugee Women and Children, *From the Field, "Can You Help Us?" Iraqi Refugees in Jordan*, 15 June 2007. www.womenscommission.org.

———, *Iraqi Refugees in Jordan: Desperate and Alone*, 11 July 2007.

———, *Iraqi Refugee Women and Youth in Jordan: Reproductive Health Findings: A snapshot from the field*, September 2007.

———, 'Overview of Iraqi Refugees in Jordan', video, November 2007. www.youtube.com/watch?v=ICI06BbD53I&eurl.

Women's International League for Peace and Freedom, *Iraq: Unemployment Forces Female Professionals Into Domestic Work*, 25 July 2006. www.peacewomen.org.

Wong, Edward, 'Sunnis find sanctuary among Iraqi Kurds', *The International Herald Tribune*, 2–3 September 2006.

———, 'Thousands of Iraqis Flee to Kurdish Region to Escape War Face Harsh Living Conditions', *The New York Times*, 21 March 2007.

The World Bank, *World Development Indicators database*, April 2007. www.worldbank.org.

———, *The World Not Traveled: Education Reform in the Middle East and Africa*, MENA Development Report, Washington DC, 2008.

World Food Programme (WFP), *The extent and geographic distribution of chronic poverty in Iraq's Center/South Region*, May 2003. www.wfp.org.

———, *WFP Food Survey Shows High Prevalence of Food Insecurity in Iraq*, 28 September 2004.

World Health Organization (WHO), *World report on violence and health*, Geneva, 2002. www.who.int.

———, *Healing Minds, Mental Health progress report 2004–2006*, 2006.

———, *Annual Report 2006, Working Together for a Healthier Iraq*, February 2007.

———, *Country Profiles: Iraq*. www.emro.who.int.

———, *Social Determinants of Health in Countries in Conflict: The Eastern Mediterranean Prospective*, Cairo, June 2007.

World Organisation Against Torture, 'Greece: Alleged ill-treatment and fear of forcible deportation of Iraqi refugees', Press Release, 5 April 2007. cm.greekhelsinki.gr.

World Vision Middle East/Eastern European Office (MEERO), *Blankets for Iraqi Refugees in Jordan*, 14 April 2008. www.meero.worldvision.org.

Wright, Robin and Baker, Peter, 'Iraq, Jordan see Threat to Election from Iran–Leaders Warn Against Forming Religious State', *The Washington Post*, 8 December 2004.

Yoshikawa, Lynn, 'Iraqi refugees in Egypt', *Forced Migration Review*, Issue 29 (December) 2007, p. 54.

Yousef, Nancy A. and Fadel, Leila, 'What Crocker and Petraeus didn't say', *McClatchy Newspapers*, 11 September 2007.

Zaiotti, Ruben, 'Dealing with non-Palestinian refugees in the Middle-East: Policies and Practices in an Uncertain Environment', *International Journal of Refugee Law*, 18/2 (2006), pp. 333–353.

Zarocastas, John, 'Exodus of medical staff strains Iraq's health facilities', *BMJ*, 334:865, 28 April 2007.

Zetter, Roger, 'Reconceptualizing the Myth of Return: Continuity and Transition Amongst the Greek-Cypriot Refugees of 1974', *Journal of Refugee Studies*, 12/1 (1999), pp. 1–22.

Zoepf, Katherine, 'The Reach of War: Exodus; Many Christians Flee Iraq, with Syria the Haven of Choice', *The New York Times*, 5 August 2004.

———, 'Iraqi Refugees Turn to the Sex Trade in Syria', *The New York Times*, 29 May 2007.

Zolberg, Aristide R., Suhrke, Astri, Aguayo, Sergio, *Escape From Violence: Conflict and the Refugee Crisis in the Developing World*, New York, Oxford University Press, 1992.

Zulal, Shwan, 'Economic successes or incompetence in Kurdistan regional government', Kurdish Media, 10 April 2008. www.kurdmedia.com.

Iraqi and Arab newspapers

Al-Arab Al-Yawm (Jordanian). www.alarabalyawm.net.

Al-Ahram Weekly (Egyptian, published in English). weekly.ahram.org.eg.

Asharq Alawsat (International Arab Daily based in London, published in English). www.asharqalawsat.com.

Azzaman (Iraqi). www.azzaman.com.

Al-Baath (Syrian). www.albaath.news.sy.

The Daily Star (Lebanese, published in English). www.dailystar.com.lb.

Al-Dustour (Jordanian). www.addustour.com.

Al-Hayat (published in Arabic and English). www.daralhayat.net.

The Jordan Times (Jordan, published in English). www.jordantimes.com.
Kurdish Globe (Kurdish, published in English). www.kurdishglobe.net.
Al-Mashriq (Iraqi). www.al-mashriq.net.
Al-Muwatin (Iraqi). www.almowaten.com.
Al-Ra'y (Jordanian). www.alrai.com.
Al-Sabaah (Iraqi). www.alsabaah.com.
Al-Sabil (Jordanian Weekly). www.assabeel.net.
Syria Times (Syrian Government newspaper, published in English).
      www.syriatimes.com.
Syria Today (Syrian Monthly). www.syria-today.com.
Al-Thawrah (Syrian). www.thawra.com.
Tishreen (Syrian). www.tishreen.info.

Western newspapers

Dagens Nyheter (Swedish, quoted in BBC Monitoring Online).
      www.bbcmonitoringonline.com.
The Economist (UK Weekly). www.economist.com.
Le Figaro (French). www.lefigaro.fr.
Financial Times (UK). www.ft.com.
The Guardian (UK). www.guardian.co.uk.
Hurriyet (Turkish, quoted in BBC Monitoring Online).
      www.bbcmonitoringonline.com.
The Independent (UK). www.independent.co.uk.
The International Herald Tribune (USA). www.iht.com.
The Los Angeles Times (USA). www.latimes.com.
The New York Times (USA). www.nytimes.com.
Swedish Press Review (Swedish, quoted in BBC Monitoring Online).
      www.bbcmonitoringonline.com.
The Times (UK). www.timesonline.co.uk.
Today's Zaman (Turkish, published in English). www.todayszaman.com.
The Washington Post (USA). www.washingtonpost.com.

News agencies and websites

Agence France-Presse (French). www.afp.com.
AlertNet (Humanitarian new network owned by Reuters). www.alertnet.org.
Associated Press. www.ap.org.
Aswat Al-Iraq (Voices of Iraq VOI, based in Baghdad). www.aswataliraq.info.
BBC Monitoring Online (UK). www.bbcmonitoringonline.com.

BBC News (UK). www.bbc.co.uk.
CNN (USA). www.cnn.com.
Iraq Directory (web guide to Iraq business). www.iraqdirectory.com.
Iraq Updates (News service that collates news on Iraq).
    www.iraqupdates.com.
Kurdish Media (Kurdish news and commentary website).
    www.kurdmedia.com.
Kuwait News Agency (KUNA). www.kuna.net.kw.
Al-Jazeera (Dubai). www.aljazeera.net
MaximsNews Network (News network for the United Nations).
    www.maximsnews.com.
Middle East Online (London). www.middle-east-online.com.
Reuters. www.reuters.com.
State House News Service (News network of the US House and Senate).
    www.statehousenews.com.
Syrian News Agency (SANA). www.sana.sy.
United Press International (UPI). www.upi.com.
Zawya (Dubai, website specializing in business). www.zawya.com.

Television stations

Al-Arabiya (Dubai).
Al-Iraqiya (Iraq).
Al-Jazeera (Dubai).
Al-Sharqiya (Dubai).

Index

abortion 40, 68
academics 23, 62, 137, 140–3, 146–8
 violence against 141–3, 147
advertising 76
Afghanistan 20, 98, 154
Africa 3, 124, 137
airports 137, 167
Al-Ali, Nadje 16
Al-Askariyya Mosque 10, 11, 27
Al-Himaya 44, 125
al-Khalidi, Ashraf and Tanner, Victor
 15
Al-Maliki, Nouri 82, 91, 136–7, 150,
 160, 165–6
Al-Qaeda 53
Al-Sadr, Moqtada 13
Albania 162
Allawi, Ali 29, 135
Alwan, Ala'din 20, 29, 145
Amnesty International 41, 62,
 68–70, 159
Anbar 13, 20, 63
Anfal campaign 9, 24
Arab League nations 96–8
Arabic 3, 23, 126, 157
Arabization 9, 24
Armenians 23, 61, 87
arms trade 79, 111, 132, 136
Asian contractors in Iraq 132
Assyrians 23–4, 26, 61, 100, 154
Australia 36, 45, 46, 59, 74, 87, 113,
 115
 donations to rebuild Iraq 122

Ba'th party
 biggest Iraqi employer 1
 expulsion 12, 24, 139
 fall of 1, 35, 115, 130–3, 140
 former members 36, 62, 97
 poverty caused by 20, 129–30
 regime 9
 violence 2–3, 14, 115, 161
Bahais 23, 26
Barakat, Sultan 134
Basra 17, 25, 99, 144, 158
 university 23, 147
Batatu, Hanna 2
begging 48
Belgium 106, 109
Bosnia 16, 113, 154, 162
brain drain 2–3, 7, 100, 140–51, 158,
 168
 of academics 23, 62, 140–2, 146–8
 causes of 129–40
 cost of 149
 of healthcare professionals 21, 34,
 47, 62, 97, 143–8
 of lawyers 62, 125, 140, 142
 reversing 145–6, 149–51
Brazil 113
Bremer, Paul 130–2
bureaucracy 135–6, 150, 159, 163

'capacity building' 29, 58
CARE 58, 115, 125–6
Caritas Internationalis 43, 58, 91,
 125–7

Chaldeans 23, 25, 100, 102, 126
Chatelard, Géraldine 34, 36, 52, 54
children 7, 9, 18–20, 125, 168–70
    child soldiers 25
    Christian 25
    deaths 18
    in Jordan 38, 40–2
    orphans 18, 20
    and return of refugees 157–8
    in Syria 65–7, 69–71
    trauma-related stress 19, 72
    as wage earners 18, 20, 38, 66, 71,
        75–6, 95
Christian Peace Association 25
Christians 23–6, 34, 36, 45, 48, 59,
        61–2, 65, 73–4, 91, 92, 101–2,
        109, 157–8
    children 25
    and healthcare 71, 73
    and Kurds 13
    NGOs 126–7
    violence against 24–6, 101–2
class 5, 12, 34, 37, 42, 47, 62, 65–6,
        100, 118, 131, 139–40, 149–51,
        166
Coalition Provincial Authority
        (CPA) 27–8, 129–34, 161
communism 61, 130
corruption 3, 21, 30, 122, 133–40,
        167–8, 170
    in Kurdistan 137
crime 15–16, 30, 48, 53, 62, 132
    see also sexual violence; violence
currency 131, 138, 140, 172

Dahuk 26
Darfur 124
death rates 15, 18, 19
demographics 14, 34, 37–8, 66, 88,
        172
Denmark 101, 106, 109, 127
Dinar (Iraqi) 131, 138, 140, 172

drainage 10
drugs 19

economics 1–7, 88–9, 94, 129–34
    banking 138
    currency 131, 138, 140, 172
    and gender 38
    inflation 13, 49, 50, 53, 77–8, 89,
        94, 130–2, 137, 139–40, 161,
        168, 172
    in Jordan 46–51
    national debt 138
    and number of refugees 4
    privatization 130, 132, 134
    reserves 166, 169
    in Syria 75–8
    upturn in 137–8
education 3, 7, 13, 22–3, 40, 111,
        120, 145–6, 150–1, 158,
        168–70
    decline in 20, 22, 70
    in Egypt 89–90
    in Jordan 33–4
    in Lebanon 93
    literacy rates 16, 22–3, 42, 70
    and NGOs 125–8
    in Sweden 102–3
    in Syria 64, 66–7, 69–70, 77–8
    teachers as refugees 34
    universities 23, 40, 42, 70–1,
        140–1, 145–8, 151
    for women 16–17, 147
Egypt
    Iraqi refugees in 5–6, 35, 44, 72,
        87–93, 128, 147, 157–60, 172
    Palestinians in 87
    and Shia 88
    signs UN Convention relating to
        the Status of Refugees, 1951 6
elderly people 25, 102, 125, 158
electricity 1, 15, 35, 44, 49, 130, 133,
        158, 159, 168

entrepreneurs 48, 51, 131, 139, 166
Ethiopia 91
ethnic cleansing 5, 9, 11, 12, 31, 45,
    74, 160–1
European Union (EU)
    donations to rebuild Iraq 122

Fafo 5, 37–8, 42–3, 45–6, 48, 59, 61,
    92, 156
Falluja 11, 19
food *see* malnutrition; rationing
France 106, 109, 127

gas 55
gender 7, 16–18
    and dress 17
    see also sexual violence
Geneva Convention 61, 87, 94–5,
    105, 118
Germany 74, 101, 105–7, 109
Greece 101, 105–6, 109, 158
Green Zone 26, 30, 134
Gulf States
    Iraqi refugees in 5, 35, 51, 56, 68,
        97, 140, 144
    political instability 6
Gulf War, 1991 1, 2, 22, 56, 129
    aftermath 3, 44, 61, 96, 98–100,
        117, 131, 140, 168

Hakki, Said 157
Hansen, Greg 121–2
health care 3, 7, 11, 19, 29, 90, 125,
    144–5, 168
    blood supplies 21
    cancer 21
    disease 18
    immunization 21
    in Jordan 33, 38, 42–4
    medical schools 145
    medical tourism 43
    mental 17, 72–3

nutrition 18, 20–1, 44, 58, 122,
    125, 169
professionals as refugees 21, 34,
    47, 62, 97, 143–8
psychology 2, 19, 22, 90, 93, 125
services, decline in 20–1
in Syria 71–3
Herzegovina 154, 162
honour 2, 16–17, 167
housing
    in Egypt 89
    IDPs 11
    in Jordan 45, 48, 55
    market 12, 48–9, 65–6
    shortage 12, 125, 160, 162–3
    in Södertälje 102–3
    in Syria 65–6, 74, 77
human rights 1, 3, 24, 62, 80, 83,
    101, 107
Human Rights Watch (HRW) 27, 40,
    47, 52, 54, 59, 75, 80, 94–5, 116,
    119
humanitarian crisis, definition of 3
Hussein, Saddam *see* Ba'th Party

inflation 49, 50, 55, 77–8, 89, 94,
    130–1, 132, 139–40, 161, 168,
    172
Integrated Regional Information
    Networks (IRIN) 17, 21, 97
interim Iraqi government 11
internally displaced persons (IDPs)
    1, 5, 166, 170, 172
    action on 27–31
    after 2003 10, 115
    under Ba'th party 9–11, 115–16
    from Baghdad 10
    categories of 12
    children 18–20, 23
    forced displacement as deliberate
        strategy 12
    IDP Working Group 13

IDPs (*cont.*)
  leave property behind 10
  literacy rates 16, 22–3
  minorities 23–7
  in north Iraq 9
  numbers of 9–10, 13, 158–9, 172
  phases of 9–14
  regulating 14, 159
  return of 158, 161
  in south Iraq 9–10
  tracking 12
  and United Nations (UN) 10–11,
    17–18, 21–3, 28–30
  women 16–18
International Catholic Migration
  Commission 58, 84, 126
International Committee of the Red
  Cross (ICRC) 115–16, 120,
  124
International Monetary Fund (IMF)
  77–8
International Organization for
  Migration (IOM) 13, 14, 29,
  121, 156–7, 161
invasion of Iraq , 2003 2–3
  cost of 167
  and economics 49–50, 130–1
  immediate effects of 10, 27,
    51–2, 62, 65, 115–17, 130–1,
    145–8
  lead-up to 34
  loss of life since 22, 167
Ipsos 65–7, 69–70, 72–3, 156
Iran 7, 63, 79, 149, 155
  Iraqi refugees in 5, 11, 33, 98–9,
    172
Iran–Iraq war 1, 2, 22, 97, 129, 138
Iraq
  army, dissolution of 132
  civil war 2, 4–5, 12, 30
  clans 1, 2, 14–15
  corruption 122, 135–9

currency 131, 138, 140, 172
death rate 15
debts 138
future of 14, 27, 139
ignores refugee crisis 166
legal system 30
militarization 1
Ministry of Displacement and
  Migration (MODM) 29, 121,
  156, 159–60
Ministry of Health 19, 21, 29,
  142–3
Ministry of Interior 28
Ministry of Planning and
  Development Cooperation
  121
Oil-for-Food 51, 56, 115, 135
parliament 27, 30, 160, 166
rebuilding 121–3, 133–4
refugees in Jordan, policy towards
  7, 57
refugees in Syria, policy towards
  7, 81–2
trade sanctions 1–3, 22, 56, 88,
  129, 134
see also brain drain; economics;
  Gulf War; invasion of Iraq ,
  2003; Iran–Iraq war; refugees,
  Iraqi
Iraq Family Health Survey (IFHS)
  17, 18
Iraqi Red Crescent Organization
  (IRCO) 12, 13, 143, 155, 157–8,
  160
Islam
  extremism 17, 24, 45–6, 62
  fatwas 26
  importance of for refugees 154
  jihadism 13
  NGOs 58, 126
  Sharia 26
  see also Shia; Sunnis

Israel 66, 87, 94, 147
  see also Palestinians

Jews 23
Jordan, Iraqi refugees in 5–7, 25,
    140, 165
  Amman 44, 45, 48–50
  children 38, 40–2
  currency 56–61
  education for 33–4, 40–2, 54
  effects of 46–51
  healthcare for 33, 38, 42–4
  history of 33–5
  housing for 48, 55
  international response to 58–60
  Iraqi policy towards 7, 57
  Jordan Red Crescent 58
  and Jordanian economy 36,
    46–51, 54–7, 170
  Jordanian policy towards 34–5,
    37, 51–7, 58
  lack of compensation for 169
  medical tourism 43
  Ministry of Education 126
  minorities 45
  and NGOs 118
  number of 33, 41–2, 51, 60, 117,
    172
  oil 56
  quality of life 37
  reasons for 35–46
  and terrorism 53–4
  as transit point 36
  and UNHCR 119–20
  US aid for 59
  wealth gap 48
  women 34, 38–40, 46
  see also Palestinians
Jordanian Hashemite Charity
    Organization 125
Jordanian National Alliance Against
    Hunger 58, 126

Juveniles 125

Kemadia 21
Kerbala 18
Kirkuk 23–4
Kosovo 30, 113, 117, 124, 162
Kurds 1, 9, 23–4, 26, 33, 61, 99, 100,
    102, 117, 129, 161, 165
  and Christians 13
  economics 137
  Faili Kurds 23–4, 98
  Iraqi professionals move to 141,
    148, 157
  Kurdistan 137–8
  no-fly zone 165
  political parties 14, 137–8
  and women 17
Kuwait 96, 122, 138
  see also Gulf War, 1991

land and property rights 160–3
land mines 2
lawyers 62, 125, 140, 142
Lebanon 157, 170
  Iraqi refugees in 5–7, 61, 92–6,
    118–19, 169, 172
  and Syria 80
legal aid 125
Libya 43

MADRE 16
Mahdi Army 15
Malley, Robert 151
malnutrition 21, 44, 72, 169
Mandeans 23, 26, 45, 62, 65, 73–4,
    84, 100, 102, 157
Maples, Michael 12–13
Marfleet, Philip 4, 15
Marsh Arabs 10, 98
Maysan 134
Medact 143–4

Médecins Sans Frontières (MSF) 21, 126
media 1, 10–11, 15–16, 19, 21, 25, 27, 30, 36–7, 50, 53, 55–6, 58, 66, 68, 74, 80, 82–3, 101, 107–8, 110, 112, 122, 133, 136, 140, 144, 165
Mercy Corps 125–6
Middle East Council of Churches 58, 115
minorities 11–12, 23–7, 45–6, 62, 73–5, 167
   see also Armenians; Assyrians; Christians; Jews; Kurds; Mandeans; Sabeans; Shabaks; Turkomans; Yazidis
Mizan 58, 125
Mosul 11, 23, 25, 26, 61, 136, 141, 147, 158

Najaf 18, 146
Nasiriya 26
Netherlands 106, 109, 127
non-governmental organizations (NGOs) 7, 58, 83–4, 115–18, 124–8, 169
   danger in Iraq 116, 128
   fail to foresee violence in Iraq post-2003 116, 117
   and UNHCR 127
nutrition 18, 20–1, 44, 58, 122, 125, 169

oil 10, 24, 56, 96, 129–31, 133, 137–8, 163, 166
   Oil-for-Food 51, 56, 115, 135
   prices 49–50, 55, 57, 78, 97, 131, 136, 168
   smuggling 135–6
Oman 97
Organization for Economic Cooperation and Development (OECD) 158

Organization of Women's Freedom in Iraq 18
Ottoman Empire 2, 24, 87

Packer, George 112
Palestine and Palestinians 1, 3, 6–7, 34, 96
   Palestinians in Brazil 113
   Palestinians in Egypt 87
   Palestinians in Iraq 27, 121
   Palestinians in Jordan 38, 43, 51–3, 56
   Palestinians in Lebanon 94
   Palestinians in Syria 61–2, 63, 74–5, 79, 121
patriotism 10
Petraeus, David H. 14
police 10, 17, 28, 62, 68, 95, 119, 136, 147, 162
poverty 18, 20, 22, 39–40, 47, 61, 66, 71, 76–8, 84, 90, 98, 132, 139, 159, 169
Première Urgence 84, 115, 127
property rights 10, 160–3
prostitution 18, 38, 39, 48, 53, 67–8, 81, 84, 94, 132, 169
psychology 2, 16, 18, 19, 22, 44, 58, 70–3, 90, 93, 125, 133

Qatar 97, 127

rape see sexual violence
rationing 1, 10, 20, 76, 125
Red Crescent Organizations 12, 43, 58, 71, 73, 83–4, 120, 127, 143, 157–8
refugees, Iraqi
   Arabic words for 3–4
   causes of 3
   definition of 3–4, 35
   economic situation 46, 48, 72, 74, 88

and exiles 4
future for 6, 169–70
history of 4, 6, 117
hostility to 6
number of 1, 4, 5–6, 165, 167,
    172
perception of 3–4
and political stability 6
rights of 6
urban 5, 37, 65, 117
see also Egypt, Iraqi refugees in;
    internally displaced persons
    (IDPs); Jordan, Iraqi refugees
    in; return of Iraqi refugees;
    Syria, Iraqi refugees in
religion 4, 5, 11, 13, 14, 17
minorities 23–7, 41
pilgrimage 18, 65
and politics 15
see also Islam
return of Iraqi refugees 6–7, 11,
    23–4, 48, 61, 70, 84–5, 95, 99,
    118, 121, 153–63
barriers to 157–8
criteria for 158–9
economics 150, 156
education 155–6
from Egypt 158–60
of IDPs 158
incentives for 157, 168
from Jordan 153, 156
land and property rights 160–3
limited numbers of 169
monitoring 162
myth of 153–5
plan not to return home 34, 36,
    46, 156, 158–60
reasons for 155–60
from Syria 153–6, 158
terrorism prevents 158
Russia 67, 98, 130, 138

Sabeans 23, 38, 45, 62, 65, 73, 157
Sadr City 158
Said, Edward 3–4
sanitation 1, 20–2
Saudi Arabia 27, 43, 51, 56, 65, 68,
    99, 122, 138
    Iraqi refugees in 5, 96–7
Save the Children 58, 126–7
segregation 13, 17, 147
sexual violence 2, 16, 39, 40, 67, 121,
    125
Shabaks 23
Shia 1, 5, 10, 18, 33, 38, 48, 54–5, 61,
    63, 65, 82, 88, 90, 91–2, 99–100,
    147–8, 154, 161
    political power 28, 62, 159
    Sunni–Shi'i dichotomy 2, 5–7, 12,
        13, 15–16, 29, 163
small businesses 132
Södertälje 101–4
Somalia 124
Stewart, Rory 134
Sudan 20, 43, 87, 89–91, 128
Sulaymaniya 13, 17, 137, 148
Sunnis 11, 26, 28, 38, 48, 57, 82, 88,
    92, 96, 98, 141, 159
    concessions to 14
    decline in population in Baghdad
        14
    fight with US forces 13
    Sunni–Shi'i dichotomy 2, 5–7, 12,
        13, 15–16, 29, 163
    unemployment among 132
Sweden
    donations to rebuild Iraq 122
    Iraqi refugees in 5, 65, 100–5, 109,
        172
    education 103
    money needed by 100–1,
    policy concerning refugees 103–5
    religious tolerance 101–2
Switzerland 109

Syria, Iraqi refugees in 5–7, 25, 165
  arms trade 79
  children 65–6, 69–71
  dangerous journeys of 64
  economics 63, 68, 71, 75–8, 80–1,
    92, 157, 172
  education for 69–70, 73
  effects of 75–78
  healthcare 44, 71–3
  history of 61–2
  international response to 83–5
  Iraqi policy towards 81–2
  lack of compensation for 169
  and Lebanon 80
  minorities in 73–4
  and NGOs 118
  number of 61, 64–5, 117, 172
  profile of 65–75
  reasons for 62–4
  return home from 153–6, 158
  and Syrian constitution 61–2
  Syrian International University 71
  Syrian policy towards 61, 63,
    79–81
  Syrian Red Crescent 71, 83–4
  and United States 111, 165
  women 67–9, 75
  see also Palestinians

Tabori, Paul 35
Telafer 24
temporary protection regime (TPR)
  118–19
Terre des Hommes 125–7
terrorism 45–6, 79, 147
  bombings 10–12, 27
  in Jordan 53–4
  kidnappings 2, 29, 140–2, 147
  prevents refugees' return to Iraq
    158–9
  suicide bombings 2, 26, 116, 158
  torture 2

Tikeyet Um Ali 125
trade sanctions 1–3, 22, 56, 88, 129,
  134
tribalism 1, 2, 14–15
Turkey 120, 127
  Iraqi refugees in 5, 67, 99, 101,
    105–6, 109
Turkomans 23–4, 99

unemployment 11–12, 20–1, 34, 46,
  49, 55, 66, 68, 75–6, 93–5, 103,
  130–3, 135, 137, 139, 156, 168
  amongst professionals 141
United Arab Emirates (UAE) 39, 83,
  97, 122, 138
United Kingdom (UK) 17, 59, 167
  British Mandate in Mesopotamia
    2
  donations to rebuild Iraq 122
  Iraqi refugees in 107–10, 154, 165
  mismanagement in Iraq 107–10
United Nations (UN)
  Convention relating to the Status
    of Refugees, 1951 6, 34, 61, 87,
    94, 105–6, 118
  and internally displaced persons
    (IDPs) 10–11, 17–18, 21–3, 28–30
  mismanagement of Iraq post-
    2003 165
  news agency 21
  UN Assistance Mission for Iraq
    (UNAMI) 17, 28
  UN Development Programme
    (UNDP) 58, 75, 78, 121, 131–2,
    172
  UN Fund for Population
    Activities (UNFPA) 44, 58, 121
  UN High Commissioner for
    Refugees (UNHCR) 5, 29,
    30–1, 34–6, 40, 43–4, 58–9, 65,
    69, 76, 84, 91–9, 107–9, 113,
    118–24, 154–7, 165, 169

UNICEF 18, 23, 44, 58, 69, 84, 120, 126
United Nations Relief and Works Agency (UNRWA) 33–4, 121
warns US-led coalition of refugee crisis 1
World Food Programme (WFP) 20, 44, 58, 76, 111, 120–1
World Health Organization (WHO) 3, 19, 20, 29, 42, 44, 58, 73, 90, 120, 121, 143
United States (US)
aid to Iraq 20, 130, 145
aid to Jordan 49, 59
cost of invasion of Iraq 167
Defence Intelligence Agency 12–13
dissolves Iraqi army 132
donations to rebuild Iraq 122, 165
economics 49
High Commissioner for Refugees (UNHCR) 11
Iraqi refugees in 5, 110–13, 154, 165, 172
mismanagement of Iraq post-2003 2–3, 27, 79, 83, 131–4, 136, 149–51, 165–8
National Intelligence Council 28
navy attacked by Al-Qaeda 53
racial bias 26
and rehousing Iraqis 162
soldiers lost in Iraq 167
and Sunni forces 13
and Syria 79, 83, 111, 165
targets Iraqi minorities for work 36
unpopularity in Iraq 11
unprepared for Iraqi invasion 2
warned of refugee crisis 1
universities 23, 40, 42, 70–1, 137, 140–1, 145–8, 151

Vietnam 113
violence
against academics 141–2, 144, 147–8
against minorities 24–6, 45, 101–2
against NGOs 116, 128
against professional classes 140, 145
against women 9
burning 16–17
causes of 14–15, 130–2
decline in 139, 155, 158
domestic 39, 93
effects of 2–4, 14–16, 18–23, 31, 35, 62, 66, 70–3, 84, 111, 131, 133, 139, 167, 168
honour killings 15–16
and internally displaced persons (IDPs) 5, 10, 115
when leaving Iraq 64, 72
murder 62
sectarian 11–12, 28–30, 62, 96, 160
sexual 2, 39, 40, 67, 121, 125, 158
and unemployment 132

water 1, 10, 20, 44, 55–6, 80, 130, 133, 146, 158
women 7, 16–18, 125, 132, 140, 147, 168
in Egypt 88
in Jordan 34, 38–40, 46
in Lebanon 95
in Syria 67–9, 75–6
Women's Commission for Refugee Women and Children 39–41, 43
World Bank 56, 172

Yazidis 23–4, 26, 38, 45, 61, 62, 157
Yemen 20, 43, 87, 97, 140
Iraqi refugees in 5, 35